Canadian Education Law and Global Comparative Studies for Teachers and Administrators

Xiaobin Li
Brock University, Canada

IGI Global
PUBLISHER of TIMELY KNOWLEDGE

A volume in the Advances in Educational Marketing, Administration, and Leadership (AEMAL) Book Series

Published in the United States of America by
IGI Global
Information Science Reference (an imprint of IGI Global)
701 E. Chocolate Avenue
Hershey PA, USA 17033
Tel: 717-533-8845
Fax: 717-533-8661
E-mail: cust@igi-global.com
Web site: http://www.igi-global.com

Library of Congress Cataloging-in-Publication Data

Names: Li, Xiaobin, 1954- author.
Title: Canadian education law and global comparative studies for teachers and administrators / auhtored by Xiaobin Li.
Description: Hershey : Information Science Reference, 2023. | Includes bibliographical references and index. | Summary: "This book provides an overview of the important elements of education law in Ontario, Canada, as education is under provincial jurisdiction in the country. It also briefly describes similar education law contents in California, the United States, as in the US education is mainly under the control of states and California is the most populous state. In addition, the book delineates corresponding contents in Chinese education law, as China has the largest education system in the world"-- Provided by publisher.
Identifiers: LCCN 2023025858 (print) | LCCN 2023025859 (ebook) | ISBN 9781668441633 (hardcover) | ISBN 9781668441671 (paperback) | ISBN 9781668441640 (ebook)
Subjects: LCSH: Educational law and legislation--Canada. | Teachers--Legal status, laws, etc.--Canada. | School administrators--Legal status, laws, etc.--Canada.
Classification: LCC KE3805 .L59 2023 (print) | LCC KE3805 (ebook) | DDC 344.71/07--dc23/eng/20230601
LC record available at https://lccn.loc.gov/2023025858
LC ebook record available at https://lccn.loc.gov/2023025859

This book is published in the IGI Global book series Advances in Educational Marketing, Administration, and Leadership (AEMAL) (ISSN: 2326-9022; eISSN: 2326-9030)

British Cataloguing in Publication Data
A Cataloguing in Publication record for this book is available from the British Library.

All work contributed to this book is new, previously-unpublished material.
The views expressed in this book are those of the authors, but not necessarily of the publisher.

For electronic access to this publication, please contact: eresources@igi-global.com.

Advances in Educational Marketing, Administration, and Leadership (AEMAL) Book Series

ISSN:2326-9022
EISSN:2326-9030

Editor-in-Chief: Siran Mukerji, IGNOU, India Purnendu Tripathi, IGNOU, India

MISSION

With more educational institutions entering into public, higher, and professional education, the educational environment has grown increasingly competitive. With this increase in competitiveness has come the need for a greater focus on leadership within the institutions, on administrative handling of educational matters, and on the marketing of the services offered.

The **Advances in Educational Marketing, Administration, & Leadership (AEMAL) Book Series** strives to provide publications that address all these areas and present trending, current research to assist professionals, administrators, and others involved in the education sector in making their decisions.

COVERAGE

- Governance in P-12 and Higher Education
- Educational Leadership
- Marketing Theories within Education
- Advertising and Promotion of Academic Programs and Institutions
- Direct marketing of educational programs
- Consumer Behavior
- Students as Consumers
- Academic Administration
- Educational Finance
- Enrollment Management

IGI Global is currently accepting manuscripts for publication within this series. To submit a proposal for a volume in this series, please contact our Acquisition Editors at Acquisitions@igi-global.com or visit: http://www.igi-global.com/publish/.

The Advances in Educational Marketing, Administration, and Leadership (AEMAL) Book Series (ISSN 2326-9022) is published by IGI Global, 701 E. Chocolate Avenue, Hershey, PA 17033-1240, USA, www.igi-global.com. This series is composed of titles available for purchase individually; each title is edited to be contextually exclusive from any other title within the series. For pricing and ordering information please visit http://www.igi-global.com/book-series/advances-educational-marketing-administration-leadership/73677. Postmaster: Send all address changes to above address.

Titles in this Series

For a list of additional titles in this series, please visit:
http://www.igi-global.com/book-series/advances-educational-marketing-administration-leadership/73677

Promoting Inclusive Education Through the Integration of LGBTIQ+ Issues in the Classroom
Francisco Javier Palacios-Hidalgo (University of Córdoba, Spain) and Cristina A. Huertas-Abril (University of Córdoba, Spain)
Information Science Reference • © 2023 • 428pp • H/C (ISBN: 9781668482438) • US $215.00

Improving Learning Through Assessment Rubrics Student Awareness of What and How They Learn
Chahna Gonsalves (King's Business School, King's College London, UK) and Jayne Pearson (King's Academy, King's College London, UK)
Information Science Reference • © 2023 • 310pp • H/C (ISBN: 9781668460863) • US $215.00

Enrollment and Retention Strategies for 21st Century Higher Education
Rayshawn L. Eastman (Mount St. Joseph University, USA)
Information Science Reference • © 2023 • 300pp • H/C (ISBN: 9781668474778) • US $215.00

Culturally Responsive Leadership for Social Equity and Academic Justice in Schools
Bethel E. Cager (Xavier University of Louisiana, USA) Jill Tussey (Buena Vista University, USA) Leslie Haas (Xavier University of Louisiana, USA) and Monica Burke (Western Kentucky University, USA)
Information Science Reference • © 2023 • 355pp • H/C (ISBN: 9781668474822) • US $215.00

Becoming and Supporting Online Adjunct Faculty in a Gig Economy
Jennifer L. Robinson (University of Arizona Global Campus, USA)
Information Science Reference • © 2023 • 300pp • H/C (ISBN: 9781668477762) • US $215.00

IGI Global
PUBLISHER of TIMELY KNOWLEDGE

701 East Chocolate Avenue, Hershey, PA 17033, USA
Tel: 717-533-8845 x100 • Fax: 717-533-8661
E-Mail: cust@igi-global.com • www.igi-global.com

Table of Contents

Preface

Educators must be aware of legal issues when they help students achieve required learning outcomes. They also need to protect their own rights in case there are disputes, particularly with the consideration that recently parents' and students' demands on teachers and schools are increasing, but educational resources are tightening. Disputes can be related to what are the most effective ways of teaching students, how to maintain order in classrooms and schools, how to work with students with different abilities, how much parents should be involved in operating schools, and what teachers' working conditions should be. Education law provides a framework that everyone in the school system shall follow for dealing with matters in an orderly way and in a way acceptable for most people. "The law is a cornerstone upon which our society is built" (Proudfoot & Hutchings, 1988, p. 13). Education law has evolved both in the courts and in legislatures to the point where there is now a substantial body of law that defines rights and responsibilities of all who are involved in education (Brown & Zuker, 2007). In Ontario, Canada, an education law course is mandatory when students complete a Bachelor of Education degree program before they can become teachers (Delaney, 2022), however, most Canadian teachers and administrators have little formal training in education law and the level of legal literacy needs improvement (Delaney, 2018).

In the preamble of its Convention on the Rights of the Child (1989), the United Nations (UN) declared that the child should grow up in an atmosphere of happiness, love, and understanding. Furthermore, the child should be brought up in the spirit of peace, dignity, tolerance, freedom, equality, and solidarity. In article 28 of the Convention the UN stipulated that States Parties recognize the right of the child to education. In Canada, according to section 93 of the Constitution Act (1982), education is exclusively under the provincial jurisdiction, except for Indigenous children and Canadian armed forces children. In the province of Ontario, the Education Act (1990) presents that a strong public education system is the foundation of a prosperous, caring, and civil society. To build such a system, knowledge in education law is essential.

Ontario is selected as the focus of this book for two reasons. The first is that the author has studied and worked in the Ontario education system for three decades, has knowledge of Ontario education law, has taught the education law course at Brock University, Ontario, and has written articles on Ontario education law. The second is that Ontario is the most populous province in Canada. What happens in Ontario is likely to have influence across the country.

While the focus of this book is Ontario education law, it will briefly describe and discuss education law in California, the United States, and education law in China, to provide an international perspective for comparison. America is selected because for a long time American education has had an influence on Canadian education. As the largest economy in the world, American education also has an influence in the world. In America education is primarily controlled at the state level. The state of California is selected because it is the most populous state in the country. What happens in California is likely to have an influence in the whole country. China is selected because as the second largest economy in the world it has the largest education system in the world with 291 million students (Chinese Ministry of Education, 2022). In addition, the author has studied and worked in China for two decades and has written articles on Chinese education law. In China most education policy is decided at the national level and there is only national education law.

This book has eight chapters. The first chapter concerns attending school. The second chapter is about roles of teachers. The third chapter focuses on discipline and safety, and the fourth chapter regards negligence, risk management, and liability. The fifth chapter provides and discusses information on special education. The sixth chapter focuses on principals' statutory responsibilities. The seventh chapter concerns collective bargaining, and the eighth chapter is about the governance of education.

Xiaobin Li
Brock University, Canada

REFERENCES

Brown, A., & Zuker, M. (2007). *Education Law* (4th ed.). Thomson Carswell.

Delaney, J. (2018). Teacher misconduct in Canada. In W. Smale (Ed.), Perspectives on Canadian Educational Law and Policy (pp. 43-66). Word & Deed Publishing Inc.

Delaney, J. (2022). *Education Law for Teachers and School Administrators* (2nd ed.). Brush Education Inc.

Education Act, RSO 1990, c E.2. https://www.canlii.org/en/on/laws/stat/rso-1990-c-e2/latest/rso-1990-c- e2.html

Proudfoot, A., & Hutchings, L. (1988). *Teacher Beware*. Detselig Enterprises Ltd.

The Chinese Ministry of Education. (2022). *2021 National Education Development Statistics* [2021年全 国教育事业发展统计公报]. http://www.moe.gov.cn/jyb_sjzl/sjzl_fztjgb/202209/t20220914_660850.html

The Constitution Act, 1982, Schedule B to the Canada Act 1982 (UK), c 11. https://www.canlii.org/en/ca/laws/stat/schedule-b-to-the-canada-act-1982-uk-1982-c- 11/latest/schedule-b-to-the-canada-act-1982-uk-1982-c-11.html

United Nations. (1989). *Convention on the Rights of the Child*. https://www.ohchr.org/en/professionalinterest/pages/crc.aspx

Chapter 1
Attending School

ABSTRACT

In this chapter, the author presents the information about attending school in the Convention on the Rights of the Child by the United Nations, the California Education Code, the Chinese Compulsory Education Act, and the Ontario Education Act. In all these three jurisdictions mentioned above a compulsory policy is implemented, but there are differences between their compulsory policies. The focus of the chapter is Ontario, as the author is more familiar with the Ontario education system than the Californian system and the Chinese system. The chapter refers to the specific sections in the Ontario Education Act on attending school, compulsory education, and the measures of implementing the compulsory education policy in Ontario.

The Convention on the Rights of the Child (UN, 1989) article 28 section 1 stipulated that States Parties recognize the right of the child to education based on equal opportunity. Clause (e) of the same section presented that States Parties should take measures to encourage regular attendance at schools and to reduce dropout rates. In California, the United States, compulsory education law requires everyone between the ages of 6 and 18 to attend school (California Legislative Information, n.d.). In China the government implements a 9-year compulsory education policy (the Chinese People's Congress, 2018).

In Ontario every person who attains the age of 6 years shall attend an elementary or secondary school on every school day until the person attains the age of 18 years. At the beginning of the Education Act (1990) in its purpose section, it states that a strong public education system is the foundation of

DOI: 10.4018/978-1-6684-4163-3.ch001

a prosperous, caring and civil society, that the purpose of education is to provide students with the opportunity to realize their potential and develop into highly skilled, knowledgeable, caring citizens who contribute to their society, and that all partners in the education sector have a role to play in enhancing student achievement and well-being, closing gaps in student achievement, and maintaining confidence in the publicly funded education systems.

Education Act (1990) Part I section 11 subsection (1) stipulates that the Minister of Education may make regulations in respect to schools established under this Act and in respect to all other schools supported in whole or in part by public money prescribing the duties of pupils. The same section subsection (8) presents that the Minister may make regulations governing the excusal of persons who are at least 14 years old from compulsory attendance at school. The following are sections in Part II of the Act related to school attendance.

Section 21 subsection (1) stipulates that unless excused under this section every person between the ages of 6 and 18 shall attend an elementary or secondary school on every school day. A person is excused from attendance if the person is receiving satisfactory instruction at home or elsewhere, is unable to attend school by reason of sickness or other unavoidable cause, transportation is not provided by a district school board for the person and there is no school that the person has a right to attend situated within a certain distance, the person has obtained a secondary school graduation diploma or has completed a course that gives equivalent standing, the person is suspended, expelled, or excluded from attendance, or the person is absent on a day regarded as a holy day by the church to which the person belongs.

Section 21 subsection (5) stipulates that the parent (guardian) of a person required to attend school shall cause the person to attend school unless the person is at least 16 years old and has withdrawn from parental control.

Section 24 subsection (1) presents that the Lieutenant Governor may appoint an officer, to be the Provincial School Attendance Counsellor, who shall, under the direction of the Minister, superintend and direct the enforcement of compulsory school attendance.

Subsection (2) stipulates that where the parent (guardian) of a child considers that the child is excused from attendance under subsection 21 (2), and the appropriate school attendance counsellor is of the opinion that the child should not be excused from attendance, the Provincial School Attendance Counsellor shall direct that an inquiry be made as to the validity of the reason for non-attendance, and for such purpose shall appoint one or more persons who are not employees of the board operating the school that the child has the right to attend to conduct a hearing and to report to the Provincial School Attendance Counsellor the result of the inquiry and may direct that the child,

(a) be excused from attendance; or
(b) attend school.

Section 25 subsection (1) stipulates that every district school board shall appoint one or more school attendance counsellors, but subsection (2) states that two or more boards may appoint the same school attendance counsellor or counsellors.

Subsection (5) provides that a school attendance counsellor has jurisdiction and is responsible for the enforcement of compulsory school attendance in respect of every child who is required to attend school.

Section 26 subsection (1) stipulates that when a school attendance counsellor has reasonable grounds for believing that a child is illegally absent from school, the counsellor may, at the written request of the parent (guardian) or of the principal of the school that the child is required to attend, take the child to the child's parent (guardian) or to the school from which the child is absent.

Subsection (2) states that the counsellor shall report to the board as required.

Subsection (3) stipulates that a school attendance counsellor is responsible to the appropriate supervisory officer and shall carry out the instructions and directions of the Provincial School Attendance Counsellor.

Subsection (4) indicates that a school attendance counsellor shall inquire into every case of failure to attend school within knowledge or when requested by the appropriate supervisory officer or the principal of a school or a ratepayer, and shall give written warning of the consequences of such failure to the parent (guardian) of a child not attending school, and shall also give written notice to the parent (guardian) to cause the child to attend school.

Section 27 stipulates that a board may make or obtain a complete census of all persons in the board's jurisdiction who have not attained the age of 21.

Section 28 subsection (1) provides that the principal of every elementary and secondary school shall, (a) report to the appropriate school attendance counsellor and supervisory officer the names, ages and residences of all pupils of compulsory school age who have not attended school as required; (b) provide the counsellor with such other information as the counsellor requires for the enforcement of compulsory school attendance; and (c) report in writing to the counsellor every case of expulsion and readmission of a pupil.

Section 29 stipulates that where it appears to the Minister that the board of an area is not providing accommodation or instruction for its resident pupils, or has in other respects failed to comply with this Act and the regulations, the Minister may authorize and direct the Provincial School Attendance Counsellor to do all things and exercise all powers necessary for the provision and maintenance of accommodation and instruction for the resident pupils of the board, and thereupon the Provincial School Attendance Counsellor has all the authority and powers vested in performing the duties of the board.

Section 30 subsection (1) states that a parent (guardian) of a person required to attend school who neglects or refuses to cause that person to attend school is guilty of an offence and on conviction is liable to a fine of not more than $200.

Subsection (2) stipulates that the court may, in addition to or instead of imposing a fine, require a parent (guardian) convicted of an offence under subsection (1) to submit to the Minister of Finance a personal bond in the penal sum of $200 with one or more sureties as required, conditioned that the parent (guardian) shall cause the person to attend school and, upon breach of the condition, the bond is forfeit to the province.

Subsection (3) stipulates that anyone who employs during school hours a person required to attend school is guilty of an offence and on conviction is liable to a fine of not more than $200.

Subsection (5) indicates that a person required to attend school refuses to attend or is habitually absent is guilty of an offence and on conviction is liable to the penalties under Part VI of the Provincial Offences Act.

Section 32 subsection (1) states that a person has the right, without payment of a fee, to attend a school in a school section in which the person is qualified to be a resident pupil.

Section 21 of the Education Act specifies that following the compulsory education policy every Ontario child between the ages of 6 and 18 shall go to school unless receiving equivalent learning elsewhere, or unless excused from attending school. Approximately 5 percent of Ontario school age children go to independent schools, private schools, or are home schooled.

While the vast majority, about 95 percent, of compulsory school age children go to publicly funded schools, there are four such school systems in the province. It is helpful for an educator in Ontario to know which of the four publicly funded school systems a child is qualified to go to: English public, English Roman Catholic separate, French public, and French Roman Catholic separate.

The first qualification to attend an elementary school is age: between 6 and 21. The second qualification is residence in the school section. Any person meeting the first and second qualifications whose parent or guardian is not a separate school or French school supporter when they pay property taxes is qualified to attend an English public school. Any person meeting the first and second qualifications whose parent or guardian is a Roman Catholic separate school supporter but not a French separate school supporter is qualified to attend an English separate school. Any French speaking person meeting the first and second qualifications whose parent or guardian is a French separate school supporter is qualified to attend a French separate school. Any French speaking person meeting the first and second qualifications whose parent or guardian is a French public-school supporter, or is not a supporter of any board, is qualified to attend a French public school (see Education Act section 33).

Section 34 subsection (1) stipulates that if a board operates a kindergarten in a school, a child who is otherwise qualified may become a resident pupil at age 5.

Section 35 prescribes that an elementary school student shall be admitted to the nearer school of the same type, where the appropriate supervisory officer for the nearer school certifies that there is sufficient accommodation for the pupil in that school, if the school the student should attend is certain distance away.

There is no age qualification listed in the Education Act for attending a secondary school. Where a pupil has been promoted from elementary school, or has not been promoted from elementary school but the principal of the secondary school is satisfied that the applicant is competent to undertake the work of the school, the pupil shall be admitted to a secondary school (see Education Act section 41). The main qualification to attend a secondary school is residence in the school section. In addition, the following are the qualifications that determine the type of school.

A person whose parent or guardian is not a separate school or French school supporter, or who is an English-language public board supporter, or who is not a supporter of any board and at least 18 years of age, is qualified to attend an English public school.

A person whose parent or guardian is an English separate school supporter, or who is an English separate school supporter, or who is not a supporter of any board and at least 18 years of age, is qualified to attend an English separate school.

A person whose parent or guardian is a French separate school supporter, or who is a French separate school supporter, or who is a French speaking person and a Catholic but not a supporter of any board and at least 18 years of age, is qualified to attend a French separate school.

A French speaking person whose parent or guardian is a French public-school supporter or is not a supporter of any board, or who is not a supporter of any board and at least 18 years of age, is qualified to attend a French public school. A French public-school supporter is also qualified (see Education Act section 36).

Section 49.1 stipulates that a person who is otherwise entitled to be admitted to a school and who is less than 18 years of age shall not be refused admission because the person or the person's parent or guardian is unlawfully in Canada.

Section 170 subsection (15) states that every board shall report to the Ministry at least once in each year the names and ages of all children of compulsory school age within its jurisdiction who are not enrolled in any school and the reasons therefore.

REFERENCES

California Legislative Information. (n.d.). *Education Code*. https://leginfo.legislature.ca.gov/faces/codesTOCSelected.xhtml?tocCode=EDC

Education Act. RSO 1990, c E.2. https://www.canlii.org/en/on/laws/stat/rso-1990-c-e2/latest/rso-1990-c- e2.html

The Chinese People's Congress. (2018). *The Chinese Compulsory Education Act* [中华人民共和国 义务教育法]. https://baike.baidu.com/item/中华人民共和国义务教育法/2342357

United Nations. (1989). *Convention on the Rights of the Child*. https://www.ohchr.org/en/professionalinterest/pages/crc.aspx

Chapter 2
Roles of Teachers

ABSTRACT

This chapter offers information concerning the roles of teachers in schools, who have the most important impact on students' learning. While mentioning the California Education Code and the Chinese Education Act, the chapter focuses on the Ontario Education Act. It provides the specific sections in the Ontario Education Act on the roles of teachers: What they shall do in schools, how they shall treat students, how they shall maintain order, how they shall conduct class, how they shall co-operate with each other, and how they shall behave in schools and in all school related activities. It lists the professional standards prescribed by the Ontario College of Teachers.

Teachers teach. In addition to teaching, contemporary teachers must also maintain order in the classroom and school and perform other duties assigned. California Education Code Title 2 Division 3 Part 25 Chapter 4 Article 1 section 44805 stipulates that every teacher in the public schools shall enforce the course of study, the use of legally authorized textbooks, and the rules and regulations prescribed for schools (California Legislative Information, n.d.). Section 44807 states that every teacher in the public schools shall hold pupils to a strict account for their conduct on the way to and from school, on the playgrounds, or during recess. The Chinese Education Act Part 4 section 33 simply stipulates that teachers enjoy their rights under the law, perform their duties according to the law, and shall be loyal to the educational cause of the people (the Chinese People's Congress, 2021).

DOI: 10.4018/978-1-6684-4163-3.ch002

The Ontario Education Act is more detailed in describing teachers' roles. The Education Act section 213 subsection (2) warns that every teacher who keeps a false school register or makes a false return is guilty of an offence and on conviction is liable to a fine of not more than $200.

Section 261 stipulates that the probationary period for teachers and designated early childhood educators when they first become employed by a district school board shall not exceed two years.

Section 262 states that no person shall be employed in an elementary or secondary school to teach or to perform any duty for which membership in the Ontario College of Teachers is required.

In terms of a teacher's contract, section 263 stipulates that when a teacher is employed by a board and a matter arises that in the opinion of the Minister adversely affects the welfare of the school where the teacher is employed, (a) the board or the teacher may, with the consent of the Minister, give the other party 30 days written notice of termination, and the teacher's employment is terminated at the expiration of 30 days from the date the notice is given; or (b) the board may, with the consent of the Minister, give the teacher written notice of immediate termination together with one-tenth of the teacher's yearly salary in addition to the amount to which the teacher would otherwise be entitled, and, on doing so, the teacher's employment is terminated.

Section 264 provides that a teacher and a temporary teacher's duty is to teach; encourage pupils to learn; inculcate respect for religion and the principles of Judaeo-Christian morality and the highest regard for truth, justice, loyalty, love of country, humanity, benevolence, sobriety, industry, frugality, purity, temperance and all other virtues; assist in developing co-operation and co-ordination of effort among the members of the staff of the school; maintain proper order and discipline in the classroom and in the school; conduct class in accordance with a timetable; participate in professional activity days; use only textbooks approved by the Minister in certain subjects and only textbooks approved by the board in all subjects; perform all duties assigned.

In addition to the Education Act, Regulation 298/1990 Operation of Schools made under the Act stipulates the duties of teachers. Section 14 subsection (3) states that a board may appoint for each organizational unit of an elementary or secondary school a teacher to direct and supervise such organizational unit.

Section 17 stipulates that a board may, in respect of one or more subjects or programs in the schools, appoint a teacher to supervise the subjects or programs, who shall hold specialist or honour specialist qualifications.

Section 19 presents that in assigning a teacher to teach in a division or to teach a subject, the principal shall have due regard for the provision of the best possible program and the safety and well-being of the pupils and that no teacher shall be assigned to teach except in accordance with the qualifications recorded on the certificate of qualification and registration.

Section 20 stipulates that a teacher shall:

a) be responsible for effective instruction, training and evaluation of the progress of pupils in the subjects assigned and for the management of the class, and report to the principal on the progress of pupils on request;
b) carry out the supervisory duties and instructional program assigned by the principal;
c) co-operate fully with other teachers and the principal in all matters related to the instruction of pupils;
d) be present in the classroom and ensure that the classroom is ready for the reception of pupils at least 15 minutes before the commencement of classes in the morning and 5 minutes before the commencement of classes in the afternoon;
e) assist the principal in maintaining close co-operation with the community;
f) prepare for use in the teacher's class such teaching plans as are required;
g) ensure that all reasonable safety procedures are carried out in courses and activities;
h) co-operate with the principal and other teachers to establish and maintain consistent disciplinary practices;
i) ensure that report cards are fully and properly completed and processed in;
j) co-operate and assist in the administration of tests under the Education Quality and Accountability Office Act 1996;
k) participate in regular meetings with pupils' parents (guardians);
l) perform duties as assigned by the principal in relation to co-operative placements of pupils; and
m) perform duties normally associated with the graduation of pupils.

Section 22.1 subsection (2) stipulates that a board may appoint an individual to a position in the board for up to one year if,

(a) the board is satisfied that the individual has a certificate granted by the teacher regulatory authority in the individual's jurisdiction that attests that the individual is qualified to practise the teaching occupation in an elementary or secondary school and is in good standing;

(b) the individual is employed as a teacher in a jurisdiction outside Ontario;
(c) the board has conducted a reference check of the individual with the individual's employer and is satisfied with the results;
(d) the board has collected a criminal background check of the individual; and
(e) the board has formally agreed to so appoint the individual in exchange for the individual's employer in the jurisdiction outside Ontario agreeing to appoint a teacher employed by the board to a teaching-related position in that other jurisdiction.

Education Act also stipulates that every district school board shall offer the new teacher induction program to each new teacher for the 12 months that follow the date on which the teacher first begins to teach for the board.

Section 268 subsection (2) states that a new teacher induction program shall contain the following elements:

1. An orientation for new teachers.
2. Mentoring for new teachers.
3. Professional development and training appropriate for new teachers.
4. Such other elements as are prescribed.

Section 269 subsection (1) provides that the principal assigned to the school to which a new teacher is assigned shall, as soon as possible, determine which elements of the new teacher induction program offered by the board are appropriate for that teacher to participate in and inform the teacher of that determination.

Subsection (2) stipulates that on determining with respect to a new teacher who was previously assigned to a different school, the principal shall consider,

(a) any elements of the new teacher induction program that the teacher participated in at the previous school; and
(b) the results of any performance appraisals conducted in respect of the teacher at the previous school.

Section 270 subsection (1) stipulates that every new teacher shall participate in the following elements of the new teacher induction program:

1. The elements that the principal has determined to be appropriate under section 269.

2. The elements in which the regulations require the teacher or a class to which the teacher belongs to participate.

Subsection (2) provides that a new teacher successfully completes the program when receiving two satisfactory ratings in performance appraisals no later than the end of the new teaching period. Subsection (3) stipulates that the principal shall take a teacher's participation in the new teacher induction program in accordance with subsection (1) into account when conducting a performance appraisal of a new teacher.

Every teacher in a publicly funded Ontario school must be a member of Ontario Teachers' Federation (see Teaching Profession Act [1990] subsection 4 [1]). Section 262 of the Education Act stipulates that no person shall be employed in a publicly funded elementary or secondary school to teach or to perform any duty for which membership in the Ontario College of Teachers is required.

The objects of the College, according to the Ontario College of Teachers Act 1996 section 3 subsection (1), are to regulate the profession of teaching and to govern its members; develop, establish and maintain qualifications for membership in the College; accredit professional teacher education programs offered by post-secondary educational institutions; accredit ongoing education programs for teachers offered by post-secondary educational institutions and other bodies; issue, renew, amend, suspend, cancel, revoke and reinstate certificates of qualification and registration; provide for the ongoing education of members of the College; establish and enforce professional standards and ethical standards applicable to members; receive and investigate complaints against members and to deal with discipline and fitness to practise issues; develop, provide and accredit educational programs leading to certificates of qualification additional to the certificate required for membership, including but not limited to certificates of qualification as a supervisory officer, and to issue, renew, amend, suspend, cancel, revoke and reinstate such additional certificates; communicate with the public on behalf of the members; and perform such additional functions as are prescribed by the regulations.

Subsection (2) stipulates that in carrying out its objects, the College has a duty to serve and protect the public interest.

To protect the public interest, according to section 4, the College Council shall be its governing body, which shall be composed of 23 persons who are members of the College and elected by the members and 14 persons who are appointed by the Lieutenant Governor in Council.

Section 13 stipulates that the College shall hold an annual meeting of the members not more than 15 months after the holding of the last preceding annual meeting of members.

Section 14 states that every person who holds a certificate of qualification and registration is a member of the College, subject to any term, condition, or limitation.

Section 15 subsection (1) states that the Council has 6 committees: Executive Committee, Investigation Committee, Discipline Committee, Registration Appeals Committee, and Fitness to Practise Committee.

Section 17 subsection (1) presents that a majority of the persons on these committees shall be persons elected to the Council.

Subsection (2) provides that the duties of a committee may be exercised by a panel satisfying certain rules:

Subsection (6) stipulates that a decision of a panel of a committee is deemed to be the decision of the committee.

Section 17.1 states that a Public Interest Committee is established. The Minister shall appoint no fewer than three and no more than five persons, who are not members of the College, to the Committee and shall designate one of those persons as the Chair of the Committee.

Section 23 presents that the Registrar shall maintain a register and any person has the right, during normal business hours, to inspect the register. The Registrar shall provide to any person, on payment of a reasonable charge, a copy of any part of the register.

The Investigation Committee shall, states section 26, consider and investigate complaints regarding the conduct or actions of a member of the College. After receiving the information, the Committee may: direct that the matter be referred, in whole or in part, to the Discipline Committee or the Fitness to Practise Committee; direct that the matter not be referred; require the person complained against to appear before the Investigation Committee to be cautioned or admonished; or take such action as it considers appropriate in the circumstances.

Section 29 stipulates that the Council or the Executive Committee may direct the Discipline Committee to hold a hearing and determine any allegation of professional misconduct or incompetence on the part of a member of the College. The Council or the Executive Committee may direct the Fitness to Practise Committee to hold a hearing and determine any allegation of incapacity on the part of a member of the College.

Section 30 states that the Discipline Committee shall hear and determine matters directed or referred to it and perform such other duties as are assigned to it by the Council. If the member has been found guilty of professional misconduct or incompetence, the Discipline Committee may make an order directing the Registrar to do one or more of the following: revoke any certificate held by the member; suspend any certificate held by the member for a stated period, not exceeding 24 months; impose specified terms, conditions or limitations on any certificate held by the member; direct that the imposition of a penalty be postponed for a specified period and not be imposed if specified terms are met within that period.

Section 31 stipulates that the Fitness to Practise Committee shall hear and determine matters directed or referred to it and perform such other duties as are assigned to it by the Council. If the Committee finds a member to be incapacitated, it may make an order directing the Registrar to do one or more of the following: revoke any certificate held by the member; suspend any certificate held by the member for a stated period, not exceeding 24 months; impose specified terms, conditions or limitations on any certificate held by the member; postpone the imposition of a penalty for a specified period and not be imposed if specified terms are met within that period. However, the Committee shall determine that an allegation of incapacity was unfounded to be published in the official publication of the College, on the request of the member against whom the allegation was made. In addition, if the Committee decides that the commencement of the proceeding was unwarranted, the Committee may order that the College reimburse the member for the costs as the Committee fixes.

Section 34 states that the Council or Executive Committee may make an order doing one or more of the following:

1. Directing the Registrar to issue a certificate to the member or former member.
2. Directing the Registrar to remove the suspension of the member's or former member's certificate.

Section 35 subsection (1) stipulates that a party to a proceeding before the Registration Appeals Committee, the Discipline Committee or the Fitness to Practise Committee may appeal to the Divisional Court from the decision of the committee.

Section 36 provides that where the Registrar believes on reasonable and probable grounds that a member has committed an act of professional misconduct or is incompetent or incapacitated, that there is cause to refuse to issue a certificate, that there is cause to suspend or revoke a certificate, or that there is cause to impose terms, conditions or limitations on a certificate, the Registrar may appoint one or more investigators to investigate whether such act has occurred, such incompetence or incapacity exists or there is such cause.

Section 37 presents that a justice of the peace may, on the application of an investigator, issue a warrant authorizing the investigator to enter and search a place and examine anything relevant to the investigation if the justice is satisfied that the investigator has been properly appointed and that there are reasonable and probable grounds for believing that the member investigated has committed an act of professional misconduct or is incompetent or incapacitated and there is something relevant to the investigation at the place. The search shall be conducted by day. An investigator entering and searching a place under the authority of a warrant shall produce identification, on request, to any person at the place. The investigator may be assisted by other persons and may enter a place by force.

Section 43.2 stipulates that an employer of a member who terminates the member's employment or imposes restrictions on the member's duties for reasons of professional misconduct shall file with the Registrar within 30 days after the termination or restriction a written report setting out the reasons. If an employer of a member intended to terminate the member's employment or to impose restrictions on the member's duties for reasons of professional misconduct but the employer did not do so because the member resigned, the employer shall file with the Registrar within 30 days after the resignation a written report setting out the reasons on which the employer had intended to act. If a member resigns while the employer is engaged in an investigation into allegations of an act or omission by the member that would, if proven, have caused the employer to terminate the member's employment or to impose restrictions on the member's duties for reasons of professional misconduct, the employer shall file with the Registrar within 30 days after the resignation a written report stating the nature of the allegations being investigated.

Section 43.3 presents that an employer shall promptly report to the College in writing when the employer becomes aware that a member employed has been charged with or convicted of an offence under the Criminal Code (Canada) involving sexual conduct and minors, or an offence indicating that students may be at risk of harm or injury, or the member has engaged in conduct that should be reviewed by a committee of the College. However, an employer who makes a report respecting a charge or conviction shall promptly report to the College in writing if the employer becomes aware that the charge was withdrawn, the member was discharged following a preliminary inquiry, the charge was stayed, or the member was acquitted.

There are 19 regulations made under the Ontario College of Teachers Act 1996. One of these regulations is Teachers' Qualifications, Ontario Regulation 176/2010, which prescribes classes of certificates of qualification and registration. Another one, Ontario Regulation 437/1997 Professional Misconduct, in its section 1, defines the following acts as professional misconduct:

1. Providing false information or documents to the College or any other person with respect to the member's professional qualifications.
2. Inappropriately using a term, title or designation indicating a specialization in the profession which is not specified on the member's certificate of qualification and registration.
3. Permitting, counselling or assisting any person who is not a member to represent the person as a member of the College.
4. Using a name other than the member's name, as set out in the register, in the course of the member's professional duties.
5. Failing to maintain the standards of the profession.
6. Releasing or disclosing information about a student to a person other than the student or, if the student is a minor, the student's parent (guardian). The release or disclosure of information is not an act of professional misconduct if,
    i. the student (or if the student is a minor, the student's parent (guardian)) consents to the release or disclosure, or
    ii. if the release or disclosure is required or allowed by law.
7. Abusing a student verbally, physically, psychologically, emotionally, or sexually.
8. Practising or purporting to practise the profession while under the influence of any substance or while adversely affected by any dysfunction,
    i. which the member knows or ought to know impairs the member's ability to practise, and
    ii. in respect of which treatment has previously been recommended, ordered or prescribed but the member has failed to follow the treatment.
9. Contravening a term, condition or limitation imposed on the member's certificate of qualification and registration.
10. Failing to keep records as required by the professional duties.
11. Failing to supervise adequately a person who is under the professional supervision of the member.

12. Signing or issuing, in the member's professional capacity, a document that the member knows or ought to know contains a false, improper or misleading statement.
13. Falsifying a record relating to the member's professional responsibilities.
14. Failing to comply with the Act or the regulations or the by-laws.
15. Failing to comply with the Education Act or the regulations made under that Act.
16. Contravening a law if the contravention is relevant to the member's suitability to hold a certificate of qualification and registration.
17. Contravening a law if the contravention has caused or may cause a student who is under the member's professional supervision to be put at or to remain at risk.
18. An act or omission that would reasonably be regarded by members as disgraceful, dishonourable or unprofessional.
19. Conduct unbecoming a member.
20. Failing to appear before a panel of the Investigation Committee to be cautioned or admonished, if required to appear.
21. Failing to comply with an order of a panel of the Discipline Committee or an order of a panel of the Fitness to Practise Committee.
22. Failing to co-operate in a College investigation.
23. Failing to take reasonable steps to ensure that the requested information is provided in a complete and accurate manner if required.
24. Failing to abide by a written undertaking given by the member or by an agreement entered into by the member.
25. Failing to respond adequately or within a reasonable time to a written inquiry from the College.
26. Practising the profession in a conflict of interest.
27. Failing to comply with the duties under the Child and Family Services Act.

In addition, Ontario College of Teachers (2018) in its bylaws section 32 prescribes professional and ethical standards applicable to members.

PROFESSIONAL STANDARDS

Commitment to Students and Student Learning

Members are dedicated in their care and commitment to students. They treat students equitably and with respect and are sensitive to factors that influence individual student learning. Members facilitate the development of students as contributing citizens of Canadian society.

Professional Knowledge

Members strive to be current in their professional knowledge and recognize its relationship to practice. They understand and reflect on student development, learning theory, pedagogy, curriculum, ethics, educational research and related policies and legislation to inform professional judgment in practice.

Professional Practice

Members apply professional knowledge and experience to promote student learning. They use appropriate pedagogy, assessment and evaluation, resources and technology in planning for and responding to the needs of individual students and learning communities. Members refine their professional practice through ongoing inquiry, dialogue and reflection.

Leadership in Learning Communities

Members promote and participate in the creation of collaborative, safe and supportive learning communities. They recognize their shared responsibilities and their leadership roles in order to facilitate student success. Members maintain and uphold the principles of the ethical standards in these learning communities.

Ongoing Professional Learning

Members recognize that a commitment to ongoing professional learning is integral to effective practice and to student learning. Professional practice and self-directed learning are informed by experience, research, collaboration and knowledge.

ETHICAL STANDARDS

Care

The ethical standard of Care includes compassion, acceptance, interest and insight for developing students' potential. Members express their commitment to students' wellbeing and learning through positive influence, professional judgment and empathy in practice.

Respect

Intrinsic to the ethical standard of Respect are trust and fair-mindedness. Members honour human dignity, emotional wellness and cognitive development. In their professional practice, they model respect for spiritual and cultural values, social justice, confidentiality, freedom, democracy and the environment.

Trust

The ethical standard of Trust embodies fairness, openness and honesty. Members' professional relationships with students, colleagues, parents, guardians and the public are based on trust.

Integrity

Honesty, reliability and moral action are embodied in the ethical standard of Integrity. Continual reflection assists members in exercising integrity in their professional commitments and responsibilities.

In addition to the Education Act and the College of Teachers Act, teachers must abide by the Child, Youth and Family Services Act to report to a children's aid society (CAS) when they have reasonable grounds to suspect that a child has suffered harm or there is a risk that a child is likely to suffer harm. The Child, Youth and Family Services Act section 125 subsection (1) stipulates that if a person, including a person who performs professional duties with respect to children, has reasonable grounds to suspect one of the following, the person shall immediately report the suspicion and the information on which it is based to a society:

1. The child has suffered physical harm inflicted by the person having charge of the child or caused by or resulting from that person's,
    i. failure to adequately care for, provide for, supervise or protect the child, or
    ii. pattern of neglect in caring for, providing for, supervising or protecting the child.

2. There is a risk that the child is likely to suffer physical harm inflicted by the person having charge of the child or caused by or resulting from that person's,
   i. failure to adequately care for, provide for, supervise or protect the child, or
   ii. pattern of neglect in caring for, providing for, supervising or protecting the child.
3. The child has been sexually abused or sexually exploited by the person having charge of the child or by another person where the person having charge of the child knows or should know of the possibility of sexual abuse or sexual exploitation and fails to protect the child.
4. There is a risk that the child is likely to be sexually abused or sexually exploited.
5. The child requires treatment to cure, prevent or alleviate physical harm or suffering and the child's parent or the person having charge of the child does not provide the treatment or access to the treatment, or, where the child is incapable of consenting to the treatment, refuses or is unavailable or unable to consent to, the treatment on the child's behalf.
6. The child has suffered emotional harm, demonstrated by serious,
   i. anxiety,
   ii. depression,
   iii. withdrawal,
   iv. self-destructive or aggressive behaviour, or
   v. delayed development,

and there are reasonable grounds to believe that the emotional harm suffered by the child results from the actions, failure to act or pattern of neglect on the part of the child's parent or the person having charge of the child.

7. The child has suffered emotional harm and the child's parent or the person having charge of the child does not provide services or treatment or access to services or treatment, or, where the child is incapable of consenting to treatment, refuses or is unavailable or unable to consent to, treatment to remedy or alleviate the harm.
8. There is a risk that the child is likely to suffer emotional harm resulting from the actions, failure to act or pattern of neglect on the part of the child's parent or the person having charge of the child.
9. There is a risk that the child is likely to suffer emotional harm and the child's parent or the person having charge of the child does not provide services or treatment or access to services or treatment, or, where the

child is incapable of consenting to treatment, refuses or is unavailable or unable to consent to, treatment to prevent the harm.

10. The child suffers from a mental, emotional or developmental condition that, if not remedied, could seriously impair the child's development and the child's parent or the person having charge of the child does not provide the treatment or access to the treatment, or where the child is incapable of consenting to the treatment, refuses or is unavailable or unable to consent to, treatment to remedy or alleviate the condition.
11. The child's parent has died or is unavailable to exercise custodial rights over the child and has not made adequate provision for the child's care and custody, or the child is in a residential placement and the parent refuses or is unable or unwilling to resume the child's care and custody.
12. The child is younger than 12 and has killed or seriously injured another person or caused serious damage to another person's property, services or treatment are necessary to prevent a recurrence and the child's parent or the person having charge of the child does not provide services or treatment or access to services or treatment, or, where the child is incapable of consenting to treatment, refuses or is unavailable or unable to consent to treatment.
13. The child is younger than 12 and has on more than one occasion injured another person or caused loss or damage to another person's property, with the encouragement of the person having charge of the child or because of that person's failure or inability to supervise the child adequately.

Subsection (2) states that a person who has additional reasonable grounds to suspect one of the matters set out in subsection (1) shall make a further report under subsection (1) even if the person has made previous reports with respect to the same child.

Subsections (5) and (6) stipulate that every person who performs professional or official duties with respect to children including a teacher, an early childhood educator, principal, social worker, family counsellor, youth and recreation worker, and operator or employee of a child care centre or home child care agency or provider of licensed child care, is guilty of an offence if the person contravenes subsection (1) or (2) by not reporting a suspicion and the information on which it was based was obtained in the course of professional or official duties, but a volunteer is excluded.

Subsection (9) states that on conviction of the offence the person is liable to a fine of not more than $5,000. Subsection (10) provides that this section applies although the information reported may be confidential or privileged, and no action for making the report shall be instituted against a person acting in accordance with this section unless the person acts maliciously or without reasonable grounds for the suspicion.

The principal and two vice-principals at C.W. Jefferys Collegiate Institute in Toronto District School Board were charged under Ontario's Child and Family Services Act with failing to report an alleged sexual assault on a student (Appleby, 2008). Although the principal and vice-principals were eventually acquitted, the case can be considered as a warning to educators as what can happen when they do not report when a child is harmed or allegedly harmed.

According to the Ontario College of Teachers (2019), anyone with a concern about a College of Teachers' member can take the steps provided by the College to go through the complaint process. The following are the steps one can take when there is a concern.

Talk to the teacher or principal to see if the issue can be dealt with at the school level. If further assistance is needed, call the College's Investigations and Hearings Department. The number is: 416-961-8800 if in Toronto, otherwise: 1-888-534-2222.

If the College can't help to resolve the issue, a formal complaint can be filed with the College's intake staff online or by mail. Complaints are screened to ensure they are neither frivolous nor an abuse of process. Anonymous complaints will not be investigated.

Complaints may be filed via letter, recording, or video and sent to:

Registrar of the College
101 Bloor Street West, Toronto
ON M5S 0A1

To file a complaint, one must include one's name, address, phone number, nature of the complaint, name of the teacher, and any other supporting evidence for consideration. If assistance is needed, call: 416-961-8800 if in Toronto, otherwise: 1-888-534-2222.

Accused members will be informed of the complaint and given 60 days to respond. Their response will be shared with the complainant.

If applicable, complaints may be settled through the College's voluntary Complaint Resolution program without an extensive investigation or hearing.

If the complaint cannot be resolved through Complaint Resolution, an investigation will be conducted, including interviews with those involved. The complainant or member can provide relevant information.

All teachers are appraised regularly. Education Act section 277 concerns teacher performance appraisals. Section 277.28 stipulates that performance appraisals of teachers, other than new teachers, shall be conducted in accordance with Ontario Regulation 99/02.

Section 277.29 subsection (1) states that every board shall ensure that each new teacher is scheduled for two performance appraisals in the first 12-month period following the teacher's beginning to teach.

Subsection (3) provides that the performance appraisals shall be conducted by the principal of the school to which the new teacher is assigned.

Subsection (5) presents that the principal shall give the teacher written notice of the rating determined for each performance appraisal.

Section 277.36 subsection (1) stipulates that when a principal conducting a performance appraisal of a teacher determines that the rating is unsatisfactory. Within 15 school days of the determination, the principal shall give the teacher written notice of the unsatisfactory rating and explain the reasons for the unsatisfactory rating to the teacher.

Subsection (3) states that within 60 school days of giving the notice of the unsatisfactory rating, the principal shall conduct a second performance appraisal.

Section 277.37 provides that when a teacher has received two consecutive unsatisfactory ratings, the principal shall give the teacher written notice of the unsatisfactory rating, place the teacher on review status and advise the teacher in writing of the review status.

If, at any time during the 120 school days starting with the day on which the teacher is advised of the review status, the principal and supervisory officer jointly determine that the delay necessitated by conducting a performance appraisal is inconsistent with the protection of the best interests of pupils, they shall promptly transmit a joint recommendation in writing to the board that the teacher's employment with the board should be terminated.

If the third performance appraisal results in an unsatisfactory rating, the principal shall promptly transmit a recommendation in writing to the board that the teacher's employment with the board should be terminated. Pending the board's decision of whether to terminate the teacher's employment, the director of education for the board shall suspend the teacher with pay or reassign the teacher to duties that are appropriate in the circumstances.

Section 277.39 stipulates that a board receiving a recommendation to terminate a teacher's employment shall determine whether the teacher is performing satisfactorily immediately before any action of the director of education. If the board determines that the teacher is not performing satisfactorily in the position, the board shall terminate the teacher's employment. If the board does not make the determination of unsatisfactory performance, the suspension or reassignment shall cease and, except where the teacher and the board agree otherwise, the teacher shall resume his or her former position.

Section 277.40 provides that when a board terminates a teacher's employment, the secretary of the board shall promptly file a complaint under the Ontario College of Teachers Act, regarding the reasons for the termination and that when a teacher employed by a board resigns while on review status, the secretary of the board shall promptly file a complaint under the Ontario College of Teachers Act, regarding the reasons for the teacher having been placed on review status.

Section 277.40.1 presents that when a principal conducting an appraisal of a new teacher determines that the first rating is not satisfactory the principal shall give the teacher written notice of the not satisfactory rating and explain the reasons for the rating, determine which elements of the new teacher induction program are appropriate for the teacher to participate in to improve performance, and develop an enrichment plan based on participation in those elements.

Section 277.40.2 states that when a principal determines that the second appraisal rating is not satisfactory the principal shall give the teacher written notice of the rating, explain the reasons for the not satisfactory rating, place the teacher on review status, and advise the teacher in writing of that fact.

Section 277.40.3 stipulates that throughout the review period the principal shall monitor the teacher's performance and provide such feedback and recommendations to the teacher as might help the teacher improve the performance. After a new teacher is advised of the review status, the principal shall conduct a third performance appraisal, which shall occur within 120 school days of the day on which the teacher is advised of the review status. In the case of a teacher on review status as a result of a not satisfactory rating in the third performance appraisal, the principal shall conduct a fourth appraisal during the 120 school days following the teacher's third performance appraisal but no later than the end of the second 12-month period following the teacher's beginning to teach. If the principal determines that the rating is not unsatisfactory, the teacher immediately ceases to be on review status and the principal shall advise the teacher in writing of that fact.

Section 277.40.3 further states that if the principal and supervisory officer jointly determine that the delay necessitated by conducting a performance appraisal is inconsistent with the protection of the best interests of pupils, they shall refrain from conducting the appraisal and shall promptly submit a joint recommendation in writing to the board that the teacher's employment with the board should be terminated. The principal shall promptly provide the teacher with a copy of the recommendation and a copy of the written reasons. The director of education for the board shall suspend the teacher with pay, pending the board's decision whether to terminate the teacher's employment.

Section 277.40.4 provides that a board receiving a recommendation to terminate a new teacher's employment shall determine whether the teacher is performing satisfactorily before any action of a director of education. The determination of the board shall be by majority vote of the members of the board present at a meeting, within 60 days of receiving the recommendation. When the board determines that the teacher is not performing satisfactorily, the board shall terminate the teacher's employment. When the board does not make the determination of the teacher's not performing satisfactorily the teacher shall resume his or her former position.

Education Act section 264 stipulates that one of the duties of a teacher is to maintain, under the direction of the principal, proper order, and discipline in the teacher's classroom and while on duty in the school and on the school ground. Section 300.4 subsection (1) prescribes that school board employees shall respond upon observing a pupil behaving in a way that is likely to have a negative impact on the school climate.

In maintaining order in classroom and school, a teacher may get into a conflict with a student. There have been cases where teachers are accused of assaulting students when teachers must deal with students who are disruptive in classroom or behave inappropriately in school. Teachers should avoid physically contacting students if possible. However, in situations where corrective force is necessary, teachers need to know that they can defend themselves by referring to section 43 of the federal statute, the Criminal Code (1985), which states that a schoolteacher is justified in using force by way of correction toward a pupil, who is under his care, if the force does not exceed what is reasonable under the circumstances.

While using force by way of correction if the force does not exceed what is reasonable can be justified, corporal punishment is unacceptable. One way of judging whether a teacher's corrective conduct is reasonable is to see if the act results in harm or the prospect of harm (Brown, 2009). Without harm or prospect of harm, another way of judging whether a teacher's corrective conduct is reasonable is to see if the teacher acts like a kind, firm, and judicious parent (see Regulation 298/1990 Operation of Schools subsection 23 [1] item [c]).

In case a teacher is sued for assault in respect of disciplinary action taken in the course of duty, the teacher may request that the employing district school board pay the cost of legal proceeding by referring to section 171 of the Education Act, which stipulates that a board may pay the costs, or any part thereof, incurred by any member of the board or by any teacher of the board in successfully defending any legal proceeding brought against him or her for libel or slander in respect of any statements relating to the employment, suspension or dismissal of any person by the board published at a meeting of the board or of a committee thereof, or for assault in respect of disciplinary action taken in the course of duty.

REFERENCES

Appleby, T. (2008, January 8). C.W. Jefferys staff charged with failing to report alleged assault. *The Globe and Mail*. https://www.theglobeandmail.com/news/national/cw-jefferys-staff-charged-w with-failing-to-report-alleged-assault/article666251/

Brown, A. (2009). *Legal Handbook for Educators* (6th ed.). Carswell.

California Legislative Information. (n.d.). *Education Code*. https://leginfo.legislature.ca.gov/faces/codesTOCSelected.xhtml?tocCode=EDC

Criminal CodeR. S. C. 1985, c C-46. https://www.canlii.org/en/ca/laws/stat/rsc-1985-c-c-46/latest/rsc- 1985-c-c-46.html

Education Act. RSO 1990, c E.2. https://www.canlii.org/en/on/laws/stat/rso-1990-c-e2/latest/rso-1990-c- e2.html

Ontario College of Teachers. (2018). *Ontario College of Teachers Bylaws*. https://www.oct.ca/about-the- college/what-we-do/legislation-regulations-and-bylaws/college-bylaws

Ontario College of Teachers. (2019). *Complaint Process*. https://www.oct.ca/public/complaints-and- discipline/complaints-process

Operation Of Schools - General. RRO 1990, Reg 298. https://www.canlii.org/en/on/laws/regu/rro-1990- reg-298/latest/rro-1990-reg-298.html

The Chinese People's Congress. (2021). *The Chinese Education Act* [中华人民共和国教育法]. http://www.moe.gov.cn/jyb_xxgk/xxgk_jyfl/flfg_jyfl/202107/t20210730_547843.html

Chapter 3 Discipline and Safety

ABSTRACT

To have a positive learning environment, schools must be safe, and students must be well-disciplined. One important task of teachers and administrators is to maintain order and discipline in schools and in school-related activities. This chapter presents the information on discipline and student safety in the California Education Code and the Chinese Education Act. Again, it focuses on the Ontario Education Act and related statutes and regulations. The chapter contains sections from the Ontario Education Act concerning consequences for inappropriate student behaviour. It also has information respecting rules administrators and teachers shall follow when they discipline students who have engaged in inappropriate activities.

Pupils are expected to comply with educational regulations. California Education Code Title 2 Division 4 Part 27 Chapter 6 section 48908 presents that all pupils shall comply with the regulations, pursue the required course of study, and submit to the authority of their teachers. The Chinese Education Act uses the expression of education receivers for all students in the Chinese education system. Chapter 5 section 44 of the Act indicates that education receivers shall comply with laws and regulations, follow the student code of conduct, respect teachers and parents, form moral behavior, study diligently, and complete prescribed learning tasks.

Part I section 11 subsection (27) of the Ontario Education Act states that the Ministry of Education may make regulations prescribing the duties of

DOI: 10.4018/978-1-6684-4163-3.ch003

pupils. Regulation 298/1990 Operation of Schools stipulates requirements for pupils.

Section 23 subsection (1) of the Regulation states that a pupil shall,

(a) be diligent in attempting to master such studies as are part of the program in which the pupil is enrolled;
(b) exercise self-discipline;
(c) accept such discipline as would be exercised by a kind, firm and judicious parent;
(d) attend classes punctually and regularly;
(e) be courteous to fellow pupils and obedient and courteous to teachers;
(f) be clean in person and habits;
(g) take such tests and examinations as are required by or under the Act or as may be directed by the Minister; and
(h) show respect for school property.

Subsection (2) stipulates that when a pupil returns to school after an absence, a parent of the pupil shall give the reason for the absence orally or in writing as the principal requires.

Subsection (3) indicates that a pupil may be excused by the principal from attendance at school temporarily at any time at the written request of a parent of the pupil. Subsection (4) stipulates that every pupil is responsible for his or her conduct to the principal of the school on the school premises, on out-of-school activities that are part of the school program, and while travelling on a school bus owned by a board or on a bus or school bus under contract to a board.

Although Regulation 298 has these requirements, there are pupils who do not meet these requirements. Education Act section 264 subsection (1) clause (e) stipulates that one of teachers' duties is to maintain, under the direction of the principal, proper order, and discipline in the teacher's classroom and while on duty in the school and on the school ground.

Regulation 298 also prescribes duties of teachers respecting discipline.

Section 20 clause (h) states that a teacher shall co-operate with the principal and other teachers to establish and maintain consistent disciplinary practices in the school. A teacher is also expected to maintain disciplinary practices during out-of-school activities that are part of the school program. For some teachers, particularly new teachers, student discipline is a challenge, but establishing and maintaining discipline in school is one important duty of teachers.

Subsection 23 (1) requires that a pupil shall exercise self-discipline, accept such discipline as would be exercised by a kind, firm, and judicious parent, be courteous to fellow pupils and obedient and courteous to teachers, and show respect for school property. However, there are students who are disruptive in class and on school premises, when teachers must consider disciplinary practices.

In the 1990s there was a perception that school discipline problems were worsening. This perception resulted in the passing of Bill 81, Safe Schools Act 2000 in the Legislative Assembly of Ontario. In the following years, the implementation of Bill 81 caused a controversy that students with special needs and racialized students were punished disproportionately, particularly where Bill 81 amended the Education Act to make certain disciplinary practices mandatory for some behaviours. The discussion that followed the controversy of disproportionately punishing certain student groups, accompanied by a change of the political party in power from the Progressive Conservatives to the Liberals, led to the introduction of Bill 212, Education Amendment Act (Progressive Discipline and School Safety) 2007, which modified the Education Act to stipulate that educators shall follow progressive disciplinary practices in considering disciplining students. Following progressive discipline practices, educators shall consider mitigating and other factors. Later, Bill 157, Education Amendment Act (Keeping Our Kids Safe at School) 2009 amended the Education Act again to make disciplinary practices more prescriptive with details stipulated in the Education Act.

Education Act Part XIII section 300.0.1 indicates that the purpose of the Part is:

1. To create schools in Ontario that are safe, inclusive, and accepting of all pupils.
2. To encourage a positive school climate and prevent inappropriate behaviour, including bullying, sexual assault, gender-based violence and incidents based on homophobia, transphobia or biphobia.
3. To address inappropriate pupil behaviour and promote early intervention.
4. To provide support to pupils who are impacted by inappropriate behaviour of other pupils.
5. To establish disciplinary approaches that promote positive behaviour and use measures that include appropriate consequences and supports for pupils to address inappropriate behaviour.

6. To provide pupils with a safe learning environment.

Section 300.2 provides that an employee of a board who becomes aware that a pupil of a school of the board may have engaged in an activity described in subsection 306 (1) or 310 (1) shall report to the principal of the school about the matter as soon as reasonably possible and a principal shall investigate any matter reported. The principal shall communicate the results of the investigation to the reporter after the investigation.

Section 300.3 presents that if the principal of a school believes that a pupil of the school has been harmed because of an activity described in subsection 306 (1) or 310 (1), the principal shall, as soon as reasonably possible, notify the parent or guardian of the pupil harmed and the parent or guardian of any pupil of the school who has engaged in the activity resulting in the harm. However, the principal shall not, without the pupil's consent, notify a parent or guardian of a pupil who is 18 years or older, or 16 or 17 years old and has withdrawn from parental control. The principal shall not notify a parent or guardian of a pupil if doing so would put the pupil at risk of harm from a parent or guardian, such that the notification is not in the pupil's best interests. When notifying a parent or guardian, the principal shall invite the parent or guardian to have a discussion with the principal about the supports that will be provided for his or her child.

To ensure all members of the school community are treated with respect and dignity, to promote responsible citizenship by encouraging appropriate participation in the civic life of the school community, and to maintain an environment where conflict and difference can be addressed in a manner characterized by respect and civility, there is a provincial code of conduct for the education sector. The code is a policy of the Minister of Education.

Education Act section 306 subsection (1) stipulates that a principal shall consider whether to suspend a pupil if the pupil has engaged in any of the following activities while at school, at a school-related activity or in other circumstances where engaging in the activity will have an impact on the school climate:

1. Uttering a threat to inflict serious bodily harm on another person.
2. Possessing alcohol or illegal drugs.
3. Being under the influence of alcohol.
4. Swearing at a teacher or at another person in a position of authority.

5. Committing an act of vandalism that causes extensive damage to school property at the pupil's school or to property located on the premises of the pupil's school.
6. Bullying.
7. Any other activity that is an activity for which a principal may suspend a pupil under a policy of the board.

However, subsection (2) states that a principal shall consider any mitigating and other factors in considering whether to suspend a pupil for engaging in any activity described above.

Subsection (3) provides that if a principal decides to suspend a pupil, the principal shall suspend the pupil from the school and from engaging in all school related activities.

Subsection (4) presents that such a suspension shall be for no less than one school day and no more than 20 school days and, in considering how long the suspension should be, a principal shall consider any mitigating and other factors prescribed by the regulations.

Subsection (5) indicates that when a principal suspends a pupil, the principal shall assign the pupil to a program for suspended pupils in accordance with any policies issued by the Minister.

Section 308 subsection (1) stipulates that a principal suspending a pupil shall inform the pupil's teacher of the suspension and make all reasonable efforts to inform the pupil's parent or guardian of the suspension within 24 hours of the suspension being imposed, unless,

(i) the pupil is at least 18 years old, or
(ii) the pupil is 16 or 17 years old and has withdrawn from parental control.

Subsection (2) states that a principal suspending a pupil shall ensure that written notice of the suspension is given promptly to the following persons:

1. The pupil.
2. The pupil's parent or guardian, unless,
    i. the pupil is at least 18 years old, or
    ii. the pupil is 16 or 17 years old and has withdrawn from parental control.
3. Such other persons as may be specified by board policy.

Subsection (3) provides that the notice must include the following:

1. The reason for the suspension.
2. The duration of the suspension.
3. Information about any program for suspended pupils to which the pupil is assigned.
4. Information about the right to appeal the suspension under section 309, including,
   i. a copy of the board policies and guidelines governing the appeal established by the board and
   ii. the name and contact information of the supervisory officer to whom notice of the appeal must be given under subsection 309 (2).

Section 309 subsection (1) stipulates that the following persons may appeal, to the board, a principal's decision to suspend a pupil:

1. The pupil's parent or guardian, unless,
   i. the pupil is at least 18 years old, or
   ii. the pupil is 16 or 17 years old and has withdrawn from parental control.
2. The pupil, if,
   i. the pupil is at least 18 years old, or
   ii. the pupil is 16 or 17 years old and has withdrawn from parental control.
3. Such other persons as may be specified by board policy.

Subsection (2) states that every board shall designate a supervisory officer for the purposes of receiving notices of intention to appeal a suspension.

Subsection (3) prescribes that a person who entitled to appeal a suspension must give written notice of the intention to appeal to the supervisory officer designated by the board within 10 school days of the commencement of the suspension. The supervisory officer may extend the deadline if the person requests an extension to accommodate a disability.

Subsection (4) indicates that after receiving a notice of intention to appeal, the board shall promptly contact every person entitled to appeal the suspension and inform him or her that it has received the notice of intention to appeal.

Subsection (5) presents that a person given notice of intention to appeal may contact the supervisory officer to discuss any matter respecting the appeal of the suspension and the supervisory officer has the powers and duties set out in board policy.

Subsection (6) provides that the board shall hear and determine the appeal within 15 school days of receiving notice, unless the parties agree on a later deadline, and shall not refuse to deal with the appeal on the ground that there is a deficiency in the notice of appeal.

Subsection (8) indicates that the parties to the appeal are:

1. The principal who suspended the pupil.
2. The pupil, if,
   i. the pupil is at least 18 years old, or
   ii. the pupil is 16 or 17 years old and has withdrawn from parental control.
3. The pupil's parent or guardian, if the pupil's parent or guardian appealed the decision to suspend the pupil.
4. The person who appealed the decision to suspend the pupil, if the decision was appealed by a person other than the pupil or the pupil's parent or guardian.
5. Such other persons as may be specified by board policy.

However, subsection (9) stipulates that a pupil who is not a party to the appeal under subsection (8) has the right to be present at the appeal and to make a statement on his or her own behalf.

Subsection (10) states that the board shall,

(a) confirm the suspension and the duration of the suspension;
(b) confirm the suspension, but shorten its duration, even if the suspension under appeal has already been served, and order that the record of the suspension be amended accordingly; or
(c) quash the suspension and order that the record of the suspension be expunged, even if the suspension under appeal has already been served.

Subsection (11) prescribes that the decision of the board on an appeal under this section is final.

Section 310 subsection (1) indicates that a principal shall suspend a pupil if the pupil has engaged in any of the following activities while at school, at a school-related activity or in other circumstances, where engaging in the activity will have an impact on the school climate:

1. Possessing a weapon, including possessing a firearm.
2. Using a weapon to cause or to threaten bodily harm to another person.
3. Committing physical assault on another person that causes bodily harm requiring treatment by a medical practitioner.
4. Committing sexual assault.

5. Trafficking in weapons or in illegal drugs.
6. Committing robbery.
7. Giving alcohol to a minor.
   7.1 Bullying, if,
      i. the pupil has previously been suspended for engaging in bullying, and
      ii. the pupil's continuing presence in the school creates an unacceptable risk to the safety of another person.
   7.2 Any activity listed in subsection 306 (1) that is motivated by bias, prejudice or hate based on race, national or ethnic origin, language, colour, religion, sex, age, mental or physical disability, sexual orientation, gender identity, gender expression, or any other similar factor.
8. Any other activity that is an activity for which a principal must suspend a pupil and investigate to determine whether to recommend to the board that the pupil be expelled.

Subsection (2) stipulates that a pupil suspended is suspended from his or her school and from engaging in all school-related activities.

Subsection (3) states that a principal may suspend a pupil for up to 20 school days and, in considering how long the suspension should be, the principal shall consider any mitigating and other factors.

Subsection (4) provides that when a principal suspends a pupil, the principal shall assign the pupil to a program for suspended pupils in accordance with any policies issued by the Minister.

Section 311 subsection (1) presents that a principal suspending a pupil shall,

(a) inform the pupil's teacher of the suspension; and
(b) make all reasonable efforts to inform the pupil's parent or guardian of the suspension within 24 hours of the suspension being imposed, unless,
   (i) the pupil is at least 18 years old, or
   (ii) the pupil is 16 or 17 years old and has withdrawn from parental control.

Subsection (2) prescribes that a principal suspending a pupil shall ensure that written notice of the suspension is given promptly to the following persons:

1. The pupil.
2. The pupil's parent or guardian, unless,
   i. the pupil is at least 18 years old, or
   ii. the pupil is 16 or 17 years old and has withdrawn from parental control.

3. Such other persons as may be specified by board policy.

Subsection (3) indicates that the notice must include the following:

1. The reason for the suspension.
2. The duration of the suspension.
3. Information about any program for suspended pupils to which the pupil is assigned.
4. Information about the investigation the principal will conduct to determine whether to recommend that the pupil be expelled.
5. A statement indicating that,
   i. there is no immediate right to appeal the suspension,
   ii. if the principal does not recommend to the board that the pupil be expelled following the investigation, the suspension will become subject to appeal, and
   iii. if there is an expulsion hearing because the principal recommends to the board that the pupil be expelled, the suspension may be addressed by parties at the hearing.

Section 311.1 subsection (1) stipulates that when a pupil is suspended, the principal shall investigate to determine whether to recommend to the board that the pupil be expelled.

Subsection (2) states that the principal's investigation shall begin promptly following the suspension and shall be conducted in accordance with the requirements established by board policy and the principal has the powers and duties set out in the policy.

Subsection (3) presents that as part of the investigation, the principal shall make all reasonable efforts to speak with the following persons:

1. The pupil.
2. The pupil's parent or guardian, unless,
   i. the pupil is at least 18 years old, or
   ii. the pupil is 16 or 17 years old and has withdrawn from parental control.
3. Any other person whom the principal has reason to believe may have relevant information.

Subsection (4) provides that in considering whether to recommend to the board that the pupil be expelled, a principal shall consider any mitigating and other factors prescribed by the regulations.

Subsection (5) indicates that if the principal decides not to recommend to the board that the pupil be expelled, the principal shall,

(a) confirm the suspension and the duration of the suspension;
(b) confirm the suspension but shorten its duration, even if the suspension has already been served, and amend the record of the suspension accordingly; or
(c) withdraw the suspension and expunge the record of the suspension, even if the suspension has already been served.

Subsection (6) prescribes that if the principal does not recommend to the board that the pupil be expelled, the principal shall ensure that written notice containing the following information is given promptly to every person to whom he or she was required to give notice of the suspension:

1. A statement that the pupil will not be subject to an expulsion hearing for the activity that resulted in the suspension.
2. A statement indicating whether the principal has confirmed the suspension and its duration, confirmed the suspension but reduced its duration or withdrawn the suspension.
3. Unless the suspension was withdrawn, information about the right to appeal the suspension, including,
   i. a copy of the board policies and guidelines governing the appeal established by the board, and
   ii. the name and contact information of the supervisory officer to whom notice of the appeal must be given.

Subsection (7) states that if, on concluding the investigation, the principal decides to recommend to the board that the pupil be expelled, he or she shall prepare a report that contains the following:

1. A summary of the principal's findings.
2. The principal's recommendation as to whether the pupil should be expelled from his or her school only or from all schools of the board.
3. The principal's recommendation as to,
   i. the type of school that might benefit the pupil, if the pupil is expelled from his or her school only, or
   ii. the type of program for expelled pupils that might benefit the pupil, if the pupil is expelled from all schools of the board.

Subsection (8) stipulates that the principal shall promptly provide a copy of the report to the board and to every person whom the principal was required to give notice of the suspension.

Subsection (9) states that the principal shall ensure that written notice containing the following is given to every person to whom the principal was required to give notice of the suspension at the same time as the principal's report is provided to that person:

1. A statement that the pupil will be subject to an expulsion hearing for the activity that resulted in the suspension.
2. A copy of the board policies and guidelines governing the expulsion hearing established by the board.
3. A statement that the person has the right to respond, in writing, to the principal's report provided.
4. Detailed information about the procedures and possible outcomes of the expulsion hearing, including, but not limited to, information explaining that,
   i. if the board does not expel the pupil, it will, with respect to the suspension imposed, confirm the suspension, shorten its duration or withdraw it,
   ii. the parties will have the right to make submissions during the expulsion hearing as to whether, if the pupil is not expelled, the suspension imposed should be confirmed, reduced or withdrawn,
   iii. any decision of the board with respect to the suspension imposed made at the expulsion hearing is final and not subject to appeal,
   iv. if the board expels the pupil from his or her school only, the board will assign the pupil to another school, and
   v. if the board expels the pupil from all schools of the board, the board will assign the pupil to a program for expelled pupils.
5. The name and contact information of a supervisory officer whom the person may contact to discuss any matter respecting the expulsion hearing.

Section 311.2 presents that if the principal does not recommend to the board that the pupil be expelled and does not withdraw the suspension, the suspension may be appealed, subject to the following:

1. A person who is entitled to appeal must give written notice of the intention to appeal within 5 school days of the date on which he or she is considered to have received the notice.

2. If the principal confirmed the suspension but reduced its duration, the appeal is from the reduced suspension and not the original suspension.

The principal may extend the deadline mentioned if the person requests an extension to accommodate his or her disability.

Section 311.3 subsection (1) provides that if a principal recommends to the board that a pupil be expelled, the board shall hold an expulsion hearing and the board has the powers and duties specified by board policy.

Subsection (2) prescribes that the expulsion hearing shall be conducted in accordance with the requirements established by board policy.

Subsection (3) states that the parties to the expulsion hearing are:

1. The principal.
2. The pupil, if,
   i. the pupil is at least 18 years old, or
   ii. the pupil is 16 or 17 years old and has withdrawn from parental control.
3. The pupil's parent or guardian, unless,
   i. the pupil is at least 18 years old, or
   ii. the pupil is 16 or 17 years old and has withdrawn from parental control.
4. Such other persons as may be specified by board policy.

Subsection (5) provides that at the hearing, the board shall,

(a) consider the submissions of each party in whatever form the party chooses to deliver the submissions;
(b) solicit the views of all the parties as to whether the pupil, if expelled, should be expelled from his or her school only or from all schools of the board; and
(c) solicit the views of all the parties as to whether, if the pupil not expelled, the board should confirm the suspension originally imposed, confirm the suspension but reduce its duration or withdraw the suspension.

Subsection (6) stipulates that after completing the hearing, the board shall decide,

(a) whether to expel the pupil; and
(b) if the pupil is to be expelled, whether the pupil is expelled from his or her school only or from all schools of the board.

Subsection (7) states that in making the decisions, the board shall take into account,

(a) all submissions and views of the parties, including their views as to whether the pupil, if expelled, should be expelled from his or her school only or from all schools of the board;
(b) any mitigating and other factors prescribed by the regulations; and
(c) any written response to the principal's report recommending expulsion that a person gave to the board before the completion of the hearing.

Section 311.4 subsection (1) presents that if a board does not expel a pupil, the board shall,

(a) confirm the suspension and the duration of the suspension;
(b) confirm the suspension, but shorten its duration, even if the suspension under appeal has already been served, and order that the record of the suspension be amended accordingly; or
(c) quash the suspension and order that the record of the suspension be expunged, even if the suspension under appeal has already been served.

Subsection (2) provides that in determining which action to take, the board shall consider,

(a) any submissions made by the parties as to whether the suspension and its duration should be confirmed, the suspension should be confirmed but its duration reduced or the suspension should be withdrawn;
(b) any mitigating or other factors prescribed by the regulations.

Subsection (3) indicates that after determining which action to take, the board shall give written notice containing the following to every person who was entitled to be a party to the expulsion hearing:

1. A statement indicating that the pupil is not expelled.
2. A statement indicating whether the board has confirmed the suspension and its duration, confirmed the suspension but reduced its duration, or withdrawn the suspension.

Subsection (4) stipulates that the decision of the board is final.

Section 311.5 prescribes that if a board expels a pupil, the board shall assign the pupil to,

(a) in the case of a pupil expelled from his or her school only, another school of the board; and
(b) in the case of a pupil expelled from all schools of the board, a program for expelled pupils.

Section 311.6 subsection (1) indicates that a board expelling a pupil shall ensure that written notice of the expulsion is given promptly to,

(a) all the parties to the expulsion hearing; and
(b) the pupil, if the pupil was not a party to the expulsion hearing.

Subsection (2) provides that the notice must include the following:

1. The reason for the expulsion.
2. A statement indicating whether the pupil is expelled from his or her school only or from all schools of the board.
3. Information about the school or program for expelled pupils to which the pupil is assigned.
4. Information about the right to appeal, including the steps that must be taken to appeal.

Section 311.7 subsection (2) presents that the following persons may appeal a board's decision to expel a pupil to the designated tribunal that hears appeals of board decisions to expel pupils:

1. The pupil's parent or guardian, unless,
   i. the pupil is at least 18 years old, or
   ii. the pupil is 16 or 17 years old and has withdrawn from parental control.
2. The pupil, if,
   i. the pupil is at least 18 years old, or
   ii. the pupil is 16 or 17 years old and has withdrawn from parental control.
3. Such other persons as may be specified by the designated tribunal.

Subsection (3) stipulates that the designated tribunal shall hear and determine an appeal and it has the powers and duties set out in the regulations.

Subsection (4) indicates that the parties to the appeal are:

1. The board.
2. The pupil, if,
   i. the pupil is at least 18 years old, or
   ii. the pupil is 16 or 17 years old and has withdrawn from parental control.
3. The pupil's parent or guardian, if the parent or guardian appealed the decision.
4. The person who appealed the decision to expel the pupil, if the decision was appealed by a person other than the pupil or the pupil's parent or guardian.

Subsection (5) prescribes that the decision of the designated tribunal on an appeal is final.

Section 312 provides that every board shall provide,

(a) at least one program for suspended pupils; and
(b) at least one program for expelled pupils.

Section 313 subsection (1) presents that an expelled pupil continues to be a pupil of the board that expelled the pupil if she or he attends a program for expelled pupils,

(a) offered by that board; or
(b) offered by another board under an agreement between that board and the board that expelled the pupil.

Section 314.5 provides that every board shall submit annual reports to the Minister respecting suspensions and expulsions.

In considering suspension or recommendation of expulsion, a principal must think about mitigating and other factors. Sections of Ontario Regulation 472/07, Behaviour, Discipline and Safety of Pupils, made under the Education Act, list these mitigating and other factors.

Section 2 lists the mitigating factors:

1. The pupil does not have the ability to control his or her behaviour.
2. The pupil does not have the ability to understand the foreseeable consequences of his or her behaviour.
3. The pupil's continuing presence in the school does not create an unacceptable risk to the safety of any person.

Section 3 lists other factors:

1. The pupil's history.
2. Whether a progressive discipline approach has been used with the pupil.
3. Whether the activity for which the pupil may be or is being suspended or expelled was related to any harassment of the pupil because of his or her race, ethnic origin, religion, disability, gender or sexual orientation or to any other harassment.
4. How the suspension or expulsion would affect the pupil's ongoing education.
5. The age of the pupil.
6. In the case of a pupil for whom an individual education plan has been developed,
   i. whether the behaviour was a manifestation of a disability identified in the pupil's individual education plan,
   ii. whether appropriate individualized accommodation has been provided, and
   iii. whether the suspension or expulsion is likely to result in an aggravation or worsening of the pupil's behaviour or conduct.

Section 4 stipulates that the Child and Family Services Review Board is designated for the purposes of the definition of "designated tribunal" to hear appeals of board decisions to expel pupils.

In dealing with behaviour, discipline, and safety of pupils Education Act section 315 subsection (1) provides that the Minister may collect and may by regulation require boards to collect such personal information as is specified by regulation from, or about, the classes of persons specified by regulation for the following purposes, and the Minister may specify or restrict the manner in which the information is to be collected:

1. To ensure the safety of pupils.
2. To administer programs, courses and services to pupils who are suspended or expelled and to determine whether an expelled pupil has successfully completed a program, course or service and as a result is eligible to return to school.

Subsection (2) stipulates that a board or other person is authorized to disclose the personal information collected under subsection (1) to the Minister for the purposes described in that subsection, and the Minister may disclose it to such persons or entities as may be prescribed by regulation for those purposes.

REFERENCES

Behaviour, Discipline and Safety of Pupils, O Reg 472/07. https://www.canlii.org/en/on/laws/regu/o-reg-472-07/latest/o-reg-472-07.html

California Legislative Information. (n.d.). *Education Code*. https://leginfo.legislature.ca.gov/faces/codesTOCSelected.xhtml?tocCode=EDC

Education Act. RSO 1990, c E.2. https://www.canlii.org/en/on/laws/stat/rso-1990-c-e2/latest/rso-1990-c- e2.html

Operation of Schools. Ontario Regulation 298. (1990). https://www.canlii.org/en/on/laws/regu/rro-1990- reg-298/latest/rro-1990-reg-298.html

The Chinese People's Congress. (2021). *The Chinese Education Act* [中华人民共和国教育法]. http://www.moe.gov.cn/jyb_xxgk/xxgk_jyfl/flfg_jyfl/202107/t20210730_547843.html

Chapter 4 Negligence, Risk Management, and Liability

ABSTRACT

This chapter focuses on the issues of negligence, risk management, and liability in schools. It contains the California Education Code and the Chinese Education Act on these issues, but its main contents are about the Ontario Education Act and related regulations concerning negligence, risk management, and liability in schools. The chapter provides sections from the Ontario Education Act and the relevant regulations on the issues mentioned above. It also has several legal cases where negligence, risk management, and liability in schools and school-related activities were discussed, explored, and analyzed by the Supreme Court of Canada and the Court of Appeal for Ontario.

DANGEROUS ACTIVITIES AND PHYSICAL EDUCATION

Children by their nature are more active than adults. Accidents happen in schools and schools related activities. California Education Code Title 2 Division 3 Part 21 Chapter 2 Article 13 subsection 35330 (a) (4) stipulates that the governing board of a school district may provide supervision of pupils involved in field trips by certificated employees. Division 4 Part 28 Chapter 5 Article 16 subsection 51879.7 states that fundamental water safety training be provided for all the children so that they will be able to enjoy water recreation while avoiding its hazards. Chapter 5.7 subsection 51940 (a) presents that the California Healthy Kids Resource Center shall review,

DOI: 10.4018/978-1-6684-4163-3.ch004

acquire, and circulate curricula focused on the prevention of brain and spinal cord injuries for use by school districts maintaining kindergarten and any of grades 1 to 12, inclusive. The Chinese Education Act does not have any section specifically on negligence, risk management, and liability.

Ontario Regulation 298 Operation of Schools (1990) subsection 19 (1) requires that educators must always keep the safety and well-being of their students in mind. Educators have a duty of care for their charge, students. In caring for their students, educators must follow practices that ensure student safety and prevent foreseeable risks. In measuring whether a teacher performs the duty of caring for students, one important standard is to see whether a teacher acts as a careful parent (Brown, 2009). Always keep an eye on students' activities to observe whether anything can go wrong. Never leave students unsupervised if possible. A teacher's presence usually has a restraining effect on the behaviour of students. If a teacher must leave students unsupervised for a short period of time, it is recommended that the teacher, before leaving, assign students a task to keep them engaged and give students very clear instruction about what they should do and should not do.

Students play during recess, lunchtime, before and after school hours in school. When they play, sometimes accidents can happen. Provide supervision whenever it is possible. Brown (2009) has a list that names the claims that allege negligence on the part of a school board and their staff. The first claim on the list is lack of adequate supervision. The following is the list of claims provided by Brown (2009, pp. 147-148):

1. lack of adequate supervision by a teacher or other staff member;
2. improper, inadequate or defective equipment;
3. failure to warn pupils of specific dangers in doing an activity;
4. failure to train pupils in the proper use of equipment or in safety proceedings;
5. failure to take reasonable precautions against injury or loss;
6. failure to hire competent staff and to provide them with the necessary training;
7. failure to properly treat an injury.

Providing adequate supervision is the most important way of preventing accidents. "The fact that a teacher permits students to participate in a potentially dangerous activity is not, in itself, negligence. However, the care taken must be appropriate to the activity, whether it be sports, outdoor education, recreation, laboratory, experiments, etc. In each case, the teacher is expected to guard against the reasonably foreseeable dangers of the activity" (Brown, 2009, p. 150).

Another important aspect is to make sure that equipment is adequate and in its proper condition. On its website, Ontario School Board Insurance Exchange has a weekly checklist and a monthly checklist for school equipment.

One case indicates the importance of teacher presence for maintaining safety when students are engaged in a potentially risky activity is the case of *Myers v. Peel County Board of Education* (1981) the Supreme Court of Canada heard. The Supreme Court stated that it cannot be said that the presence of a teacher among six to eight students in the exercise room would not have had a restraining effect upon the students, which might have influenced the course of events and prevented the accident, that it cannot be an answer for the school authorities to say that even the presence of a supervising teacher would not have prevented the accident. The following is an adapted version of the judgment the Supreme Court of Canada delivered.

Myers v. Peel County Board of Education

Date: 1981-06-22

Gregory Jan Myers, an infant by his next friend, Edward Percival Myers, and Edward Percival Myers, in his personal capacity *(Plaintiffs) Appellants;*

and

Peel County Board of Education and Walter Jowett *(Defendants) Respondents.*
Present: Laskin C.J. and Dickson, Estey, McIntyre and Lamer JJ.
On appeal from the Court of Appeal for Ontario.

This appeal concerned an accident suffered by a 15-year old boy in attempting to dismount from the rings in a gymnastic class at high school. The accident occurred in an exercise room, an area opening on to the gymnasium but at a somewhat higher level, where supervision from the main floor was impossible. The teacher for the period was responsible for a combined class and had given Myers and a friend permission to practise their gymnastic manoeuvres in the exercise room. The friend acted as Myers' spotter, a person positioned to catch a person or at least to break his fall in the event of an accident. When Myers dismounted, the spotter considered him finished working on the rings and turned to leave. Myers, however, remounted, attempted a difficult manoeuvre for the first time, and fell breaking his neck; his claim that he told the spotter of his intention to do so was rejected by the trial judge.

At trial, the manoeuvre was found to be suitable for a student of Myers' age and condition if given suitable coaching and supervision. The supervision incumbent was found to be lacking and the mats in place under the rings at the time of the accident inadequate. Liability was apportioned, the defendant being 80% liable, and Myers 20% liable. The Court of Appeal allowed an appeal finding that there was no evidence that other mats would have avoided the injury and that it could not be assumed that a teacher's presence would have avoided the accident.

Held: The appeal should be allowed.

The trial judge's finding of liability against respondent was supported on only two bases, the failure to provide adequate matting, and the failure to supervise. There was evidence of the former, that of an expert witness. As to the second, no supervision was provided as far as events leading up to the accident were concerned. An appellate court, because other evidence to the contrary existed, was not justified in relying on that evidence to reach a conclusion different from that of the trial judge in the absence of some error in principle.

The standard of care to be exercised by school authorities in providing for the supervision and protection of students for whom they were responsible—that of a careful parent—was not met. A prudent parent would not be content to provide the protective matting used when other, more protective mats were available or to permit his son to leave the gymnasium to practise potentially dangerous manoeuvres in a room without adult supervision.

Myers showed that respondent's failures caused or contributed to the accident which resulted in the injuries. It was not necessary to prove positively that the presence of the crash mat would have prevented the injury but merely, on the balance of probabilities, that the failure of the school authorities to provide more adequate matting and insist on its use contributed to the accident. Further, it could not be said that the presence of a teacher among six to eight students in the exercise room would not have had a restraining effect on the students and so could have influenced the course of events and prevented the accident.

Myers was contributorily negligent as found by the trial judge.

APPEAL from a decision of the Court of Appeal for Ontario, allowing an appeal from the judgment of O'Driscoll J. Appeal allowed.

The judgment of the Court was delivered by

MCINTYRE J.—This appeal concerns an accident suffered by a 15-year-old boy. At trial the defendants were found negligent, as was the plaintiff, the division of liability being 80% to the defendants and 20% to the plaintiff.

Damages were awarded and after the allowance for the shared liability the plaintiff obtained judgment for $64,000 and one-half of his costs. His father, who had been the plaintiff's next friend at the commencement of the action, received judgment for $2,656.30. An appeal was taken to the Ontario Court of Appeal by the defendants. The Court of Appeal allowed the appeal and dismissed the action. The appellant appeals to this Court by leave and seeks the restoration of the trial judgment.

The accident occurred on December 6, 1972. The appellant was a member of the Grade XI physical education class for boys at the Erindale Secondary School under the Peel County Board of Education. The course had commenced in the autumn with the commencement of the school year. The accident occurred almost at the end of the course. The gymnastic program was conducted generally in the school gymnasium. In addition to the gymnasium, there was an exercise room on a level somewhat higher than the gymnasium but opened on to it, which was used on occasion. While there was an unobstructed opening between the two rooms, the different levels of their floor surfaces made it impossible for a person in the gymnasium to see into the exercise room to observe the activities carried on within.

On the day of the accident there were from 25 to 30 students in Myers' class. The Grade XII class was also in session using the gymnasium or part of it, and the presence of this class raised the number of participating students to about 40. The Grade XII teacher responsible for the Grade XII students was ill and not in the school. Supervision of both classes for this period, which commenced about 2:00 p.m. and was to last until shortly before 3:00 p.m., was left to the one Grade XI teacher, a Mr. Jowett. Shortly after the commencement of the class, Myers and a classmate asked permission of Jowett to leave the gymnasium and go to the exercise room to practise their gymnastic manoeuvres. Permission was granted and they went to the exercise room. This was not an unusual occurrence and frequently such permission was given. On the date in question, 15 boys according to Myers, 6 to 8 according to Jowett, were allowed to go to the exercise room. While they were there, they were expected to practise their gymnastic manoeuvres in preparation for testing, which would establish their marks. They were without any supervision from faculty members during the time they were in the exercise room and, they were out of sight of the teacher who remained in the gymnasium.

In the exercise room Myers commenced the performance of some manoeuvres on the rings. This apparatus consists of two wooden rings suspended from the ceiling on parallel wires about 8 feet from the floor and being about 2 feet apart. His classmate was standing by as a spotter whose function was to be present during the manoeuvre and to assist the person on the rings and, in the event of a fall, to catch the performer or at least to make contact with him and break the force of fall. This function and the importance of spotters generally had been stressed by Jowett, and all witnesses called to give evidence on gymnastic matters agreed that spotters are essential to the safe conduct of these activities. There was evidence that Myers' class had been warned of the necessity of spotters and had received some instruction in their duties. They had also been told that a performer was to tell his spotter what he proposed to do from time to time, so that the spotter could be of service if required. Myers finished his manoeuvre and dismounted from the rings. The spotter, who said that he considered Myers was finished working on the rings, turned to leave and had moved away about 15 feet when he saw "out of the corner of his eye" Myers fall from the rings on his head. Myers said that after finishing one manoeuvre and dismounting he had told the spotter that he intended to do a straddle dismount and, assuming that the spotter had heard and would be in a position to assist, he proceeded to do so. It should be noted that the trial judge rejected that aspect of Myers' evidence. He had never attempted such a dismount before—a manoeuvre that requires the performer, while swinging from the rings, to bring his legs up over his head and execute a backward somersault, releasing the rings at the appropriate moment, and to land on his feet on the mats below. He fell from the rings during the manoeuvre and broke his neck, immediately becoming a quadraplegic. Fortunately, after some time in hospital, he made a very substantial recovery and was able to return to school and is now gainfully employed but no doubt with substantial disabilities.

The trial judge found that, although the manoeuvre described as a straddle dismount was suitable to Myers' age and condition if he had received suitable coaching and instruction for such a manoeuvre, the defendants had not provided that degree of supervision which it was incumbent upon them to provide, and that there had been insufficient protective matting available and in place beneath the rings at the time of the accident. The defendants were therefore liable to Myers. He rejected the evidence of *volenti non fit injuria* advanced by the defendants, and it was not pursued in this Court, and he concluded as well that Myers was guilty of contributory negligence in attempting the straddle dismount without proper experience and precautions. He found the defendant 80% liable and Myers 20%.

He considered the question of suitability of the exercise to a young man of the plaintiff's age and condition and concluded that the manoeuvre was suitable for the appellant in that he had been taught the dangers of the rings generally, and the straddle dismount in particular, and that he has been informed about spotters and their necessity. He considered, as well, the question of training and coaching in preparation for the manoeuvre and found upon the evidence that Myers had been properly coached and instructed. He found, however, that the equipment provided by the respondent school board for use by the students was not adequate nor suitably arranged. He believed that the placing of two or three slab mats on a vinyl floor did not meet the reasonable requirements of safety in the circumstances and, finally, he found that there was a total absence of supervision at the time of the accident. This last conclusion was inevitable because it was never suggested by the respondent that any supervising teacher was in the exercise room when the accident occurred. He concluded that failure to provide adequate matting and the failure to supervise the activities in the exercise room contributed to the accident causing the injury suffered by Myers.

In the Court of Appeal Arnup J.A., for the majority, considered that there was no evidence that the injury suffered by the plaintiff could have been avoided if a different type of matting had been in use and he considered that it could not be assumed that the presence of a teacher in the exercise room at the vital time would have prevented the injury. He considered that the finding of improper supervision was not based on credible evidence, and he considered that a careful father would not have hesitated to let his son go to the exercise room without further supervision.

The trial judge limited the issues in this case to a very narrow compass. The whole finding of liability against the respondent is supported on only two bases, the failure to provide adequate matting, and the failure to supervise.

It is necessary to consider the record and see whether there was evidence on which the finding of the inadequacy of the mats could rest and whether the conclusion, that the absence of supervision at the time of the accident was a contributing factor to the damage suffered by Myers, is sustainable.

The trial judge could reasonably conclude that the use of crash mats for inexperienced students was a necessary precaution. It was clear that there was evidence upon which the trial judge could base his finding of inadequacy in protective matting.

As to the other finding of fault on the part of the respondent, the failure to supervise, as far as the events leading up to this accident are concerned, no supervision was provided.

The standard of care by school authorities in providing for the supervision and protection of students is that of the careful parent. It is not, however, a standard applied in the same manner and to the same extent in every case. Its application will vary from case to case and will depend upon the number of students being supervised at any given time, and a host of other matters which may be widely varied but which may affect the application of the prudent parent-standard to the conduct of the school authority in the circumstances.

Was the standard of care so described met in the case at bar? It was not. It was common ground that training in gymnastics and, particularly, gymnastic exercises upon the rings carried with it a potential for danger. The danger is that the student may fall to the floor and, because of the nature of the exercises he is performing and the position of his body during such performance, he is apt to fall in such manner that the possibility of serious injury will be increased, and that indeed occurred in the case. There can be no doubt that injury was foreseeable and indeed it was foreseen. All the witnesses gave evidence of the necessity for steps and precautions to be taken to guard against injury and it was accepted that students would from time to time fall from the rings. Against this background I am unable to conclude that a prudent parent would be content to provide as protective matting only the compressed slab mats when other and more protective mats could be obtained. I am also unable to conclude that, considering the nature of the activity which was contemplated in the gymnastics course, a prudent parent would have been content to have his son permitted to depart from the gymnasium into a room where there would be no adult supervision to practise gymnastic manoeuvres on the rings which could involve the straddle dismount with its potential dangers.

The respondents, as found by the trial judge, failed to meet the required standard by failing to fulfil the requirement of supervision and in failing to provide and insist upon the use of adequate matting for the protection of students working on the rings.

The appellant fell with some force from a height in the neighbourhood of 8 feet. All gymnastic experts called recognized that mats were a necessary protective feature. The evidence was to the effect that when the danger of falling was greatest, *i.e.* in the early stages of training, the use of a crash mat was required. This would have at least doubled the protective material beneath the appellant and because of the nature of the crash mat, it could have lessened the effect of the fall and it was a reasonable inference to be drawn by the trial judge, from the evidence that additional protection would be provided by the use of a crash mat. The plaintiff is bound to prove, according to a balance of probabilities, that the failure of the school authorities to provide more adequate matting and insist upon its use contributed to the accident.

On all the evidence before him the trial judge reached the conclusions that such proof had been made and, he was justified in that finding.

On a balance of all the probabilities it was the opinion of the trial judge that the absence of supervision contributed to the cause of the accident. It cannot be said that the presence of a teacher among 6 to 8 students in the exercise room would not have had a restraining effect upon the students which could have influenced the course of events and prevented the accident. The respondent should have anticipated reckless behaviour from at least some of the young boys sent off by themselves to work on gymnastic equipment. The evidence revealed that it was a recurring problem to keep students from attempting gymnastic exercises without spotters and the proclivity of young boys of high school age to act recklessly in disregard, if not in actual defiance, of authority is well known. The manoeuvre attempted by the appellant is admittedly one of some danger. He had not been told not to try it. In fact, he had been virtually invited to do so, since higher marks could be obtained by the performance of Level 2 exercises. He was permitted to go to the exercise room without any supervision and with no inquiry as to what was contemplated on his arrival there. What happened was that he foolishly tried for the first time a dangerous manoeuvre and did himself serious injury. According to the evidence of the teacher, there were about 3 or 4 couples in the exercise room. This evidence was accepted by the trial judge. It would be more than mere speculation to conclude that the presence of a teacher in the exercise room could have influenced the situation.

While I am of the view that negligence has been shown on the part of the respondent, I also accept the trial judge's finding of contributory negligence on the part of the appellant.

The learned trial judge correctly found that there was contributory negligence on the part of Greg Myers in performing a difficult manoeuvre, fraught with danger, without announcing his move and without the presence of a spotter in position to break his fall.

I would accordingly allow the appeal with costs to the appellant in this Court and in the Court of Appeal, and restore the judgment at trial, leaving intact the finding of contributory negligence against the appellant, which is well supported in the evidence, the apportionment of damages, and the disposition of costs at trial.

Appeal allowed with costs.

Sometimes it is impossible for a teacher to be present every minute in the classroom or on the playground, or even when a teacher is present every minute, but the teacher is not able to pay attention to everything that is going on. When an accident happens, whether a teacher in charge of students is liable depends on whether causation can be established with evidence between the absence, or inadequacy, of supervision and the happening of the accident.

In one case the trial jury and the Court of Appeal for Ontario found Board of Education for Toronto and a teacher liable for the injury of a student, but the Supreme Court of Canada dismissed the claim for the initial injury. The following is an adapted version of the judgment the Supreme Court delivered.

Board of Education for Toronto v. Higgs et al.

Date: 1959-12-21

The Board of Education for the City of Toronto and J.C. Hunt (Defendants) Appellants;

and

William Higgs by his next friend, John Cecil Lowings, and Helen Higgs (Plaintiffs) Respondents.
On appeal from the Court of Appeal for Ontario.

During the school recess period, the plaintiff infant was injured when another pupil, known as a boy who indulged in rough play, lift him off his feet and carried him over to a rink where he dropped him on the ice. None of the four teachers supervising the recess saw the incident. One was called over by other pupils and ran across the ice. The boy refused help, and another teacher ordered him into line and into class although he was limping and complaining. Ultimately, he was sent to see the nurse and then sent home in a taxi. The initial injury was found to have been a hip bone displacement which was aggravated when the boy was required to walk.

The action alleged negligence in (1) failure to provide adequate supervision; (2) permitting rough play which the defendants knew or ought to have known would cause injury; and (3) failure to intervene when they saw or ought to have seen that the rough play was likely to cause serious injury. At trial and in this Court liability for the initial injury was treated separately from liability for the aggravation. The jury found that the initial injury was the result of the failure of the defendants to supervise the activities of the pupils because there was not a sufficient number of teachers on duty, in view of the winter conditions, the number and ages of the children and the fact that ice being on such a large area would limit the access of the teachers to the scene of the accident. On the second branch of the case, the jury found negligence which had aggravated the injury. The action was accordingly maintained, and this judgment was affirmed by the Court of Appeal.

Held: The appeal should be allowed in part by dismissing the claim for the initial injury.

The omission as found by the jury did not constitute the breach of a duty owing to the injured boy by both or either of the defendants. Neither inadequate supervision of the rough boy nor failure to see him pick up and carry the injured boy formed any part of the failure found. The finding of the jury raised the question of the adequacy of the system for supervising the break period used by the school principal. That system had been employed satisfactorily by the principal for several years, and he had no reason to believe that it did not constitute a reasonable safe system having regard to the number and ages of the children, and there were not any unusual circumstances that day which made it reasonably foreseeable that a greater number of teachers would be required. The winter conditions specified by the jury did not constitute such an unusual circumstance. Even if the "failure" as found by the jury had constituted a breach of duty, it had not been shown to be probable that any of the ingredients of that "failure" caused or contributed to the injury. Even on the view that the jury's answers included a finding of "inadequate supervision," it is not the duty of school authorities to keep pupils under supervision every moment while they are at school.

As to the aggravation of injury. The Public Schools Act imposes upon every teacher a duty "to give assiduous attention to the health and comfort of the pupils…". There was evidence to support the jury's answers as to the negligence of the two teachers particularly having regard to the requirement of "assiduous attention", and the Board must bear the responsibility for their subsequent actions.

APPEAL from a judgment of the Court of Appeal for Ontario, affirming a judgment given at a jury trial. Appeal allowed in part.

The judgment of the Court was delivered by

Ritchie J.: — This is an appeal by the defendants from a judgement delivered by Laidlaw J.A. on behalf of the Court of Appeal for Ontario dismissing an appeal from the judgment of McLennan J., sitting with a jury. The plaintiff (respondent) in this action was a student in the academic and vocational class of the Maurice Cody School in the City of Toronto and in the month of January 1957 was 15 years of age. He was apparently a normal boy, and while there is some evidence that he was subjected to ridicule from time to time by other students, there is nothing to suggest that he was in any way markedly different from his fellows or that he required any special attention from the authorities. He had an association with a boy by the name of Taylor who was a fellow student in the same class which involved lunching together and a certain amount of horse play which Higgs himself describes by saying "We used to fall around all the time".

On January 31, 1957, Higgs appears to have spent the greater part of the morning break talking to some girls in the neighbourhood of a large patch of ice generally referred to as the "pleasure rink" which had been cleared away in the school yard for the purpose of sliding and skating and which was played on to some extent during the break. Towards the end of the break, while Higgs was still in conversation with the girls, Taylor appears to have come up from behind, and lifting him off his feet, carried him a distance of about 20 feet and dropped him on the ice.

Taylor was a boy about the same size as Higgs but apparently a good deal stronger. He was known to the school authorities to be a boy who indulged in rough play. He had been warned and disciplined for his behaviour on more than one occasion in the past, and indeed his behaviour on this morning bears out the character of a rough and overbearing youth. After he dropped Higgs on the ice, he proceeded to kick snow in his face from the pile of snow that had been cleared off around the ice-covered area.

Although 5 students, who had been close to the boys at the time of the incident, gave evidence, none of them was able to testify to seeing Higgs being picked up, although 2 say that they saw him being carried and 2 others that they saw him being dropped on the ice.

The school yard consisted of an area of about 250 feet in length and approximately 400 feet in width although the width varied. At the north end of the yard a substantial area consisted of a hockey rink and in approximately the middle of the yard there was the pleasure rink above referred to and at the southern end of the yard there was a concrete area in front of the L-shaped school building itself. The evidence discloses that there were 4 teachers out of doors on duty supervising the break period. One of them, Mr. Hunt, was stationed in the northwest portion of the yard and his area of operations ran from the southwest corner of the hockey rink down the western side of the pleasure rink to approximately the point where the concrete surface began. Mr. Herlick fulfilled a similar function on the east side of the yard and there is some evidence to the effect that both these masters were directing their attention more to the students on the hockey rink than to those in the central part of the playground. There were also 2 female teachers stationed on the concrete surface outside the school who covered the southern area of the playground and one of whom was only about 35 feet away from the scene of the accident. None of the teachers saw this happening or knew anything about it until Herlick, who was then standing at the southeast corner of the hockey rink, was alerted by some boys who came across the ice to draw his attention to it. Herlick appears to have acted quickly because he ran across the ice and reached Higgs before he had got up. Higgs' own estimate was that Herlick was there in 2 or 3 minutes while other say that it only took him 1 minute.

Herlick found the boy with tears in his eyes and gained the impression that he was hurt and very much aggrieved, but the boy refused his offer of assistance and Herlick did not insist on taking him in to the school nurse. Shortly after this Mr. Hunt also came to the scene, and although there is some conflict as to exactly how Higgs reached the school it is apparent that when he got there he hung up his coat and hat, and although he was limping quite obviously and complaining, Mr. Hunt ordered him into line and into class. The boy says that Hunt struck him, but in any event he was required to walk into the classroom, and having reached it he appears to have shown very apparent signs of pain and disturbance as a result of which Mr. Hunt ultimately sent him to the nurse. The treatment he received from the nurse was somewhat superficial, and the upshot of it all was that he was sent home in a taxi and on arrival there was put to bed where the family physician attended him that evening. Upon X-rays being taken, it appeared that the boy's hip bone was dislocated and it was the opinion of his doctors that the original injury sustained by being dropped on the ice would probably not have resulted in more than a 20 per cent displacement which could have been cured by manipulation, but that the fact that he had been required to put his weight on his leg was likely to have caused the more severe condition which required hospitalization.

Higgs, by his next friend, sued the Board of Education and Mr. Hunt claiming general damages and Mrs. Higgs joined in the action asserting her claim for special damages.

The statement of claim alleges that the injuries to the plaintiff were caused by the negligence of the defendant in the manner following:

(a) failure to provide reasonable or adequate supervision during the recess period:
(b) allowing and permitting rough play of such a nature that they knew or ought to have known that it was likely to cause serious injury to pupils;

(c) failure to intervene when they saw or ought to have seen that the actions hereinbefore related were likely to cause serious injury to the plaintiff.

In putting this matter to the jury and indeed to this Court, the question of liability for the initial injury sustained when the boy was dropped on the ice was treated separately from that of liability for the events which succeeded and allegedly aggravated it.

On the first branch of the case the following questions were submitted to the jury and answered in the manner indicated:

1 (a) Were the injuries suffered by the Infant Plaintiff the result of the failure of the defendants to supervise the activities of the students?

Answer "Yes" or "No" Answer: YES

(b) If your answer to Question 1(a) is "Yes", then in what respect did the defendants fail to supervise such activities. *Answer fully.* There was not a sufficient number of teachers on duty in the playground, in view of the winter conditions, the number and ages of the children and the fact that ice being on such a large area of the yard would limit the access of teachers to the scene of any accident.

It is to be noted that the learned trial judge, in directing the jury to answer question 1(b) "fully", had this to say:

I should tell you now, when I say "Answer fully", it is not sufficient to say the defendants failed to supervise, but the Court requires you to give the facts on which you say there is no supervision, if that is the conclusion you come to.

These are the submissions of counsel for the plaintiff:

In the circumstances there were not enough teachers supervising;

There was, secondly, an inadequate supervision of Taylor that day;

And thirdly, there was a failure of the particular supervisors to see Taylor pick up Higgs and carry him the 20 feet and dump him on the ice, which could have been stopped by a single word.

Counsel for the defendant, on the other hand, says you should answer Question 1(a), "No", and he says that there was adequate supervision-two men teachers over these boys on the north end of the school yard—and that teachers are not bound to watch Taylor every minute; and I think there is undoubtedly something in that submission. If a person is so dangerous a character that he has to be watched every minute, then he should not be in the school at all. Then, as to the defendants' third point, he says there was no time to do anything because it happened so quickly.

When the answers to questions 1(a) and 1(b) are read together in light of these instructions and of the pleadings, neither "inadequate supervision of Taylor" nor "failure of any particular supervisor to see Taylor pick up Higgs and carry him twenty feet and drop him" forms any part of the "failure" which the jury found to have resulted in the respondent's injury, which "failure" is confined to not having "a sufficient number of teachers in the playground in view of:

(1) The winter conditions;
(2) The number and ages of the children;
(3) The fact that ice being on a large area of the yard would limit the access of teachers to the scene of any accident.

In rendering the decision of the Court of Appeal for Ontario, Laidlaw J.A. said, "The omission constituting a breach of duty consisted in not having sufficient teachers on duty in the particular circumstances as found by the jury". I have the greatest difficulty in agreeing that the "omission" as so found did indeed constitute the breach of a duty owing to the infant respondent by both or either of the appellants.

The primary responsibility for the manner in which the pupils in this school are to be supervised while at play lies upon the Board of Education for the City of Toronto (hereinafter called the "Board") itself as distinct from its employees, but the regulations which it had promulgated to this end were excluded from the evidence by the learned trial judge and there is no evidence respecting the steps taken by the Board as such in this regard.

At the other end of the chain of responsibility are the teacher-supervisors (including the appellant, Hunt) who were seized with the task of actual supervision but who had neither the power nor the responsibility of controlling the number of teachers to be on duty in the playground. The law does not contemplate the existence of a duty in an individual who is powerless to discharge it, and it must be concluded that these findings cannot apply to the appellant, Hunt, and that the order appealed from should be set aside insofar as it relates to his responsibility for the initial injury to the respondent.

The school principal, Mr. Macpherson, was the person vested with authority to control the matter of "having sufficient teachers on duty in the playground", and it is the nature of the duty resting upon him which must be examined to determine whether there was such a failure as to make the Board liable for the injury.

In the decision appealed from, Laidlaw J.A. has this to say on the subject: The duty is to take such care as a careful father would take in the circumstances. He must guard the pupils against danger that could reasonably be foreseen.

There can be no disagreement with the views of the learned judge in this regard except that it seems to me that the analogy between the duty of a school master to his pupils and that of a parent to his children cannot be related with the same validity to the responsibilities of organization and administration which rested on Mr. Macpherson as principal of a school with an enrolment of 750 pupils. If the jury had found any "failure" on the part of an individual supervisor, then other considerations might apply, but the jury did not find this and their answers to questions 1(a) and 1(b) are directed solely to the "failure" to so organize the break period as to have more than 4 teachers on duty in the playground. It is, therefore, a question of what standard of organization the law requires of a school authority under such circumstances which must be determined.

It is really the "system" employed by Mr. Macpherson for supervising the break period which is in question, and it is a factor to be considered that exactly the same number of teachers had been stationed in the same area of the same playground in both winter and summer ever since Mr. Macpherson came to the school in 1952.

There does not appear to be anything unreasonable about the system which was employed. As the burden of proving that the system was defective lay upon the respondents, it can be taken that Mr. Macpherson had no reason to believe that the teachers allocated to the various areas of the playground specified by him constituted anything less than a reasonably safe system of supervision having regard to the number and ages of the children unless there existed on the day in question any unusual circumstances which made it reasonably foreseeable that a greater number of teachers would be required.

The winter conditions specified by the jury did not constitute such an unusual circumstance. The evidence in this regard is to the effect that the pupils might be a little more excitable in wintertime and that the attention of the supervisors at the north end of the yard might be somewhat more engaged with the activities on the hockey rink than on the centre of the playground but that there was about the same amount of activity in both areas throughout the year. This does not indicate a condition which would cause a prudent school principal to anticipate danger to his pupils, and certainly gives no ground for anticipating such an accident.

Nor does the fact that ice would limit the access of teachers to the scene of any accident indicate any such condition. The relevant evidence in this connection is that when the accident in question happened one of the pupils ran over and brought Mr. Herlick back across the ice to the scene within 1 or at most 2 or 3 minutes, and in any event before Higgs had got up from the ice.

There was a teacher on duty at each corner of the playground and indeed Higgs himself stated that one of the women teachers was within 35 feet of him. The only evidence to suggest that this number was inadequate was the fact that the accident happened. It is said that this was an event which the principal was under a duty to foresee and guard against, but even if this had been so it was not a duty to which any of the matters specified in the answer to question 1(b) gave rise.

Looking at another aspect of these same facts, I have also concluded that even if the "failure" as found by the jury had constituted a breach of duty, it has not been shown to be probable that any one of the ingredients of that "failure" as specified in the answer to question 1(b) caused the respondent's injury which was occasioned by the sudden and unheralded action of the boy Taylor.

It would not be proper to leave this branch of the case without taking note of the fact that the decision appealed from is based in large measure on the assumption that the jury's answers were capable of being construed as including a finding that the school authorities were negligent in failing to provide against the foreseeable danger represented by the Taylor boy. Even if this element were deemed to form a part of the jury's answers, it would have to be remembered that not only did none of the teachers see the incident but that of the 750 pupils in the playground, some of whom were only 10 feet away, not one of them saw its inception and only two even saw Higgs being carried.

It is true that the rough habits of Taylor made him a pupil to be watched, but the facts do not seem to make it probable that having additional teachers on duty would have resulted in his being seen and stopped before the damage was done, and the fact that the presence of a teacher within 30 or 40 feet at the time of the incident did not deter him strongly suggests that the presence of additional persons in authority would not have affected his conduct.

Even on the view that the jury's answers included a finding of "inadequate supervision of Taylor" as a cause of the accident, I am still far from satisfied that this accident would not have happened whether additional supervisors had been there or not.

As to the second branch of the case, the following questions were put to the jury and answered in the manner indicated below:

2. (a) After the Infant Plaintiff was thrown to the ice, was there any negligence or improper conduct on the part of

    (1) Herlick "Yes"
    (2) Hunt "Yes"

which aggravated the Plaintiff's original injury?

(b) If your answer to Question 2(a) is "Yes", state the particulars with respect to each; Answer fully

(1) Herlick should have taken Higgs, personally and carefully, straight to the nurse, despite the protestations of Higgs. In the alternative, Herlick should have immediately informed Hunt as to the obvious suffering of Higgs. By these omissions we hold him to be partially responsible for the aggravation.
(2) By ignoring the plea from Higgs that he could not walk and following his admitted observance of Higgs in the playground, he caused further aggravation of the injury by insisting that Higgs walk into the class room.

The Public Schools Act, R.S.O. 1950, imposes upon every teacher a duty "to give assiduous attention to the health and comfort of the pupils". The master, Herlick, came promptly to the aid of the respondent as he lay on the ice and his offer of further assistance was refused, but it cannot be said that there was no evidence to support the jury's answer to question 2(b) (1) particularly having regard to the requirement of "assiduous attention" which is prescribed in the statute and the Board must bear the responsibility for his actions. These latter considerations apply with even greater force to the conduct of Hunt, and there is no reason to disturb the finding of the jury contained in the answers to the questions.

I am of opinion that the appeal should be allowed insofar as the first branch of this case is concerned and the order of the trial judge should be set aside insofar as it attributes responsibility to either of the appellants for the initial injuries sustained by the respondent, but as to the second branch of the case the appeal is dismissed. In the result the adult respondent will recover $510.95 and the infant respondent $10,000.

In the special circumstances of this case, the respondents will have their costs of this appeal.

Appeal allowed in part.

In determining whether teachers and school boards are liable when a student is injured in school, judges often apply the test of "but for" to see whether a causality between teachers' action and a student's injury can be established, which means whether a student will be injured but for the negligence of a teacher. One case where the judges in the Supreme Court of Canada clarified the "but for" test was Resurfice Corp. v. Hanke, [2007].

Citation: Resurfice Corp. v. Hanke

McLachlin C.J. (Bastarache, Binnie, LeBel, Deschamps, Fish, Abella, Charron and Rothstein JJ. concurring)

Resurfice Corp. Appellant
v.
Ralph Robert Hanke Respondent
and
LeClair Equipment Ltd. Appellant
v.
Ralph Robert Hanke Respondent
2006: December 12; 2007: February 8.

On appeal from the court of appeal for Alberta

Hanke, the operator of an ice-resurfacing machine, was badly burned when hot water overfilled the gasoline tank of the machine, releasing vapourized gasoline which was then ignited by an overhead heater, causing an explosion and fire. H sued the manufacturer and distributor of the machine for damages, alleging that the gasoline and water tanks were similar in appearance and placed close together on the machine, making it easy to confuse the two. The trial judge dismissed the action. He found that H did not establish that the accident was caused by the negligence of the manufacturer or distributor. The Court of Appeal set aside the judgment and ordered a new trial, concluding that the trial judge had erred in both his foreseeability and causation analyses.

Held: The appeal should be allowed and the trial judgment restored.

No error of law has been established in the trial judge's approach on this issue. There was evidence supporting his finding that H was not confused by the two tanks, notably H's own admission, and the seriousness of H's injury and the relative financial positions of the parties were not matters relevant to foreseeability.

With respect to causation, the trial judge did not need to engage in a contributory negligence analysis because he found, not only that H's carelessness was responsible for his injuries, but also that the alleged design defects were not responsible for these injuries. Further, the Court of Appeal erred in holding that the trial judge should have applied the "material contribution" test to determine causation. The basic test remains the "but for" test. This test ensures that a defendant will not be held liable for the plaintiff's injuries where they may very well be due to factors unconnected to the defendant and not the fault of anyone.

APPEAL from a judgment of the Alberta Court of Appeal. Appeal allowed.

The judgment of the Court was delivered by

The Chief Justice — This case involves a tragic injury that befell a young man, Mr. Hanke, when a water hose was placed into the gasoline tank of an ice-resurfacing machine rather than the water tank. When hot water overfilled the gasoline tank, vapourized gasoline was released into the air. It was ignited by an overhead heater, causing an explosion and fire. Mr. Hanke was badly burned.

Mr. Hanke sued the manufacturer and distributor of the ice-resurfacing machine for damages, alleging design defects. He contended that the gasoline tank and the water tank were similar in appearance and placed close together on the machine, making it easy to confuse the two.

The trial judge dismissed Mr. Hanke's action (2003). He found that Mr. Hanke had not discharged the plaintiff's burden of establishing that the accident was caused by the negligence of the manufacturer or distributor. First, he had not established that it was reasonably foreseeable that an operator of the ice-resurfacing machine would mistake the gas tank and the hot water tank. Second, he had not shown that the defendants caused the accident. The trial judge concluded that the accident had been caused by Mr. Hanke's decision to turn the water on when he knew, or should have known, that the water hose was in the gasoline tank, knowing full well, by his own admission, the difference between the two tanks. He found as a fact that Mr. Hanke was not confused by the placement and character of the tanks, and consequently that this had not caused the accident.

On appeal, the judgment was set aside and a new trial ordered (2005). The Court of Appeal concluded that the trial judge had erred in both his foreseeability and causation analyses.

First, the basic test for determining causation remains the "but for" test. This applies to multi-cause injuries. The plaintiff bears the burden of showing that "but for" the negligent act or omission of each defendant, the injury would not have occurred.

The "but for" test recognizes that compensation for negligent conduct should only be made "where a substantial connection between the injury and the defendant's conduct" is present. It ensures that a defendant will not be held liable for the plaintiff's injuries where they "may very well be due to factors unconnected to the defendant and not the fault of anyone".

The Court of Appeal erred in failing to recognize that the basic test for causation remains the "but for" test. It further erred in applying the material contribution test in circumstances where its use was neither necessary nor justified.

Conclusion

I would allow the appeal, set aside the order of the Court of Appeal and restore the trial judgment, with costs throughout.

LIABILITY IN SCHOOL SPORTS

There are situations when people are engaged in activities that they know involve risks. They take part in these activities assuming that if they are careful, they can avoid accidents. When accidents do happen, the injured may sue the occupiers of the premises alleging that the occupiers have not fulfilled their statutory duty of care. In these cases, the court gives more weight to the statutory duty than a local custom. One will not be successful in defense by referring to the local custom and by saying that everybody does this and the injured assumes risk when the person comes to the premises. The case of *Waldick v. Malcolm* (1991) indicates that the courts give more weight to the statutory duty than a custom. The following is an adapted and significantly shortened version of the judgment the Supreme Court of Canada delivered.

Waldick v. Malcolm

Date: 1991-06-27

Marvin Malcolm, Roberta Malcolm, Betty Stainback and Harry Hill Appellants
v.
Norman Edward Waldick and Janet Marie Waldick Respondents

1991: February 26; 1991: June 27.
on appeal from the court of appeal for Ontario

Waldick was seriously injured when he fell on the icy parking area of the Malcolms' rented farmhouse. The parking area and laneway had not been salted or sanded; apparently few people in that rural region did so. Waldick was aware that the laneway was slippery and acknowledged that its condition could be seen without difficulty. At issue here was whether the Malcolms failed to meet the statutory duty of care imposed by the Occupiers' Liability Act on occupiers of premises to persons coming onto those premises and whether Waldick had willingly assumed the risks of the injury. Also involved was the issue of whether Waldick had been contributorily negligent.

The Malcolms were found liable for Waldick's personal injuries, and the Court of Appeal dismissed the appeal from that judgment. The action and cross-claim against the other appellants, Betty Stainback and Harry Hill, were dismissed because they had rented the property to the Malcolms and were not the occupiers of the farmhouse.

Held: The appeal should be dismissed.

The Malcolms, notwithstanding the alleged local custom, breached s. 3(1) of the Act. The existence of customary practices which are unreasonable in themselves, does not oust the duty of care owed by occupiers under the Act. This statutory duty to take reasonable care in the circumstances to make the premises safe does not change but the factors which are relevant to an assessment of what constitutes reasonable care will necessarily be very specific to each fact situation. Local custom is one such circumstance. It can inform the court's assessment of what is reasonable in any given set of circumstances. Where an alleged custom is raised, however, the party who relies on his compliance with it must prove the custom is in effect. Only in the rarest and most patently obvious of cases will the courts take judicial notice of a custom.

No amount of general community compliance will render negligent conduct reasonable in all the circumstances. If it is unreasonable to do absolutely nothing to one's driveway in the face of clearly treacherous conditions, it matters little that one's neighbours also act unreasonably. The Act was meant to discourage this type of generalized negligence. It was far from self-evident that the "practice" of not sanding or salting parking areas and driveways in the area should earn the acceptance of the courts.

The Act promotes and requires positive action on the part of occupiers to make their premises reasonably safe.

This Court was not presented with any new arguments on the issue of contributory negligence that could in any way lead to the conclusion that the trial judge made a "palpable and overriding" error in his appreciation of the evidence.

APPEAL from a judgment of the Ontario Court of Appeal (1989), dismissing an appeal from a judgment of Austin J. (1987). Appeal dismissed.

The judgment of the Court was delivered by

Iacobucci J. -- The defendants, Marvin and Roberta Malcolm ("the Malcolms"), appeal from a judgment of the Ontario Court of Appeal dismissing their appeal from the judgment at trial finding the Malcolms liable for personal injuries suffered by the plaintiff, Norman Waldick ("Waldick").

The appeal involves the interpretation of the nature and extent of the duty of care under the Ontario Occupiers' Liability Act, R.S.O. 1980, c. 322 (the "Act"). In general terms, the Act sets out the duty of care owed by occupiers of premises to persons who come onto those premises and specifies certain exceptions to the prescribed duty of care. As this appeal is the first involving the Act to reach this Court and as several provinces have similar statutory regimes, it is important to clarify the scope of the duties owed by occupiers to their visitors.

Waldick was seriously injured in a fall on the premises occupied by the Malcolms. It was in this context that the questions arose as to whether the Malcolms had failed to fulfil their statutory duties under the Act, and whether Waldick had willingly assumed the risks of the injury. Also involved is an issue of contributory negligence of Waldick. But before going further, a further elaboration of the facts giving rise to this appeal is warranted.

Facts

On February 7, 1984, Waldick suffered a fractured skull when he fell on the icy parking area of the rural residential premises near Simcoe, Ontario occupied by the Malcolms. Waldick is Mrs. Malcolm's brother. Mrs. Malcolm worked as a hairdresser, but she often cut hair at her home for friends and relatives without receiving any remuneration. The property, which consisted of a farmhouse and barn on approximately three acres of land, was owned by the other appellants, Betty Stainback and Harry Hill. The Malcolms rented the premises from them. Since they were not the occupiers of the farmhouse, the action and cross-claim against Stainback and Hill were dismissed on consent in June, 1986.

On the premises was a gravel laneway that ran for about 200 to 300 feet from the road, past the house, and to the barn. Opposite the house, the laneway widened to form a parking area which could accommodate three or four vehicles at any one time. The house had a small wooden porch with two steps. Leading from the steps toward the laneway was a walk made of cement slabs which was about six feet long, but which did not reach the laneway. The rest of the distance between the walk and the laneway was grass-covered. The trial judge noted that there was "a perceptible grade downwards from the house to the parking area."

At the time of the injury, the porch and steps of the house had been shovelled and, while the walk and grassy area had also been shovelled, these were still snow-covered. The laneway had not been salted or sanded. The appellant, Roberta Malcolm, testified that she did not consider it necessary and reasonable to do so. She also testified that few of the residents in that rural region salted or sanded their laneways in winter. Four days before the accident, the region had experienced an ice storm. Waldick was aware that the laneway was "slippery, very icy with a dusting of snow on it" and acknowledged that its condition could be seen without difficulty. Because of the ice, he took exceptional caution in driving up the laneway. He parked about 20 feet from where the gravel laneway met the grassy stretch, and entered the house, walking very carefully because of the ice. Some time later, he went out to his car to get a carton of U.S. cigarettes which he had purchased for his sister. He put on his winter boots, turned on the porch light, and got the cigarettes. As he was walking back to the house, he slipped on the ice, fell backwards in the parking area, and fractured his skull.

Waldick commenced an action in the Supreme Court of Ontario under the Act, alleging negligence on the part of the Malcolms and the owners of the premises; as noted above, the action against the owners was dismissed on consent. The trial judge found the Malcolms liable for the injuries sustained by Waldick and by agreement of the parties deferred the determination of damages.

Malcolms' appeal was dismissed by the Ontario Court of Appeal.

Relevant Statutory Provisions

Occupiers' Liability Act, R.S.O. 1980, c. 322

1. … the provisions of this Act apply in place of the rules of the common law that determine the care that the occupier of premises at common

law is required to show for the purpose of determining his liability in law in respect of dangers to persons entering on the premises.

2. (1) An occupier of premises owes a duty to take such care as in all the circumstances of the case is reasonable to see that persons entering on the premises are reasonably safe while on the premises.
3. (1) The duty of care provided for in subsection 3 (1) does not apply in respect of risks willingly assumed by the person who enters on the premises, but in that case the occupier owes a duty to the person to not create a danger with the deliberate intent of doing harm or damage to the person and to not act with reckless disregard of the presence of the person.

Decisions Below

Supreme Court of Ontario

1987

Austin J. began by considering the statutory standard of care owed by occupiers of premises under s. 3(1) of the Act.

... the effect of the Act is twofold. Firstly, it does away with the difference between invitees and licensees and puts both invitees and licensees into the common defined class of visitor.... Secondly, and more importantly, the statute now imposes an affirmative duty upon occupiers to take reasonable care for the safety of people who are permitted on the premises. ... *Now, the occupier has to make the premises reasonably safe. That does not absolve the visitor of his duty to take reasonable care but does place an affirmative duty on each occupier to make the premises reasonably safe.*

Applying the "reasonableness" standard, in light of all the facts before him, Austin J. said:

The ice storm had occurred four days prior to the accident, followed by above and below freezing temperatures. In other words, the condition of the [Malcolms'] parking area on February 7th was not unexpected. The [Malcolms] did nothing to render their parking area less dangerous. The question is, by doing nothing under these conditions, do the [Malcolms] meet the standard of care required of them under the Act? In my opinion they do not.

"Doing nothing at all under the circumstances was not reasonable care", and he accordingly found the Malcolms in breach of s. 3(1).

Austin J. noted that the effect of s. 4(1) of the Act is to restrict the usual duty of care owed under s. 3(1). As to the application of s. 4(1) to the facts, Austin J. said:

The issue here then is what is meant by "risks willingly assumed"? Does it mean proceeding in the face of knowledge of the risks involved or is s. 4(1) intended to be a codification of the doctrine volenti non fit injuria?

If the former, Austin J. was of the view that Waldick must fail, because the evidence showed that he was fully aware of the ice and the attendant risks of slipping. If the latter were the correct interpretation, then s. 4(1) would not bar the claim as there had been no agreement waiving legal rights. He noted that the volenti doctrine requires such an agreement.

He concluded that Waldick's mere knowledge of the conditions did not constitute "risks willingly assumed" within the meaning of s. 4(1).

In the result, the Malcolms were found liable, but by consent damages were not assessed.

Ontario Court of Appeal
(1989)

Blair J.A. noted that this was the first occasion that the Court had considered the Act. One of the principal purposes of the legislation was to replace the somewhat obtuse common law of occupiers' liability by a generalized duty of care based on the "neighbour" principle.

Blair J.A. stated that section 3(1) of the Act requires a court to determine the scope of an occupier's duty "in all the circumstances of the case". It would be contrary to the scheme of the Act to fragment the duty of occupiers by the imposition of arbitrary judge-made rules applicable to different kinds of premises, such as those suggested by counsel for the appellants for residential or commercial premises located in rural or urban settings.

Blair J.A. agreed with the trial judge's holding that by doing nothing, the appellants breached the standard prescribed by s. 3(1).

The Malcolms submitted that the evidence at trial showed that Waldick had been contributorily negligent. In particular, it was urged that the evidence showing that Waldick was not wearing a coat at the time of the accident proved that he was hurrying and being less than prudent. Blair J.A. reviewed the thorough comments of the trial judge on this point, and noted that a number of decisions of this Court establishes that, in the absence of palpable error, an appellate court should not interfere with a trial judge's finding of negligence. Blair J.A. was of the view that no such palpable error was present in this case.

Consequently, the appeal was dismissed.

Points in Issue

1. Whether the Court of Appeal of Ontario erred in holding that the Malcolms breached the duty of care imposed by s. 3(1) of the Occupiers' Liability Act;
2. Whether, in the event that the Court of Appeal of Ontario was correct that the Malcolms did not meet the duty of care, Waldick willingly assumed the risks of walking over the icy parking area, thus relieving them from liability, pursuant to s. 4(1) of the Act;
3. Whether the trial judge made a palpable error when he found that Waldick was not contributorily negligent.

Analysis

1. Did the Court of Appeal of Ontario err in holding that the Malcolms breached the duty of care imposed by s. 3(1) of the Occupiers' Liability Act?

The courts below concluded that the Malcolms breached the duty of care owed under the Act by doing nothing to render the parking area entrance to their house less slippery. Austin J. was of the view that doing nothing fell short of the reasonable care requirement. Blair J.A. agreed, noting the duty was limited only to salting or sanding that part of the parking area next to the entrance and adding that it was undeniable that the Malcolms knew this part would be used by visitors like Waldick.

I am unable to agree with the Malcolms' submissions for several reasons. I do not agree with the premise of their argument, viz., that the lower courts failed to consider local custom. Both Austin J. and Blair J.A. considered all the factors which could enter an assessment of what constitutes reasonable care, including the alleged custom in the rural community involved. A close reading of the judgments below reveals that the learned judges considered: the weather, the time of year, the size of the parking area, the cost of preventive measures, the quality of the footwear worn by Waldick, the length of the pathway, and the fact that these were rural and residential premises.

The mere fact that the alleged custom was not decisive of the negligence issue does not in any way support the conclusion that it was not considered. After all, the statutory duty on occupiers is framed quite generally, as indeed it must be. That duty is to take reasonable care in the circumstances to make the premises safe. That duty does not change but the factors which are relevant to an assessment of what constitutes reasonable care will necessarily be very specific to each fact situation -- thus the proviso "such care as in all circumstances of the case is reasonable". One such circumstance is whether the nature of the premises is rural or urban. Another is local custom, which Blair J.A. explicitly mentions and I view his reasons as considering and rejecting the alleged custom.

Secondly, there are proof problems that complicate the Malcolms' argument in this regard. It would be preferable for courts to demand evidence of the general practice or not to rely on custom at all.

Thirdly, even if there had been adequate evidence in the record of a general local custom of not salting or sanding driveways, such a custom would not necessarily be decisive against a determination of negligence in the case.

In short, no amount of general community compliance will render negligent conduct "reasonable ... in all the circumstances". Presumably it is exactly this type of generalized negligence that the Act is meant to discourage.

The existence of customary practices which are unreasonable in themselves… in no way ousts the duty of care owed by occupiers under the Act. That duty is to take such care as is reasonable in the circumstances, and … both Austin J. and Blair J.A. correctly stated and applied the law in this regard. They both considered "all the circumstances of the case". I would accordingly agree that the Malcolms breached the statutory duty of care imposed by the Act.

2. In the event that the Court of Appeal of Ontario was correct that the Malcolms did not meet the duty of care, did Waldick willingly assume the risks of walking over the icy parking area, thus relieving them from liability, pursuant to s. 4(1) of the Act?

At issue under this ground of appeal is the scope of the defence which s. 4(1) offers to occupiers. They will be absolved of liability in those cases where the losses suffered by visitors on their premises come as a result of "risks willingly assumed" by those visitors. There are two quite distinct and conflicting trends in the jurisprudence as to the proper interpretation of this term. In essence, they reflect two standards of what assuming a risk means: the first involves merely knowing of the risk that one is running, whereas the second involves not only knowledge of the risk, but also a consent to the legal risk, or in other words, a waiver of legal rights that may arise from the harm that is being risked. The latter standard is captured by the maxim volenti non fit injuria whereas the former is sometimes referred to mere "knowing" as opposed to actually "willing".

The goals of the Act are to promote, and require where circumstances warrant, positive action on the part of occupiers to make their premises reasonably safe. The occupier may, however, wish to put part of his property "off limits" rather than to make it safe, and in certain circumstances that might be considered reasonable. Where no such effort has been made, the exceptions to the statutory duty of care will be few and narrow.

The legislature's intention in enacting s. 4(1) of the Act was to carve out a very narrow exception to the class of visitors to whom the occupier's statutory duty of care is owed. This exception shares the same logical basis as the premise that underlies volenti, i.e., "that no wrong is done to one who consents. By agreeing to assume the risk the plaintiff absolves the defendant of all responsibility for it".

Both Austin J. and Blair J.A. were of the view that Waldick did not consent to the legal risk or waive any legal rights that might arise from the negligence of the Malcolms. I agree with their disposition of this ground of appeal and conclude that Waldick is not barred from recovery by the operation of s. 4(1) of the Act.

3. Did the trial judge made a "palpable and overriding error" when he found that Waldick was not contributorily negligent?

Blair J.A. refused to revisit the findings of Austin J. as to the issue of contributory negligence. The Malcolms before this Court simply reargued a point that was explicitly rejected by Blair J.A. They contest the failure of the trial judge to draw an inference of carelessness from the proof that Waldick was not wearing a winter coat. There have been no new arguments presented before this Court that could in any way lead to the conclusion that Austin J. made a "palpable and overriding" error in his appreciation of the evidence or in his finding on the contributory negligence issue.

CONCLUSION

For the foregoing reasons, I would dismiss the appeal with costs.

Appeal dismissed with costs.

With the consideration of the *Waldick v. Malcolm* (1991) case, school administrators must be very careful in making school premises, including sidewalks surrounding schools, safe for students, parents, staff, and the public.

Sometimes accidents happen when students are engaged in sports in schools or in sports organized by schools, where dangers are inherent, particularly in contact sports. In participating in sports activities, students assume risks after they and their parents sign a consent form. When accidents happen during these activities and students are injured, how do educators know whether they are liable? One case illustrates the principles judges applied in determining the liability of school coaches and school board when a student was injured in a high school football game. In the case, *Thomas v. Hamilton (City), Board of Education* (1994), the judges of Court of Appeal for Ontario dismissed an action against the school board and coaches for damages for negligence. The following is an adapted version of the judgment.

Thomas v. Hamilton (City), Board of Education

Date: 1994-10-26

On October 26, 1982, Thomas, then age 16, broke his neck while making a tackle in a high school football game. He and members of his family sued his three coaches and the Hamilton Board of Education, which ran the curricular and extra-curricular football programs. The action was dismissed, and he appealed. The appeal raised the issues of the appropriate standard of care, whether the trial judge misapprehended the evidence, and whether the risk of injury came within the ambit of the "Interscholastic Athletic Permission Form", the consent given by T and his mother.

Held, the appeal should be dismissed.

The trial judge made no error in applying the standard of the careful parent to the discharge of the duty owed by the Board and the coaches to Thomas. In particular, the judge's rejection of the allegation that the coaches failed to recognize that Thomas was not in a condition to play was reasonable and supported by the evidence as was the finding that there was no breach of duty in the coaches' instructions about tackling techniques. There was no error in the trial judge's rejection of the "long, lean swan neck" theory which alleged that the school board and the coaches ought to have been aware of a connection between an athlete's neck configuration and neck injury vulnerability. Under this theory, it was argued that Thomas, because of his neck configuration, ought to have been warned about his risk of injury and ought not to have been permitted to play or permitted to play only at low risk positions. The evidence supported the trial judge's findings that the long, lean swan neck theory was not widely known and that there was no reason why the board or the coaches should have undertaken a search of the sports medicine literature concerning serious neck injuries or warned Thomas of the alleged increase of his vulnerability to a serious neck injury. It was also open to question whether the theory was valid and whether Thomas had a long, lean swan neck. The trial judge was correct in concluding that neither the board nor the coaches were negligent and that Thomas and his mother consented to the normal risks of the game, which included the injury suffered by him. The injury was sustained during a routine play and, although the consequences of the injury were devastating, the injury came within the ambit of those risks inherent in a contact sport such as football.

APPEAL from a judgment of the General Division dismissing an action for damages for negligence.

The judgment of the court was delivered by

OSBORNE J.A.: On October 26, 1982, Jeffry Thomas, then 16, made what appeared to be a routine tackle in a high school football game. In making the tackle he broke his neck and is a quadriplegic. He and members of his family sued a number of defendants, including the respondent Hamilton Board of Education and his team's coaches. His action was dismissed after a lengthy non-jury trial before Steele J. Jeffry Thomas (the appellant) and his stepfather Terry Wilkinson (a Family Law Act claimant), have appealed from the trial judge's findings on the general issue of the respondents' liability.

Thomas also appeals from the decision of the trial judge to reduce, by two years, the period over which prejudgment interest would be calculated. In addition, Terry Wilkinson, Jeffry Thomas' stepfather, appeals from the trial judge's assessment of damages of $1,000 for his loss of care, guidance and companionship, occasioned by the appellant's injuries.

The appeal on liability raises the issues of the appropriate standard of care to be required of the Board of Education and team coaches, whether the trial judge misapprehended the evidence, and whether the trial judge erred in concluding that the risk of injury in issue came within the ambit of the consent given by Thomas and his mother. For purposes of this appeal, the respondents are the Board of Education for the City of Hamilton (the "Board") and the appellant's three coaches, Di Liberto, Bell and MacLean.

The Evidence

(i) High School Football Programs and the Hamilton Board of Education

In 1982, football was a part of both curricular and extra- curricular programs in Hamilton high schools. Hamilton high school football programs were run under the control of the Board. Individual, football-related skills, and skills related to other sports, were taught in the classroom as a part of the high school's physical education program.

Football was also an extra-curricular sport in which all Hamilton high schools participated. The eligibility of student football players was determined by age. Each high school had a senior and junior team. A player could not be older than 15 at the commencement of the school year to be eligible to play junior football. Thomas was 15 when the 1982 school year began. He turned 16 on September 23, 1982, one day before his team's first game. He was one of the oldest, the best, and most experienced players on the 1982 junior football team.

The Board was responsible for ensuring that playing facilities and conditions were safe and for establishing a contact with each high school's sports convenor. The Board established the junior and senior football schedules and provided game officials and other personnel required for high school football games.

The Board also made relevant football information available to the schools through the offices of its supervisor of physical and health education and each school's sports convenor. It had final authority with respect to the rules under which football was played. It did not, however, have a role in the selection of high school football coaches.

High school football coaches did not have to be certified by the Board. They were selected by each high school's principal after consultation with the head of the school's physical education department and its staff. The Board encouraged football coaches to come from within the school, that is from the faculty. Scott Park Secondary School's coaches were all teachers.

Apart from the junior age eligibility restriction, the high school football program was open to any students who wanted to participate, subject to the requirement that each participating student provide an "Interscholastic Athletic Permission Form" signed by his parent or guardian and a medical report which certified that the student was fit to play football.

Scott Park's junior football team was coached by three teachers, the respondents, John Di Liberto, Orval Bell and Brian MacLean. No issue is taken with the authority under which the three coaches operated.

(ii) The Appellant's Football and Other Athletic Experience

This is an area of the evidence in which there is little dispute. Thomas was an active teenager. In the summer of 1980, after he had completed Grade 8, he played on a football team in the Steel City Peewee League. That team started its practices in July 1980 and completed its season in October 1980. Thomas was a runningback on his peewee team. At the end of the season, he was named the most valuable player (offence) in the league.

In the 1980 season, Thomas wore shoulder pads to which a "horse collar" was attached. A horse collar is a tubular neck pad which extends around the back and sides of the neck. It is intended to limit extension and lateral movement of the neck. It is of no assistance in limiting neck flexion. He was wearing a similar collar when he was injured on October 26, 1982.

Because of his involvement with a non-school football team, Thomas could not play for his high school's junior football team in the 1980 season. He did, however, play midget basketball for his high school team after the conclusion of the football season.

In 1981 Thomas tried out for and made Scott Park's junior football team. Before the 1981 football season began, he attended a preliminary meeting with about 20 other candidates for the junior football team. At that meeting, he was given a consent to play form to be executed by one of his parents and he was told that he would require a doctor's certificate before he could play. In due course Thomas' mother signed the consent to play form and he provided his coaches with the required medical certificate. He played in all six games, on offence, defence and on special teams.

During the 1981 season, Thomas' coaches provided tackling instruction and required all players to participate in tackling drills. The coaches instructed their players to make contact with their shoulders and with their heads up, that is with their necks extended to a limited degree. Thomas did not recall the coaches connecting improper tackling methods with an increased risk of injury. They said nothing to him about any relationship between his neck configuration (width and length) and the risk of a neck injury.

At Christmas 1981 Thomas received a set of weights as a gift. He played basketball in the 1981-82 junior basketball season. He was named to the all-star team. He said that he used his weights about three times a week during the winter of 1981-82.

In the summer of 1982 Thomas played recreational basketball, frequently rode his bike, jogged one or two times a week over distances which sometimes reached four miles and lifted weights four times a week. He also enjoyed water skiing. He undertook these activities because, as he put it, "I enjoyed doing them."

By the fall of 1982 Thomas was 6 feet tall and weighed about 145 to 150 lbs. His neck measured about 15 inches around. Pictures of Thomas filed at trial suggest to me that he had a long, but reasonably well muscled neck.

Thomas decided to return to junior football, instead of playing senior football, for the 1982 season for one reason. He thought that he would play more on the junior team than he would if he were on his high school's team.

Football practices began once school started after Labour Day in 1982. Thomas was one of the best and fastest players on his team. In 1982, he played "both ways", on offence and defence. He was a flanker on offence, and a defensive halfback, and sometimes a linebacker, on defence. He also played on the "special teams", that is to say he was on the field for kickoffs and punts both by, and to, his team. He spent very little time on the bench. What limited time he did spend on the bench was simply to provide him with a short breather.

The Scott Park junior team played its first game of the 1982 season on September 24, 1982. During that game Thomas injured a finger on his left hand and his left wrist. After the game Terry Wilkinson, his stepfather, took him to a Hamilton hospital where he was fitted with a splint for his finger and an aluminum brace for his lower arm and wrist. His injury was not serious, and he was not admitted to the hospital.

Because of this injury, he had to obtain a medical clearance to play before he could rejoin his team. He obtained that clearance on October 7, 1982. At that time, he was examined by his family doctor, who signed a note dated October 7, 1982, confirming that Thomas was fit to play football. He delivered the medical clearance to his coaches shortly after he received it. Thomas played in his team's fifth game on October 19, on offence, defence and on special teams.

(iii) The October 26, 1982 Game

Scott Park junior football team's sixth and last game of the 1982 season took place on October 26, 1982 at Brian Timmis Stadium against Glendale

Secondary School. Once again Thomas played on offence, defence and special teams. Late in the third quarter his team punted from about its 20-yard line. His assignment on that occasion, and generally in punting situations, was to be the "contain" man. Thomas' responsibility was to attempt to ensure that the punt returner, after catching the punt, was turned inside, that is towards the centre of the field where, in theory, he could be more easily tackled.

The opposing team had made some modest punt return scheme adjustments at half time of the October 26 game, the main purpose of which was to avoid Thomas. The punt returner was supposed to return Scott Park's punt by following blockers set up to his right, that is on the other side of the field from that occupied by Thomas. Unfortunately, as it turned out, the punt returner ran the wrong way. He proceeded to return the punt to the side of the field on which Thomas had "contain" responsibility. Because he was returning the punt not according to plan, the punt returner was unaccompanied by blockers. In the result, something akin to a one-on-one confrontation developed between the punt returner and Thomas. According to Thomas' evidence, it became apparent to him that the punt returner was attempting to go to his right, that is, outside his position and toward the sideline. It was Thomas' responsibility to see that that did not happen.

As the Glendale punt returner attempted to go between Thomas and the sideline, Thomas tackled him. It is not clear whether he left his feet. He may have done so. In any case, in making the tackle Thomas' body was extended, and the impact between Thomas and the punt returner was substantial. The impact of the tackle drove the punt returner back a number of yards. The estimates vary as to how far. The punt returner required the on-field assistance of his team's trainer, and he had to be helped from the field.

At the moment of the impact Thomas was running at jogging speed, or faster. The punt returner was running at full speed. The point of contact is not entirely clear. There is no doubt that from Thomas' standpoint the initial point of contact was his helmet. Indeed, the opposing coach expressed the opinion that as the tackle was made, Thomas unintentionally committed the rule infraction of "spearing". However, no penalty was called, or in the tragic circumstances, called for.

Thomas said that the last thing he could remember seeing before he made contact with the punt returner was his hip. The evidence would suggest that the top of Thomas' helmet made initial contact with the punt returner in the general area of his mid torso. One of the opposing coaches, who had a reasonably good view of the tackle, said the punt returner lowered his shoulder at the moment of impact and may have attempted to fend off the imminent contact by use of a straight arm. It is not clear whether the punt returner's arm came into contact with Thomas' helmet. If it did, the contact was momentary, but it may have resulted in Thomas' head and neck being positioned at a more dangerous angle immediately before the impact. It is apparent that Thomas' head was not up, that is his neck was not extended, at the moment of contact.

The play developed very quickly. Not all witnesses to it agree as to what happened. All witnesses, however, agree that the contact was substantial and that Thomas' body was extended as he made what turned out to be his last tackle as a football player. There is no suggestion that the punt returner committed any rules infraction during the play. It is apparent that Thomas' head was not up at the point of contact. Indeed, his neck was slightly flexed when the top of his helmet struck the punt returner.

(iv) Thomas' Injury and Subsequent Treatment

Thomas was placed on a fracture board and quickly removed from the field to an ambulance which took him to hospital. He received expert medical treatment within 45 minutes of his injury. Because the trial judge's assessment of damages is not in issue, I propose to deal very briefly with Thomas' injuries and treatment.

Shortly after Thomas arrived at hospital, he was seen by a neurologist who immediately recognized the severity of his injuries and referred him to Dr. Hansebout, a neurosurgeon. X- rays very quickly established that he had a fracture dislocation of his cervical spine at the C-4-5 level. The C-4 vertebra was displaced one centimetre forward on his C-5 vertebra. Both facet joints were locked. The lamina of his C-5 vertebra was fractured. The trauma and its resulting consequence resulted in the narrowing of the space for the spinal cord from a normal width of about 14 millimetres to 6 millimetres.

Dr. Hansebout and an orthopaedic surgeon immediately operated on Thomas. His cervical spine was stabilized by a fusion at the C-4-5-6 level. His locked facet joints were unlocked and his fractured lamina was removed. The treatment that Thomas received was excellent. The results of that treatment were not. Thomas is a quadriplegic.

The Issues

(i) The Standard of Care

It is not disputed that the respondent Board and coaches owed a duty of care to Thomas. Thus, the issue that must be addressed is what was required of the respondent to discharge that duty.

Mr. Morphy, for the appellant, submits that the trial judge erred in resorting to a standard of care which was too low. He contends that the trial judge should not have applied a "prudent parent" standard of care, but rather should have resorted to a higher standard, that is a "supraparental" standard of care, in assessing the acts and omissions of the Board and the coaches.

The trial judge was alert to the "qualifications" imposed upon the "prudent parent" standard of care to which he resorted. I see no error in his characterization and application of the standard of care. In any case, in these circumstances, it seems to me that the important issue is not how the standard of care is defined, but rather how it is to be applied.

(ii) Misapprehension of the Evidence

The appellant's position is that the respondents' conduct consisted of both misfeasance and non-feasance in four discrete areas, fell below the standard of care which the law requires, and that the respondents accordingly breached the duty of care that they owed to the appellant. The appellant's argument identifies, under the general heading of "misapprehension of the evidence", the following:

(a) The failure of the coaches to recognize that on October 26, 1982, Thomas was not in condition to play football and that at the time of his injury their failure to recognize that his level of fatigue was such that he should not have been playing. This is the de-conditioning and fatigue issue.
(b) The respondent coaches' failure to instruct Thomas on the appropriate techniques to be used when tackling. Thomas contends that he was not "properly and progressively coached".
(c) The respondent Board's failure to extract from the sports-medicine and other literature information and opinions suggesting that athletes with a particular neck configuration should not play football, at least

in high risk positions where the athlete would be required to tackle extensively. Thomas also contends that the coaches were negligent because they were unaware of the suggested connection between an athlete's neck configuration and neck injury vulnerability. This is what was referred to at trial as the "long, lean swan neck" issue. Thomas also contends that the Board owed a duty to him to warn him that because of his neck configuration, he was particularly vulnerable to serious neck injury.

(d) The trial judge's conclusion that Thomas and his mother consented to the normal risks of football, including the risk of injury as serious as that suffered by him. Thomas dealt with consent as a separate issue, however, it seems to be related to his broader submission that the trial judge misapprehended the evidence.

(a) Conditioning and Fatigue

The trial judge found that Thomas was in condition to play football on October 26, 1982, when he was injured.

There was ample evidence to support this conclusion and I see no basis upon which to interfere with it. Thomas was an active athletic teenager. He was engaged in physical activities on a year-round basis. While he was unable to play due to his finger injury, he participated in his team's practices. Thomas' own evidence would suggest that he was physically fit to play football when he was injured. The trial judge took the competing evidence of the defence witnesses into account in reaching the conclusion.

It was open to the trial judge to give the evidence of those experts little weight when he dealt with the issue of Thomas' conditioning. The trial judge was entitled to conclude that on October 26, 1982 Thomas was fit from the standpoint of his cardiovascular conditioning, his strength and his flexibility.

In dealing with the somewhat related issue of Thomas' level of conditioning, the trial judge took the evidence of Drs. Johnson, Bull and Bishop into account. Junior football games were not long. They consisted of four 12-minute quarters in which the clock was stopped only in the last three minutes of each half. The trial judge's conclusion that Thomas was not fatigued when he was injured was a reasonable one and a conclusion which was supported by the evidence, including Thomas' evidence. I would not give effect to this ground of appeal.

(b) The Coaches' Instructions on Tackling Techniques

Thomas contends that the duty of care imposed upon his coaches in respect of their obligation to teach their players appropriate tackling techniques was not met.

The evidence is clear that as a regular part of practices the coaches had the team break up into three groups, one of which worked on tackling and blocking techniques. It does support the conclusion that the tackling techniques that were taught were drilled into the players to a sufficient degree. In addition, the 1982 season was Thomas' third season of organized football. He had been taught to tackle by keeping his head up and to make contact with his shoulders in all three seasons.

The trial judge accepted the evidence of Thomas' three coaches, all of whom said that all players were taught to keep their heads up when making a tackle. He accepted the coaches' evidence over that of some former Scott Park players who gave evidence for Thomas at trial. In addition, it seems to be significant that Thomas testified that he knew that he should keep his head up when making a tackle.

It is apparent that if Thomas' head had been up when he made his last tackle, the neck injury he sustained would not have occurred. This was made clear in the uncontradicted evidence of Drs. Upton and Hansebout. They explained that Thomas' injury was caused by "axial loading". Axial loading occurs when, in the circumstances of a tackle, the contact between the tackler's head (helmet) and a punt returner's body, results in the transmission of compression forces from the point of original contact directly through the tackler's cervical spine. Dr. Upton referred to axial loading in terms of the application of a top to bottom force; he said that if the point of contact during a tackle was at an angle so that the compression forces generated by the tackle were transmitted directly down the tackler's spine there is a risk of a serious neck injury. He added that, in this case, the fact that Thomas' facet joints were locked and his lamina fractured suggested that his neck was in a flexed position at the point of contact, to some limited degree.

Thomas testified that he was taught to tackle with his shoulders, not his head. He knew that he should have his head up, that is he should have his neck slightly extended at contact, and that he should make his initial contact with his shoulder. This is what his coaches had taught him. It is manifest that he would not have sustained the injury he did had he made his October 26, 1982 tackle in a manner consistent with the instructions of the respondent coaches.

Two further tackling related issues remain. Thomas contends that the coaches' tackling instructions were deficient in that they taught him to tackle "low", and did not teach him to "bull" his neck when making a tackle.

The evidence is less than clear as to what is meant by "low" in reference to tackling. In any case, Thomas was not attempting to tackle the Glendale player "low". Thomas' tackle was not, and was not intended to be, "low".

The evidence of Thomas' head coach, which the trial judge accepted, was that if the coaches' tackling instructions were followed, a tackler's neck would be "bulled" at the time of contact. The head coach said "bulling your neck" was achieved if the tackler's head was up when making a tackle.

This is consistent with the evidence of Dr. Johnson, an orthopaedic surgeon, who specializes in sports medicine. Dr. Johnson said that "bulling" the neck minimizes neck flexion. From the standpoint of avoiding serious neck injury, it is common ground that a tackler should not have his neck in a flexed position at contact. Apart from the advantage to a player of being able to see what he is doing when making a tackle, one of the principal benefits to be derived from the head-up (neck-extended) tackling position is that it eliminates the prospect of contact being made with the player's neck in the very dangerous flexed position. Dr. Johnson related bulling the neck to keeping one's head up when tackling, although he added that bulling the neck also involves contracting the neck muscles. He viewed bulling the neck "as a little more specific in terms of protection". In any case, in reacting to the circumstances with which he was confronted, Thomas extended his body and to some -- perhaps limited degree -- flexed his neck. He made contact with the player he wanted to tackle with his head (not his shoulders) in that flexed position. "Bulling" his neck, an element of the "head-up" tackling technique taught, was ignored.

The trial judge's findings on the "tackling" issue were supported by the evidence. I see no merit in this ground of appeal.

(c) The Long, Lean Swan Neck Theory

Thomas submits that, because of his neck configuration, he should not have been permitted to play football at all, or that he should have been permitted to play only at low risk positions, where he would not be required to do much tackling. He also submits that the respondents should have been aware of, and warned him (and his parents) about the risk of, serious injury generally, and the risk to which he was exposed because of his neck configuration in particular.

The dual premises that tackling is the most dangerous football-related activity and that players with long, lean swan necks have an increased exposure to neck injuries when making a tackle are at the core of Thomas' position on this issue. He contends that the school authorities were negligent because they were unaware of what was referred to as the long, lean swan neck theory of neck injury vulnerability, and thus did not inform high school coaches about it. Had the Board advised the respondent coaches of the sports-medicine and other literature concerning this theory, Thomas contends that at the critical time in the third quarter of the October 26, 1982 game, Thomas "wouldn't have been there". I took that to mean that he would not have been permitted to play junior football at all, or that he would, at least, not have been permitted to play when his team was punting or kicking-off where he would, in both cases, be expected to make tackles.

For the purpose of an analysis of the long, lean swan neck theory I will accept the premise that tackling is the football activity which exposes football players to the greatest risk of neck injuries. It follows that players who make tackles in games, or in practices, are statistically more likely to sustain neck injuries than those who do not. I would add that because football is a contact sport, it carries with it an obvious risk of a variety of injuries. The exposure to a particular kind of injury may to some degree be related to the position played. For example, anecdotal evidence would suggest that running backs are more exposed to knee injuries than those who tackle them. The risk of a particular injury is activity, and thus position dependent, to some unquantified degree. Mr. Morphy takes account of the relationship between the position played and the risk of a serious neck injury, in his alternative submission that Thomas should have been played at a position where he would not be required to tackle.

The idea that there is a relationship between neck injuries of the sort sustained by Thomas and a football player's neck configuration was referred to in the Canadian Amateur Football Association ("CAFA") Coaching Certification Manual and in a paper by Joseph C. Maroon, published in the November 1981 issue of the Physician and Sports Medicine.

The CAFA certification manual, in a part titled "Balanced Competition", referred to a football player's neck configuration as follows:

Every coach is aware of the difference in sizes of various players and I think it is the coach's responsibility to advise the long, lean swan neck type of individual, that perhaps football is not his game. These are the individuals who are very prone to serious and devastating neck injuries. It should be obvious to the coach that some players are just not the football build, and they are very prone to injury if they are put in this situation.

This part of the CAFA coaching certification manual was written by Dr. Johnson in about 1974. Dr. Johnson gave evidence for the appellant. The CAFA had no direct involvement with Hamilton high school football. Hamilton football coaches were not required to take the CAFA coaching certification program. It would appear that apart from what Dr. Johnson wrote in the "Balanced Competition" part of the CAFA manual, the CAFA made no specific effort to alert coaches of the theory that players with "long, lean swan" necks are particularly vulnerable to serious neck injuries. There is no evidence that any special directive or warning came from the CAFA office that players with long, lean swan necks should play football, or not play in positions where they would be required to tackle.

The reference to players with long, lean swan necks was removed from the CAFA manual in about 1989, according to the evidence of Douglas Hargreaves, the head football coach of Queen's University.

The respondent Board's failure to be aware of the long, lean swan neck theory, and its concomitant failure to advise the coaches of it, are central to Thomas' position on this issue.

The trial judge found that the long, lean swan neck theory was not generally known to football coaches in 1982. The evidence of the respondents, as well as the evidence of Vickers (the opposing coach on October 26, 1982) and Hargreaves fully support that conclusion. In addition, Thomas' family doctor knew nothing about the long, lean swan neck theory. I note in passing that the CAFA manual, on which Thomas relies, states: "The family doctor is usually the best to determine the player's physical health and his verification is usually the most reliable."

The trial judge noted that Mr. Parnell, who was a co-author of the CAFA manual, had no idea how many high school football coaches had taken the CAFA program. The trial judge also found that there were other courses and seminars available to coaches, several of which were attended by the respondent coaches. He noted that there was no evidence that any of these courses or seminars made reference to the long, lean swan neck theory.

Douglas Hargreaves, the head football coach at Queen's University, gave evidence for the respondents. He said that the CAFA Coaching Certification Program began in the early 1970s. He became involved in 1977 or 1978. In respect of the manual's reference to players with long, lean swan necks, Mr. Hargreaves said:

I read the phrase in the book. I'm aware that there are people with longer necks than others, yes, but I don't know the classification of what is a long neck person.

He noted that as a coach of a university team, he did not screen players based on their neck configuration. He also stated, as a member of the coaches committee that revised the CAFA manual in 1989, that in July 1989, reference to the long, lean neck was removed. Once that happened, Mr. Hargreaves said that to his knowledge no coaching manuals referred to the long, lean neck theory.

In the mid 1970s, Dr. Maroon became concerned about the number of serious neck injuries sustained by high school football players in western Pennsylvania. In result, he examined a sample group consisting of seven Western Penn high school football players who had sustained serious neck injuries. His paper set out the information he gathered under six headings: date of injury, age, weight, height, neck size and position played.

Dr. Maroon, a professor of neurosurgery at the University of Pittsburg did not testify at trial. However, I read his paper, published in the November, 1981 edition of The Physician and Sports Medicine. He reached a number of conclusions in his analysis of his seven-student sample group and of interviews he had with their parents and coaches which I summarize as follows:

1. In respect of neck injuries, tackling is the most dangerous football-related activity. No issue is taken with that conclusion.
2. Serious football-related neck injuries are typically caused by axial loading with a flexion component. This is consistent with the evidence of Drs. Hansebout and Upton, both of whom described the mechanics of Thomas' neck injury in their evidence.
3. The players most at risk are lightweight "thin-necked" players who are most likely to be played at defensive back positions.
4. Dr. Maroon concluded that his generally lightweight sample group were often mismatched in the sense that they were frequently required to tackle "much larger and stronger offensive players". There is no evidence of mismatching, that is of any significant size disparity, in this case.
5. Dr. Maroon recognized that improper blocking and tackling techniques are a major contributing factor in catastrophic neck injuries. He added that, "improperly fitted or defective equipment particularly helmets may result in serious injury, as suggested by the mother of one of the players in this series".

The trial judge's finding that the long, lean swan neck theory of special vulnerability was not generally known is amply supported by the evidence.

Thomas, however, takes it further in submitting that had the Board investigated to a reasonable degree, it would have been made aware of the long, lean swan neck theory.

I do not think the Board was required to make the general inquiries suggested by the appellant. There were no data available in 1982, or before, that suggested that there was a neck injury trend at Scott Park, or in other Hamilton high schools, which required an investigation. The statistical evidence relied upon included head injuries. It did not reflect anything resembling a trend with respect to serious neck injuries. Indeed, there had not been a high school football injury resulting in paralysis in Hamilton before Thomas' injury.

The Board had no information on file in respect of the long, lean swan neck theory. There was no reason for the Board to have embarked on an unfocused sports medicine literature search. In any case, the trial judge found that if the Board had done a specific neck injury literature search, a logical source would have been the Sports Information Resource Centre (SIRC) in Ottawa. Since 1974, SIRC has published a monthly sports bibliography that was available for a fee. The SIRC bibliography has been in the Hamilton Board's library since 1987; however, the trial judge found that it was not in the Board's library in 1982 and that the CAFA coaching certification manual was not in the SIRC bibliography in 1982. This is consistent with the evidence that the CAFA manual was available only to those who took the CAFA coaching certification program.

In summary, the evidence supports the trial judge's findings that the long, lean swan neck theory was not widely known, particularly to coaches, and that there was no reason why the Board should have undertaken a search of the sports medicine literature concerning serious neck injuries.

I have assumed that Thomas had a long, lean swan neck and accepted the validity of the long, lean swan neck theory. Both assumptions seem to me to be open to question. I will deal with Thomas' neck configuration first.

A number of witnesses were asked if they thought that Thomas in fact had a long, lean neck. Some knew him in 1982 and before; his coaches, the opposing coach on October 26, 1982, his stepfather, the appellant Terry Wilkinson, and his family doctor are in that group. Others did not know Thomas before he was injured and expressed their opinion on his neck configuration based on photographs of him taken in the summer and early fall of 1982. Drs. Bull, Bishop and Johnson are in that group.

There are no objective criteria by which to determine whether an athlete's neck fits within the long, lean swan neck configuration. Thomas had a long neck. Most of the witnesses agreed on that point, although Dr. Upton expressed the opinion that Thomas' neck was "completely normal".

The trial judge found that Thomas had a long, lean neck, but that the evidence did not establish that his neck came within the long, lean swan neck category.

It seems that the trial judge was not satisfied that the evidence established that Thomas came within the category of football players with a neck configuration that was referred to in the CAFA Manual as a "long, lean swan neck". I see no basis upon which to interfere with his findings on this issue.

This brings me to the issue of validity of the long, lean swan neck theory. The trial judge did not deal with this issue directly because he rejected the submission that the school authorities were negligent because they were unaware of the notion that football players with long, lean swan necks were particularly vulnerable to neck injuries.

Apart from Dr. Maroon's study of seven high school football players who had sustained serious neck injuries, there was no empirical evidence in support of the neck configuration theory on which Thomas relies. Dr. Maroon's study was relatively superficial and it seems that it did not establish anything more than a possible connection between the neck injuries sustained in his seven-player sample group and the five factors he identified -- size differential, inadequate equipment, poor tackling or blocking techniques, the position played and, finally, neck configuration.

Dr. Maroon did not attempt to come to grips with the issue whether players with long, lean necks sustain a disproportionate number of serious neck injuries because they have that neck profile, who because of their slim physiques, play in positions where they are required to tackle, the activity in football which seems to be directly related to many serious neck injuries.

There is no evidence which provides a basis for concluding that there is a correlation between serious axial loading neck injuries and the athlete's neck configuration.

It seems that the submission that the school authorities did not measure up to the standard of care imposed upon them by their failure to warn Thomas and his mother of the long, lean swan neck theory somewhat begs the question in the sense that the very existence of the asserted duty is based upon an assumption the validity of which has not been established. I do not find it surprising that references to the neck configuration theory relied upon by Thomas were removed from the CAFA Coaching Certification Manual in 1989.

Finally on this issue, Thomas' position is that because of his neck configuration, as an alternative to not playing at all, the coaches should have played him on offence as a flanker, the idea being that in that position he would not be required to make tackles. It seems that this option sheds some light on the precarious assumption that a specific neck configuration increases the risk of a serious neck injury. If Thomas had a long, lean, swan neck, I query how the duty of care imposed upon the school authorities could be discharged by permitting him to play football at all, given the obvious risk that at some point in the ebb and flow of a football game, all players may be required to tackle or make contact with an opposing player while blocking in a way giving rise to the potential of an axial loading neck injury if proper tackling or blocking techniques are not used.

I agree with the trial judge's conclusion that the Board and coaches were not negligent for not having known of, and warned Thomas of, the alleged increase of his vulnerability to a serious neck injury because of his neck configuration.

(d) Consent

Thomas does not take the position that football is so inherently dangerous a game that high school students should not be permitted to participate in it. Nor does he contend that his high school should not have participated in junior and senior football programs. This latter issue arose because many of Scott Park's players have part-time employment with the result that they are not available for practice on Fridays.

Thomas participated in his high school's junior football program of his own free will. He was aware of the risk of injury, even serious injury, that is inherent to participation in a contact sport such as football. However, he did not, through his consent to participate (and that of his mother), assume all risk of injury to the extent that the school authorities were relieved of the duty of care that they owed to him.

Thomas was not incapacitated, let alone obviously incapacitated. He had his mother's consent, and his family doctor's certificate stating that he was fit to play football. He knew football was a contact sport which carried with it the risk of serious injury. He wore a "horse collar" because he knew his neck was exposed to injury. He said that even if he had specifically contemplated the risk of a catastrophic neck injury, he would probably have continued to play.

Thomas was appropriately and progressively coached. He was an excellent athlete who excelled in a number of sports, including football. His equipment was adequate. The injury he sustained occurred during a routine play and, although the consequences of his injury were devastating, the injury came within the ambit of those risks inherent in a contact sport such as football. He did not, of course, give a consent which would overcome negligent conduct on the part of the Board or his coaches. However, I agree with the trial judge that neither the Board nor the coaches were negligent and that the appellant and his mother "consented to the normal risks of the game". I am not prepared to say that the trial judge was wrong in reaching that conclusion.

Conclusion

For these reasons, subject to the minor variations in the trial judgment in respect of the appellant Terry Wilkinson's Family Law Act claim and prejudgment interest, I would dismiss the appeal with costs, if demanded. I would limit the respondents to one set of costs.

Appeal dismissed.

ACTIVITIES OUTSIDE SCHOOL HOURS AND OUTSIDE SCHOOL

Educators have a duty of taking care of students as their prudent parents not only in schools but also in activities outside schools that are organized by schools. These activities include field trips and extracurricular activities (Brown, 2009, p. 154). In 2004 four-year-old Allyceea Ennis died on a school bus while being transported to a day-care centre. Her parents filed a notice of intent to sue the Thunder Bay Catholic District School Board in the Superior Court of Justice (Suit in the Works, 2006). In July 2017 Jeremiah Perry, a 15-year-old student from C. W. Jefferys Collegiate Institute in Toronto District School Board, drowned in a field trip, and the teacher organizing the trip, Nicholas Mills, was charged of criminal negligence causing death (Shum, September 11, 2018). Although Mr. Mills was eventually found not guilty (Hasham, 2021), the case can be considered as a warning to educators as what can happen when death occurs because of school organized activities.

REFERENCES

Board of Education for Toronto v. Higgs et al. [1960] SCR 174, 1959 CanLII 24 (SCC). https://www.canlii.org/en/ca/scc/doc/1959/1959canlii24/1959canlii24.html

Brown, A. (2009). *Legal Handbook for Educators* (6th ed.). Carswell.

California Legislative Information. (n.d.). *Education Code*. https://leginfo.legislature.ca.gov/faces/codesTOCSelected.xhtml?tocCode=EDC

Education Act. RSO 1990, c E.2. https://www.canlii.org/en/on/laws/stat/rso-1990-c-e2/latest/rso-1990-c- e2.html

Hasham, A. (2021). Toronto teacher should have foreseen drowning risk but is not guilty in death of Jeremiah Perry, 15, judge rules. *Toronto Star*. https://www.thestar.com/news/gta/2021/10/06/verdict-coming-in-toronto-teachers-trial-over- drowning-of-jeremiah-perry-15-in-algonquin-park.html

Myers v. Peel County Board of Education [1981] 2 SCR 21, CanLII 27 (SCC). https://www.canlii.org/en/ca/scc/doc/1981/1981canlii27/1981canlii27.html

Operation of Schools. Ontario Regulation 298. (1990). https://www.canlii.org/en/on/laws/regu/rro-1990- reg-298/latest/rro-1990-reg-298.html

Resurfice Corp. v. Hanke [2007] 1 SCR 333, SCC 7 (CanLII). https://www.canlii.org/en/ca/scc/doc/2007/2007scc7/2007scc7.html

School Bus Fleet Forums. (2006). *Suit in the Works*. https://www.schoolbusfleet.com/forum/topic.asp?TOPIC_ID=12655

Shum, D. (2018, September 11). Teacher charged in death of teen who drowned in Algonquin Park has court case put over. *Global News*.

The Chinese People's Congress. (2021). *The Chinese Education Act* [中华人民共和国教育法]. http://www.moe.gov.cn/jyb_xxgk/xxgk_jyfl/flfg_jyfl/202107/t20210730_547843.html

Thomas v. Hamilton (City), Board of Education 1994 CanLII 739 (ON CA). https://www.canlii.org/en/on/onca/doc/1994/1994canlii739/1994canlii739.html

Waldick v. Malcolm [1991] 2 SCR 456, CanLII 71 (SCC). https://www.canlii.org/en/ca/scc/doc/1991/1991canlii71/1991canlii71.html

Chapter 5
Special Education

ABSTRACT

Students need support to succeed in school, and students with exceptionalities need more support to succeed. This chapter offers information on special education from the California Education Code, the Chinese Compulsory Education Act, and the Ontario Education Act. It contains sections from the Ontario Education Act and related regulations on special education, as well as information respecting several cases the Supreme Court of Canada heard that dealt with the issue of special education, particularly when it concerned the question of whether special education for students with exceptionalities was a right or privilege. The determinations of the Supreme Court have had a decisive influence on provincial education policies.

The support provided to students with exceptional needs has been increasing in California, China, and Ontario. California Education Code Title 2 Division 4 Part 30 Chapter 1 Article 1 subsection 56000 (a) states that the Legislature declares that all individuals with exceptional needs have a right to participate in free appropriate public education and special educational instruction and services for these persons are needed to ensure the right to an appropriate educational opportunity to meet their unique needs. The Chinese Compulsory Education Act Chapter 7 section 57 stipulates that no school shall refuse to admit into the regular classroom children and youth with exceptionalities who have the ability of receiving the general education. For those with exceptionalities that have difficulty to study together with the average students there are special schools and classes.

DOI: 10.4018/978-1-6684-4163-3.ch005

Ontario Ministry of Education's (2009) Equity and Inclusive Education Strategy defines equity as a state of fair, inclusive, and respectful treatment of all students. While treating students similarly without considering their different socio-economic, racial, and ethnic backgrounds is an important policy of equity and inclusiveness strategy, students with different learning needs must be treated differently so that they are provided the necessary opportunities to achieve similar required learning outcomes. Supporting students with exceptionalities is one of the three common vertical equity measures in financing elementary and secondary education in North America (Imazeki & Reschovsky, 2006; Li, 2016). These three common vertical equity measures are extra financial supports provided to learners from low social-economic families, English language learners, and learners with exceptionalities. The Ontario funding mechanism provides support to all three groups, but the support to students with exceptionalities is the most significant one. The European Agency for Special Needs and Inclusive Education's (2015) vision for inclusive education stated that all learners be afforded meaningful, high-quality educational opportunities in their local community, alongside their peers. The United Nations Educational, Scientific and Cultural Organization (2017) indicated that every learner mattered and mattered equally. Slee suggested six areas of indicators for inclusive education development. Two were the most relevant here: (a) education jurisdictions' legislation and regulations for inclusive education and (b) increasing government budgets for inclusive education (Meijer & Watkins, 2019, p. 708).

The Ontario government expects all students to attend school, when possible, as required by the relevant sections in the Education Act concerning compulsory education. If there are students with exceptionalities, these exceptional needs should be accommodated, whenever possible, through special education programs and services offered through district school boards and schools (Ontario Ministry of Education [OME], n.d., p. 5). Regulation 181/1998 required school boards to consider placing exceptional students into regular classes with appropriate support before the consideration of placing them in a special education class. Where students were placed in special education classes as needed, reasons for doing so must be provided (OME, 2014, p. 10). The same regulation also introduced the individual education plan (IEP), which became the centre piece for offering special education programs and services to students with exceptionalities (OME, 2014, p. 10).

In addition to the Education Act and Regulation 181/1998, district school boards must also follow the Ontarians with Disabilities Act (2001), the Accessibility for Ontarians with Disabilities Act (2005), and the Ontario

Human Rights Commission's (2018) Policy on Accessible Education for Students with Disabilities, as applicable. Providing extra support to students with special needs required resources. How the laws and regulations determined financing had an impact on decision-making in relation to critical issues of supporting some students' needs (Meijer & Watkins, 2019).

Students need support to succeed in school, but some students need additional support to meet their specific learning needs. Support for students with exceptionalities may include extra programs, services, and equipment (OME, 2018). They have complex and unique educational needs. Data obtained from the School Information System indicated that in 2018-2019, 17.7 percent of students in Ontario's school system received special education programs and services (Osgoode Hall Law School, [OHLS], 2020). District school boards reported a total count of 360,450 students receiving special education programs and services out of 2,040,432 students (OHLS, 2020).

School boards were required to establish an identification, placement, and review committee (IPRC), which was responsible for deciding whether a student should be identified as exceptional, identifying the exceptionality according to the categories and definitions set out by the OME, deciding whether to put the student in a regular class or special class, and reviewing the identification and placement generally once in a school year (OME, 2018). Students identified by an IPRC with exceptionalities were normally put into one of five categories and 12 definitions: (a) behavioural; (b) intellectual—giftedness, mild intellectual disability, developmental disability; (c) communication—autism, deaf and hard-of-hearing, language impairment, speech impairment, learning disability; (d) physical—physical disability, blind and low vision; or (e) multiple exceptionalities (OME, 2018, p. 2). These categories were designed to address the wide range of conditions that might affect a student's learning ability but did not exclude any condition that could lead to a specific type of learning challenges. Students with demonstrable needs were entitled to proper support in the form of special education programs and services, including accommodations, modifications, and alternative expectations.

Special teaching and assessment strategies, human supports, and individualized equipment were among the most frequently used accommodation measures. When there was modification, expectations differed somewhat from the regular grade level. Alternative learning was developed to help students acquire knowledge not represented in the provincial curriculum expectations (OME, 2018, p. 16). About 86% of all students receiving special programs and services were placed in regular classrooms for more than half of the instructional day (OHLS, 2020).

Students with exceptionalities are one group that are often at risk of lower educational achievement. In many countries, the concept of inclusive education is embedded in legislation and policy that provide extra support to this group of students (Meijer & Watkins, 2019). Ontario Ministry of Education allocates funding for students with exceptionalities through the special education grant in its funding formula to ensure that all students will be included to be inspired to reach their full potential equitably. The special education grant provided to support students with exceptionalities has been increasing significantly since the Education Amendment Act 1980 made the provision of education to students with exceptionalities mandatory (Li, 2023).

The increase of funding for students with exceptionalities proportionately surpassed the increase in the overall funding for elementary and secondary education. The special education grant increased from $1.6 billion in 2002-2003 to $3.25 billion in 2022-2023, representing a 103% increase (OME, 2022), while the overall number of students in Ontario decreased 113,590, a decrease of approximately 5% (OME, 2003, 2022). At the same time, the consumer price index in Ontario increased almost 53% from 2002 to 2022 (Statistics Canada, 2023). More funding is provided to support students with exceptionalities. Meanwhile determining this funding becomes more complex.

The Education Act (1990) requires that all district school boards provide special education programs and services for students with exceptionalities, which includes students receiving special education programs and services that have been identified as exceptional by an Identification, Placement, and Review Committee (IPRC) and students receiving special education programs and services that have not been identified as exceptional by an IPRC. All students receiving special education programs and services, whether identified as exceptional, should have an Individual Education Plan (IEP)—a written plan describing the special education programs or services needed by the student, based on a thorough assessment of his or her strengths and needs (OME, 2018).

In 2022-2023 the special education grant for elementary and secondary students was approximately 12.4% of the overall education funding, which was the second largest grant, next only to the pupil foundation grant (OME, 2022). In the category of funding for special purpose grants, the special education grant accounted for the largest proportion (OME, 2018). Even with the increasing support to students with exceptionalities, there are still demands to increase the support for them (Luke et al., 2018; People for Education, 2019). As such a significant amount is committed to providing support to students with exceptionalities, there are three sections in the Education Act that concern special education.

In the Act section 1 subsection (1) stipulates that "exceptional pupil" means a pupil whose behavioural, communicational, intellectual, physical, or multiple exceptionalities are such that he or she is considered to need placement in a special education program by a committee,

(a) of which the pupil is a resident pupil,
(b) that admits or enrols the pupil other than pursuant to an agreement with another board for the provision of education, or
(c) to which the cost of education in respect of the pupil is payable by the Minister.

The same subsection also states that "special education program" means, in respect of an exceptional pupil, an educational program that is based on and modified by the results of continuous assessment and evaluation and that includes a plan containing specific objectives and an outline of educational services that meets the needs of the exceptional pupil. It further prescribes that "special education services" means facilities and resources, including support personnel and equipment, necessary for developing and implementing a special education program.

Section 57 subsection (1) stipulates that the Lieutenant Governor in Council shall establish one or more Special Education Tribunals.

Subsection (3) provides that where a parent or guardian of a pupil has exhausted all rights of appeal under the regulations in respect of the identification or placement of the pupil as an exceptional pupil and is dissatisfied with the decision in respect of the identification or placement, the parent or guardian may appeal to a Special Education Tribunal for a hearing in respect of the identification or placement.

Subsection (4) presents that the Special Education Tribunal shall hear the appeal and may,

(a) dismiss the appeal; or
(b) grant the appeal and make such order as it considers necessary with respect to the identification or placement.

Subsection (5) indicates that the decision of the Special Education Tribunal is final and binding on the parties to the decision.

Section 57.1 subsection (1) stipulates that every district school board shall establish a special education advisory committee.

Subsection (2) states that the Lieutenant Governor in Council may make regulations requiring school authorities to establish special education advisory committees.

Subsection (3) prescribes that the Lieutenant Governor in Council may make regulations governing,

(a) the establishment and composition of special education advisory committees;
(b) practices and procedures relating to special education advisory committees;
(c) the powers and duties of special education advisory committees;
(d) the duties of district school boards or school authorities in relation to special education advisory committees.

Section 170 subsection (1) indicates that every board shall provide or enter into an agreement with another board to provide special education programs and special education services for its exceptional pupils.

In addition to the Education Act, Regulation 298/1990 Operation of Schools specifies the provision of special education. Its section 30 presents that a hearing-handicapped child who has attained the age of two years may be admitted to a special education program for the hearing-handicapped.

Its section 31 stipulates that the maximum enrolment in a special education class shall depend upon the extent of the exceptionalities of the pupils in the class and the special education services that are available to the teacher, but in no case shall the enrolment in a self-contained class exceed,

(a) in a class for pupils who are emotionally disturbed or socially maladjusted, for pupils who have severe learning disabilities, or for pupils who are younger than compulsory school age and have impaired hearing, 8 pupils;
(b) in a class for pupils who are blind, for pupils who are deaf, for pupils who have developmental disabilities, or for pupils with speech and language disorders, 10 pupils;
(c) in a class for pupils who are hard of hearing, for pupils with limited vision, or for pupils with orthopaedic or other physical handicaps, 12 pupils;
(d) in a class for pupils who have mild intellectual disabilities, 12 pupils in the primary division and 16 pupils in the junior and intermediate divisions;
(e) in an elementary school class for pupils who are gifted,
    (i) 20 pupils, if the class consists only of pupils in the primary division,

(ii) 23 pupils, if the class includes at least one pupil in the primary division and at least one pupil in the junior division or intermediate division, and
(iii) 25 pupils, if the class consists only of pupils in the junior division or intermediate division;

(f) in a class for aphasic or autistic pupils, or for pupils with multiple handicaps for whom no one handicap is dominant, 6 pupils; and
(g) on and after the 1st day of September, 1982, in a class for exceptional pupils consisting of pupils with different exceptionalities, 16 pupils.

Section 32 states that where it is practical to do so and if the pupil understands American Sign Language or Quebec Sign Language, a teacher or temporary teacher may use American Sign Language or Quebec Sign Language,

(a) in the classroom; and
(b) as a language of instruction and in communications in regard to discipline and management of the school.

Under the Education Act, two regulations were made concerning special education: Identification and Placement of Exceptional Pupils, Ontario Regulation 181/98, and Special Education Programs and Services, RRO 1990, Regulation 306. The following are some of the important contents of Regulation 181/98.

Regulation 181/98 section 1 subsection (1) stipulates that "committee" means a special education identification, placement and review committee, and "designated representative" means,

(a) in relation to a board that has a director of education, the director of education, and
(b) in relation to a board that does not have a director of education, the secretary or equivalent of the board;

"parent" includes a guardian.

Subsection (2) prescribes that a reference to the category and definition of an exceptionality is a reference to the category and definition of the exceptionality as established under subsection 8 (3) of the Education Act.

Section 5 subsection (1) provides that a parent of a pupil and, where the pupil is 16 years of age or older, the pupil, are entitled,

(a) to be present at and participate in all committee discussions about the pupil; and
(b) to be present when the committee's identification and placement decisions are made.

Subsection (2) states that a parent of a pupil and, where the pupil is 16 years of age or older, the pupil, are entitled to be present at and participate in all discussions about the pupil at the meeting held by the special education appeal board.

Section 6 subsections (1) and (2) prescribe that when a board implements a placement decision the board shall promptly notify the principal of the school at which the special education program is to be provided of the need to develop an individual education plan for the pupil in consultation with the parent and, where the pupil is 16 years of age or older, the pupil.

Subsection (3) states that the individual education plan must include,

(a) specific educational expectations for the pupil;
(b) an outline of the special education program and services to be received by the pupil; and
(c) a statement of the methods by which the pupil's progress will be reviewed.

Subsection (4) stipulates that where the pupil is 14 years of age or older, the individual education plan must also include a plan for transition to appropriate post-secondary school activities, such as work, further education and community living.

However, subsection (5) states that subsection (4) does not apply in respect of a pupil identified as exceptional solely on the basis of giftedness.

In developing the individual education plan the principal shall,

(a) consult with the parent and, where the pupil is 16 years of age or older, the pupil; and
(b) take into consideration any recommendations made by the committee or the Special Education Tribunal, regarding special education programs or services.

Subsection (7) prescribes that in developing a transition plan, the principal shall consult with such community agencies and post-secondary educational institutions the principal considers appropriate.

Subsection (8) provides that within 30 school days after placement of the pupil in the program, the principal shall ensure that the plan is completed and a copy of it sent to a parent of the pupil and, where the pupil is 16 years of age or older, the pupil.

Section 7 subsections (1) and (2) present that the board shall promptly notify the principal of the school at which the special education program is to be provided of the need to review the pupil's individual education plan to determine whether it needs to be updated when a board implements a change in placement, or an existing placement is confirmed.

Subsection (3) prescribes that in reviewing the plan, the principal shall,

(a) consult with the parent and, where the pupil is 16 years of age or older, the pupil; and
(b) take into consideration any recommendations of the committee or the Special Education Tribunal, regarding special education programs or special education services.

Subsection (4) indicates that where an individual education plan does not include a plan for transition to appropriate post-secondary school activities and the pupil has attained the age of 14 or will attain the age of 14 within the school year, the principal shall ensure that a transition plan is developed and included in the individual education plan.

Subsection (5) provides that subsection (4) does not apply in respect of a pupil identified as exceptional solely on the basis of giftedness.

Subsection (6) stipulates that in reviewing an individual education plan that includes a transition plan or in developing a transition plan, the principal shall consult with such community agencies and post-secondary educational institutions as the principal considers appropriate.

Subsection (7) states that within 30 school days of an implementation of a change in placement or, where the placement is confirmed, within 30 schools days of receiving the notice, the principal shall ensure that,

(a) the plan has been reviewed and updated as appropriate;
(b) a transition plan has been added to the individual education plan where required; and
(c) a copy of the individual education plan has been sent to a parent of the pupil and, where the pupil is 16 years of age or older, the pupil.

Section 8 prescribes that the principal shall ensure that the individual education plan for a pupil is included in the record kept in respect of the pupil, unless a parent of the pupil has objected in writing.

Section 9 subsection (1) indicates that no pupil is to be denied an education program pending a meeting or decision under this Regulation.

Subsection (2) presents that where an education program is provided to a pupil pending a meeting or decision under this Regulation,

(a) the program must be appropriate to the pupil's apparent strengths and needs;
(b) the placement for the program must be consistent with the principles underlying section 17; and
(c) appropriate education services must be provided to meet the pupil's apparent needs.

Section 13 subsection (1) states that each board shall prepare a guide for the use and information of parents and pupils that,

explains the function of a committee on a referral;
outlines the procedures set out in this Regulation that a committee must follow in identifying a pupil as exceptional and in deciding the pupil's placement;
explains the committee's duty to describe pupils' strengths and needs and to include, in its statements of decision, the categories and definitions of any exceptionalities it identifies;
explains the function of a special education appeal board and the right of parents to appeal committee decisions to it;
lists the parent organizations that are local associations of the board;
includes the names, addresses and telephone numbers of the provincial and demonstration schools in Ontario;
indicates the extent to which the board provides special education programs and special education services and the extent to which it purchases those programs and services from another board;
explains that no committee placement decision can be implemented unless,
a parent has consented to the decision, or
the time limit for filing a notice of appeal in respect of the decision has expired and no such notice has been filed.

Subsection (2) prescribes that the board shall ensure that copies of the guide are available at each school in the board's jurisdiction and at the board's head office.

Subsection (3) indicates that the board shall, at the request of a parent or pupil, provide the parent or pupil with a guide in a braille, large print, or audio-cassette format.

Section 14 subsection (1) stipulates that the principal of the school at which a pupil is enrolled,

(a) may on written notice to a parent of the pupil; and
(b) shall at the written request of a parent of the pupil,

refer the pupil to a committee established by the board, for a decision as to whether the pupil should be identified as an exceptional pupil and, if so, what the placement of the pupil should be.

Subsection (2) provides that where a decision is made that a pupil is to leave a demonstration school and enter a school of a board, the superintendent of the demonstration school shall so notify the designated representative of the board.

Subsection (3) presents that on receiving the notice, the designated representative of the board shall ensure that the pupil is referred to a committee established by the board, for a decision as to what the placement of the pupil should be.

Subsection (4) states that the superintendent of the demonstration school acting under subsection (2) and the designated representative of the board acting under subsection (3) shall use their best efforts to ensure that the committee meets as soon as possible after the decision is made to move the pupil from the demonstration school to the school of the board.

Subsection (5) prescribes that where more than one committee has been established by the board, the referral shall be to the committee that the principal or the designated representative considers to be the most appropriate for the pupil, having regard to the jurisdiction of the committees.

Subsection (6) stipulates that within 15 days of giving a notice or receiving a request, the principal shall provide the parent with,

(a) a copy of the guide prepared;
(b) a written statement of approximately when the principal expects that a committee will meet for the first time to discuss the pupil; and
(c) in the case of a request, a written acknowledgement of the request.

Subsection (7) states that within 15 days of receiving a notification under subsection (2), the designated representative shall provide the parent with,

(a) a copy of the notification under subsection (2);
(b) a copy of the guide prepared; and
(c) a written statement of approximately when the designated representative expects that a committee will meet for the first time to discuss the pupil.

Section 15 subsection (1) indicates that a committee that has received a referral under section 14 shall obtain and consider an educational assessment of the pupil.

Subsections (2) and (3) stipulate that subject to the Health Care Consent Act, 1996, the committee shall also obtain and consider a health assessment of the pupil by a qualified medical practitioner and a psychological assessment of the pupil if the committee determines that the assessments are required to enable it to make a correct identification or placement decision.

Subsections (4) and (5) indicate that where the committee determines that it would be useful to do so and the pupil is less than 16 years of age, the committee shall, with the consent of a parent, interview the pupil. The parent has a right to be present at the interview.

Subsections (6) and (7) prescribe that the committee shall also consider any information about the pupil submitted to it by a parent of the pupil and, where the pupil is 16 years of age or older, the pupil. In addition, the committee shall consider any information submitted to it that it considers relevant.

Subsection (8) presents that as soon as possible after the chair of the committee obtains any information relating to the pupil, the chair shall provide the information to,

(a) a parent of the pupil; and
(b) the pupil, where the pupil is 16 years of age or older.

However, subsection (9) provides that subsection (8) does not apply to oral information submitted at a meeting that the committee holds in respect of the pupil in accordance with this Regulation.

Section 16 subsections (1) to (3) stipulate that the committee may discuss any proposal for special education services or special education programs and shall do so at the request of a parent or a pupil who is 16 years of age or older. The committee may make recommendations regarding special education programs and special education services. The committee may recommend that an exceptional pupil who is 21 years of age or older remain in a secondary day school program.

However, subsection (4) prescribes that the committee shall not make decisions about special education services or special education programs.

Section 17 subsection (1) states that when making a placement decision on a referral under section 14, the committee shall, before considering the option of placement in a special education class, consider whether placement in a regular class, with appropriate special education services,

(a) would meet the pupil's needs; and
(b) is consistent with parental preferences.

Subsection (2) indicates that if, after considering all the information obtained by it, the committee is satisfied that placement in a regular class would meet the pupil's needs and is consistent with parental preferences, the committee shall decide in favour of placement in a regular class.

Section 18 subsection (1) provides that as soon as possible after making its decisions on a referral under section 14, the chair of the committee shall send a written statement of decision to,

(a) a parent of the pupil;
(b) the pupil, where the pupil is 16 years of age or older;
(c) the principal who made the referral; and
(d) the designated representative of the board that established the committee.

Subsection (2) presents that in the case of a referral by a principal, the statement of decision shall,

(a) state whether the committee has identified the pupil as an exceptional pupil;
(b) where the committee has identified the pupil as an exceptional pupil, include,
    (i) the committee's description of the pupil's strengths and needs,
    (ii) the categories and definitions of any exceptionalities identified by the committee,
    (iii) the committee's placement decision, and
    (iv) the committee's recommendation, if any; and
(c) where the committee has decided that the pupil should be placed in a special education class, state the reasons for that decision.

Subsection (3) stipulates that in the case of a referral by a designated representative, the statement of decision shall,

(a) include,
  (i) the committee's description of the pupil's strengths and needs,
  (ii) the categories and definitions of any exceptionalities identified by the committee,
  (iii) the committee's placement decision, and
  (iv) the committee's recommendation, if any; and
(b) where the committee has decided that the pupil should be placed in a special education class, state the reasons for that decision.

Section 19 subsection (1) prescribes that a parent who receives a statement of decision may, by written notice within 15 days of receipt of the statement of decision, request a meeting with the committee.

Subsections (2) and (3) stipulate that the notice shall be delivered to the principal, or the designated representative, who, on receiving the request, shall arrange for the committee to meet as soon as possible with the parent and, where the pupil is 16 years of age or older and wishes to attend, the pupil, to discuss the statement of decision.

Subsections (4) and (5) indicate that as soon as possible following a meeting, the chair of the committee shall send a written notice to each of the persons involved, stating whether any changes in its decisions were made because of the meeting. If changes in the committee's decisions were made as a result of the meeting, the notice shall be accompanied by a revised statement of decision, together with written reasons for the changes.

Section 20 subsection (1) provides that a board shall implement a placement decision made by a committee when one of the following two events occurs:

1. A parent of the pupil consents in writing to the placement.
2. The time period provided for filing a notice of appeal from the decision expires without a notice of appeal being filed.

Subsection (2) stipulates that the board shall implement a placement decision made by a committee as soon as possible after an event described in paragraph 1 or 2 of subsection (1) occurs.

Subsection (3) states that a board implementing a placement decision made by a committee without the written consent of a parent of the pupil shall give written notice of the implementation to a parent of the pupil.

Section 21 subsection (1) prescribes that the principal of the school at which a pupil's special education program is being provided,

(a) may on written notice to a parent of the pupil;
(b) shall at the written request of a parent of the pupil; and
(c) shall, at the written request of the designated representative of the board providing the special education program to the pupil,

refer the pupil to a committee established by the board providing the special education program to the pupil, for a review of the identification or placement of the pupil.

Subsection (2) provides that a request by a parent may be made at any time after a placement has been in effect for three months.

Subsection (5) indicates that within 15 days of giving a notice or receiving a request, the principal shall provide the parent with a written statement of the approximate time when the review meeting will take place.

Section 23 subsection (1) presents that sections 15 and 16 apply with necessary modifications to a committee engaged in a review.

Subsection (2) states that with the written permission of a parent of the pupil, a committee conducting a review shall consider the pupil's progress with reference to the pupil's individual education plan.

Subsection (3) prescribes that as soon as possible after a committee engaged in a review decides that it is satisfied with the identification and placement of a pupil, the chair of the committee shall send a written statement of decision confirming the identification and placement to,

(a) a parent of the pupil;
(b) the pupil, where the pupil is 16 years of age or older;
(c) the principal of the school at which the pupil's special education program is being provided;
(d) the designated representative of the board providing the special education program to the pupil; and

Subsection (4) stipulates that as soon as possible after a committee engaged in a review decides that the identification or placement or both should be changed, the chair of the committee shall send a written statement of decision to the persons involved.

Subsection (5) indicates that a statement of decision shall state,

(a) the reasons for the committee's decision that the pupil's identification or placement or both should be changed;

(b) whether the committee considers that the pupil should continue to be identified as an exceptional pupil;
(c) where the committee considers that the pupil should continue to be identified as an exceptional pupil,
    (i) the committee's placement decision,
    (ii) the committee's description of the pupil's strengths and needs, and
    (iii) the categories and definitions of any exceptionalities identified by the committee; and
(d) where the committee considers that the pupil should be placed in a special education class, the reasons for that decision.

Section 24 subsection (1) prescribes that a parent receiving a confirmation, or a statement of decision may request a meeting with the committee by written notice to the principal of the school.

Subsection (2) states that on receiving the request, the principal shall arrange for the committee to meet as soon as possible with the parent and, where the pupil is 16 years of age or older and wishes to attend, the pupil, to discuss the statement of decision.

Subsection (3) provides that as soon as possible following a meeting, the chair of the committee shall send a written notice to each of the persons involved, stating whether any changes in its decisions were made because of the meeting.

Subsection (4) presents that if changes in the committee's decisions were made as a result of the meeting, the notice shall be accompanied by a revised statement of decision, together with written reasons for the changes.

Section 25 subsection (1) stipulates that a board shall implement a change in placement because of a decision made by a committee when one of the following two events occurs:

1. A parent of the pupil consents in writing to the placement.
2. The time provided for filing a notice of appeal from the decision expires without a notice of appeal being filed.

Subsection (2) states that a board shall implement a change in placement as a result of a decision made by a committee as soon as possible after an event described in paragraph 1 or 2 of subsection (1) occurs.

Subsection (3) prescribes that a board that, without the written consent of a parent of the pupil, implements a change in placement because of a decision made by a committee shall give written notice of the implementation to a parent of the pupil.

Section 26 subsection (1) presents that a parent of a pupil may, by filing a notice of appeal, require a hearing by a special education appeal board in respect of,

(a) a committee decision that the pupil is an exceptional pupil;
(b) a committee decision that the pupil is not an exceptional pupil; or
(c) a committee decision on placement of the pupil.

Subsection (2) indicates that a notice of appeal in respect of a committee decision shall be filed with the secretary of the board,

(a) if no meeting is held, within 30 days of receipt of the statement of decision by the parent seeking to appeal; or
(b) if a meeting is held, within 15 days of receipt of the notice by the parent seeking to appeal.

Subsection (3) provides that a notice of appeal in respect of a committee decision shall be filed with the secretary of the board,

(a) if no meeting is held, within 30 days of receipt of the confirmation or the statement of decision by the parent seeking to appeal; or
(b) if a meeting is held, within 15 days of receipt of the notice by the parent seeking to appeal.

Subsection (4) stipulates that a notice of appeal shall indicate which of the decisions the parent disagrees with and shall include a statement that sets out the nature of the disagreement.

Subsection (5) prescribes that the special education appeal board shall not reject or refuse to deal with an appeal by reason of any actual or alleged deficiency in the statement or by reason of the failure of the parent to accurately indicate in the notice of appeal the subject of the disagreement.

Section 28 subsection (1) states that the chair of the special education appeal board shall arrange for a meeting of the members of the special education appeal board to discuss the matters under appeal and shall give notice of the meeting to a parent of the pupil and, where the pupil is 16 years of age or older, the pupil.

Subsection (2) indicates that the meeting shall be arranged to take place at a convenient place and at a time that is no more than 30 days after the day on which the chair is selected and shall be conducted in an informal manner.

However, subsection (3) presents that with the written consent of the parents of the pupil and the designated representative of the board, the meeting may be scheduled for a time that is more than 30 days after the day on which the chair is selected.

Subsection (4) stipulates that any person who in the opinion of the chair may be able to contribute information with respect to the matters under appeal shall be invited to attend the meeting.

Subsection (6) provides that where the special education appeal board is satisfied that the information bearing on the appeal have been sufficiently presented to it, the board shall end the meeting and, within three days of ending the meeting, shall,

(a) agree with the committee and recommend that its decisions be implemented; or
(b) disagree with the committee and make a recommendation to the board about the pupil's identification, placement or both.

Section 29 subsection (1) indicates that the special education appeal board shall send a written statement of its recommendations to,

(a) a parent of the pupil;
(b) where the pupil is 16 years of age or older, the pupil;
(c) the chair of the committee;
(d) the principal of the school in which the pupil is placed;
(e) the designated representative of the board in which the pupil is placed.

Section 30 subsection (1) prescribes that within 30 days of receiving the special education appeal board's written statement, the board shall consider the special education appeal board's recommendations, shall decide what action to take with respect to the pupil and shall give notice in writing of the decision to each of the persons involved.

Subsection (2) presents that in deciding what action to take with respect to a pupil, the board is not limited to the actions that the special education appeal board recommended or could have recommended.

Subsection (3) states that the notice to a parent shall include an explanation of the further right of appeal provided by section 57 of the Education Act.

Section 31 subsection (1) provides that the board shall implement a decision when one of the following events occurs:

1. A parent of the pupil consents in writing to the decision.
2. Thirty days have elapsed from receipt of the notice by a parent of the pupil and no appeal has been commenced in respect of the decision.
3. An appeal from the decision is dismissed or abandoned.

Subsection (2) stipulates that in accordance with an agreement between the board and a parent of the pupil, the board may change a decision made by it,

(a) while an appeal is pending; or
(b) before the end of the period referred to in paragraph 2 of subsection (1).

Subsection (3) states that where the board changes a decision, the board shall give notice in writing of the change in decision to each of the persons involved.

Support for students with special needs is an important aspect of education. In Ontario the special education grant is the second largest grant in the overall funding for elementary and secondary education, however, there are situations when the budget is tightening, one area negatively affected is funding for students with special needs. The Charter of Rights and Freedoms became part of Canadian Constitution in 1982, with the equality provisions coming into effect in 1985. The Supreme Court of Canada is often placed in the position of interpreting and applying the Charter to cases in the absence of established precedents (Manley-Casimir & Manley-Casimir, 2009). In one case the Supreme Court heard the Court determined that special education support is the ramp with which students with special needs require to access the general education, to which every child is entitled. The following is an adapted version of the judgment the Supreme Court of Canada delivered.

Moore v. British Columbia (Education)

Date: 2012-11-09

Between:

Frederick Moore on behalf of Jeffrey P. Moore
Appellant
and

Her Majesty the Queen in Right of the Province of British Columbia, as represented by the Ministry of Education, and Board of Education of School District No. 44 (North Vancouver), formerly known as The Board of School Trustees of School District No. 44 (North Vancouver)

Respondents

- and -

Attorney General of Ontario, Justice for Children and Youth, British Columbia Teachers' Federation, Council of Canadians with Disabilities, … British Columbia Human Rights Tribunal, First Nations Child and Family Caring Society of Canada

Interveners

2012: March 22; 2012: November 9.

on appeal from the court of appeal for British Columbia

Human rights — Discrimination — Prohibited grounds — Mental or physical disability — Education — Student with dyslexia attending public school — School district cancelling special education program requiring student to enrol in specialized private school — Whether school district discriminating against student by failing to provide necessary remediation — Human Rights Code, R.S.B.C. 1996, c. 210, s. 8.

Education law — School regulation and administration — Curriculum and education programs — Obligations of school authorities — What constitutes meaningful access to education for students with learning disabilities — School Act, S.B.C. 1989, c. 61.

Jeffrey suffered from severe dyslexia for which he received special education at his public school. In Grade 2, a psychologist employed by the school district recommended that since he could not get the remedial help he needed at his school, he should attend the local Diagnostic Centre to receive the necessary remediation. When the Diagnostic Centre was closed by the school district, J transferred to a private school to get the instruction he needed. His father filed a complaint with the B.C. Human Rights Tribunal on J's behalf against the school district and the Province, on the grounds that J had been denied a "service . . . customarily available to the public" under s. 8 of the B.C. Human Rights Code. The Tribunal concluded that there was discrimination against J by the District and the Province and ordered a wide range of sweeping systemic remedies against both. It also ordered that the family be reimbursed for the tuition costs of J's private school. The reviewing judge set aside the Tribunal's decision, finding that there was no discrimination. A majority of the Court of Appeal dismissed the appeal.

Held: The appeal is substantially allowed.

The purpose of the School Act in British Columbia is to ensure that "all learners . . . develop their individual potential and . . . acquire the knowledge, skills and attitudes needed to contribute to a healthy, democratic and pluralistic society and a prosperous and sustainable economy". Adequate special education, therefore, is not a dispensable luxury. For those with severe learning disabilities, it is the ramp that provides access to the statutory commitment to education made to all children in B.C.

The "service" to which J is entitled under s. 8 of the B.C. Human Rights Code is education generally. To define special education as the service at issue risks descending into a kind of "separate but equal" approach. If J is compared only to other special needs students, full consideration cannot be given to whether he had meaningful access to the education to which all students in B.C. are entitled. This risks perpetuating the very disadvantage and exclusion the Code is intended to remedy.

To demonstrate prima facie discrimination under s. 8, complainants must show that they have a characteristic protected from discrimination; that they have experienced an adverse impact with respect to a service customarily available to the public; and that the protected characteristic was a factor in the adverse impact. Once a prima facie case has been established, the burden shifts to the respondent to justify the conduct. If it cannot be justified, discrimination will be found to occur.

There is no dispute that J's dyslexia is a disability. There is equally no question that any adverse impact he suffered is related to his disability. The question then is whether J has been denied meaningful access to the general education available to all children in B.C. based on his disability.

Prima facie discrimination was made out based on the insufficiently intensive remediation provided by the District for J's learning disability for him to get access to the education he was entitled to. J received some special education assistance until Grade 3, but the Tribunal's conclusion that the remediation was far from adequate to give J the education to which he was entitled, was fully supported by the evidence. The Tribunal found that the family was told by District employees that J required intensive remediation. As a result of the closing of the Diagnostic Centre, a private school was the only alternative that would provide the intense remediation that J required.

The Tribunal found that when the decision to close the Diagnostic Centre was made, the District did so without knowing how the needs of students like J would be addressed, and without undertaking a needs-based analysis to consider what might replace the Diagnostic Centre. It was the combination of the clear recognition by the District, its employees and the experts that

J required intensive remediation in order to have meaningful access to education, the closing of the Diagnostic Centre, and the fact that the family was told that these services could not otherwise be provided by the District, that justified the Tribunal's conclusion that the failure of the District to meet J's educational needs constituted prima facie discrimination.

The finding of discrimination against the District is therefore restored.

APPEAL from a judgment of the B.C. Court of Appeal, 2010 BCCA 478, affirming a decision of Dillon J., 2008 BCSC 264, reversing a decision of the B.C. Human Rights Tribunal, 2005 BCHRT 580. Appeal substantially allowed.

The judgment of the Court was delivered by

Abella J. — This case is about the education of Jeffrey Moore, a child with a severe learning disability who claims that he was discriminated against because the intense remedial instruction he needed in his early school years for his dyslexia was not available in the public school system. Based on the recommendation of a school psychologist, Jeffrey's parents enrolled him in specialized private schools in Grade 4 and paid the necessary tuition. The remedial instruction he received was successful and his reading ability improved significantly.

Jeffrey's father, Frederick Moore, filed a human rights complaint against the School District and the B.C. Ministry of Education alleging that Jeffrey had been discriminated against because of his disability and had been denied a "service . . . customarily available to the public", contrary to s. 8 of the Human Rights Code, R.S.B.C. 1996, c. 210 ("Code").

The Human Rights Tribunal held 43 days of hearings, receiving evidence about the funding and administration of special education in the District and Province, the District's budgetary constraints at the relevant time, dyslexia generally, and Jeffrey's circumstances in particular.

The Tribunal concluded that the failure of the public school system to give Jeffrey the support he needed to have meaningful access to the educational opportunities offered by the Board, amounted to discrimination under the Code. I agree.

The preamble to the School Act stated that the purpose of the B.C. school system is to enable all learners to develop their individual potential and to acquire the knowledge, skills and attitudes needed to contribute to a healthy, democratic, and pluralistic society and a prosperous and sustainable economy. Adequate special education, therefore, is not a dispensable luxury. For those with severe learning disabilities, it is the ramp that provides access to the statutory commitment to education made to all children in B.C.

Background

At the relevant time, public school funding in B.C. was approved annually by the Province but administered by districts under the School Act. As of the 1990/91 school year, the Province instituted a block funding system, whereby an overall amount of money was made available for education and then allocated among the various districts by the Minister. The block amount, as determined in the base year, was adjusted annually to allow for changes in enrolment, mandated services, and economic indicators such as changes in the cost of resources. For a short period, the Province provided equalization grants to ease the transition for districts which had historically earned significant supplementary funds through local taxation.

When Jeffrey entered kindergarten in 1991, students with special needs in the District were supported in several ways, and a small number of them were placed in the Diagnostic Centre for more intensive assistance.

Following the implementation of the block funding model, there were significant financial pressures on Jeffrey's home district, School District No. 44. From 1991/92 to 1994/95, the District consistently faced budgetary shortfalls. It had relied on supplementary funds in the past and received declining equalization grants until 1992/93. Despite requests, it did not get additional funding from the Province but got permission to run temporary deficits. Consistent deficits during this period led to wide-scale budget cuts in the District between 1991/92 and 1994/95, including a reduction of almost $1.5 million in spending for high incidence/low cost students with learning disabilities.

In the 1994/95 budgetary process, possible solutions to the financial difficulties included restricting the availability of Aides or closing the District Diagnostic Centre, a program which provided intensive services and individualized assistance to students with severe learning disabilities. The District limited its cuts to Aide allocation because of the terms of its Collective Agreement with the teachers' association, which required a minimum of two hours a week of Aide time once a student was designated as being in a high incidence/low cost category. Other proposed cuts were implemented, including the closing of the Diagnostic Centre in 1994. In February 1996, the Province fired the Board of the District and replaced it with an Official Trustee.

Jeffrey Moore started kindergarten in September 1991 at Braemar Elementary School, his North Vancouver neighbourhood school in the District. While he was happy and energetic in nursery school, it quickly became apparent in kindergarten that Jeffrey needed extra support to learn to read. After scoring low on a screening test, Jeffrey was referred to the Elementary Learning Resource Team, a group of specialists who provided support and assistance to students in the District who had severe learning disabilities, including dyslexia.

After his first assessment in kindergarten, Jeffrey was observed in the classroom and given 15 minutes of individual help from an Aide three times a week. He was assessed twice by the Elementary Learning Resource Team in Grade 1 because he continued to fall behind in literacy skills. He started attending the Learning Assistance Centre three times a week, for half-hour individual sessions with Barbara Waigh, a learning assistance teacher. He also had two 40-minute sessions in the Learning Assistance Centre with a volunteer tutor. Because he still made poor progress, Jeffrey's parents, at the school's recommendation, hired a private tutor to work with Jeffrey.

In January 1994, while Jeffrey was in Grade 2, his parents, concerned about his worsening headaches, took him to a neurologist. They were told that Jeffrey was under significant stress which could be improved by addressing his learning difficulties. The next month, Jeffrey was again referred to the Elementary Learning Resource Team, with his teachers reporting slow academic progress and immature behaviour. He received a full psycho-educational assessment on April 1, 1994, a prerequisite to his designation as a Severe Learning Disabilities student. Following the assessment, Mary Tennant, a psychologist employed by the District, concluded that Jeffrey needed more intensive remediation than he had been receiving and suggested that he attend the Diagnostic Centre.

Ms. Tennant, Ms. Waigh, and Bryn Roberts, Braemar's principal, met with the Moores soon after this assessment. Ms. Tennant and Ms. Waigh told the Moores that because the Diagnostic Centre was being closed, Jeffrey could not obtain the intensive remediation he needed in the District's public schools. The necessary instruction was available only at Kenneth Gordon School, a private school specializing in teaching children who had learning disabilities.

Jeffrey could not enrol in Kenneth Gordon School until Grade 4. His pre-referral form to that school confirmed a serious lack of progress in reading and spelling as well as his poor self-esteem. Every week during Grade 3 at Braemar, he received two 30-minute sessions of individual assistance in the Learning Assistance Centre, two 40-minute periods of individual assistance with a tutor in the Learning Assistance Centre, and four 40-minute sessions with an Aide, primarily in the classroom.

Jeffrey attended Kenneth Gordon School from Grade 4 to Grade 7. When he left, he was reading at a Grade 5 level and was at Grade 7 level in math. He began Grade 8 in September 1999 at Fraser Academy, another private school specializing in children with learning disabilities. He remained there until the time of the hearing and eventually completed high school there.

Prior Proceedings

The Tribunal chair, Heather MacNaughton, found that there was general agreement among the experts about the significant, negative long-term consequences for students with unremediated learning disabilities. The experts also agreed that children with reading disabilities should be identified early and provided with intensive supports.

Based on this evidence, the Tribunal concluded that a range of services was necessary for these students, from a modified program within the classroom to full-time placement in a special program for Severe Learning Disabilities students.

The Tribunal accepted the evidence of experts and of District employees like Ms. Tennant that Jeffrey could not get sufficient services within the District after the closure of the Diagnostic Centre in 1994. Only one expert, who was called by the District, said that Jeffrey had received the services he needed at his public school and that the interventions had been of appropriate intensity.

The Tribunal concluded that there was both individual discrimination against Jeffrey and systemic discrimination against Severe Learning Disabilities students in general. It grounded its finding of discrimination against Jeffrey in the District's failure to assess Jeffrey's learning disability early, and to provide appropriately intensive instruction following the closing of the Diagnostic Centre. It ordered that the Moores be reimbursed for the costs related to Jeffrey's attendance at private schools, as well as $10,000 in damages for pain and suffering.

The finding of systemic discrimination against the District was based on the underfunding of Severe Learning Disabilities programs and the closing of the Diagnostic Centre. While accepting that the District's financial circumstances were compelling, the Tribunal found that there was no evidence that the District had considered any reasonable alternatives for meeting the needs of Severe Learning Disabilities students before cutting available services such as the Diagnostic Centre. It ordered a wide range of sweeping systemic remedies against both the District and the Province.

In the Supreme Court of B.C., Dillon J. allowed the application for judicial review. She found that Jeffrey's situation should be compared to other special needs students, not to the general student population as the Tribunal had done. There was no evidence about this comparison, nor was there evidence about how students with special needs were affected by funding mechanisms such as the high incidence/low cost cap or the closing of the Diagnostic Centre. The failure to identify and compare Jeffrey with the appropriate comparator group tainted the entire discrimination analysis. As a result, she set aside the Tribunal's decision.

A majority in the Court of Appeal dismissed the appeal, agreeing that Jeffrey ought to be compared to other special needs students. To compare him with the general student population was to invite an inquiry into general education policy and its application, which it concluded could not be the purpose of a human rights complaint.

Analysis

Section 8 of British Columbia's Human Rights Code states that it is discriminatory if a person without a bona fide and reasonable justification denies to a person any accommodation, service customarily available to the public based on a prohibited ground. That means that if a service is ordinarily provided to the public, it must be available in a way that does not arbitrarily exclude individuals by virtue of their membership in a protected group.

A central issue throughout these proceedings was what the relevant "service customarily available to the public" was. While the Tribunal and the dissenting judge in the Court of Appeal defined it as "general" education, the reviewing judge and the majority defined it as "special" education.

For students with learning disabilities like Jeffrey's, special education is not the service, it is the means by which those students get meaningful access to the general education services available to all of British Columbia's students:

It is accepted that students with disabilities require accommodation of their differences to benefit from educational services. Jeffrey is seeking accommodation, in the form of special education through intensive remediation, to enable him equal access to the "mainstream" benefit of education available to all. In Jeffrey's case, the specific accommodation sought is not an extra "ancillary" service, but rather how meaningful access to the provided benefit can be achieved. Without such special education, the disabled simply cannot receive equal benefit from the underlying service of public education.

The answer is that the 'service' is education generally. Defining the service only as 'special education' would relieve the Province and District of their duty to ensure that no student is excluded from the benefit of the education system by virtue of their disability.

If Jeffrey is compared only to other special needs students, full consideration cannot be given to whether he had genuine access to the education that all students in B.C. are entitled to. This risks perpetuating the very disadvantage and exclusion from mainstream society the Code is intended to remedy.

Most students do not require intensive remediation to learn to read. Jeffrey does. He was unable to get it in the public school. Was that an unjustified denial of meaningful access to the general education to which students in B.C. are entitled and, as a result, discrimination?

As the Tribunal properly recognized, to demonstrate prima facie discrimination, complainants are required to show that they have a characteristic protected from discrimination under the Code; that they experienced an adverse impact with respect to the service; and that the protected characteristic was a factor in the adverse impact. Once a prima facie case has been established, the burden shifts to the respondent to justify the conduct, within the framework of the exemptions available under human rights statutes. If it cannot be justified, discrimination will be found to occur.

There is no dispute that Jeffrey's dyslexia is a disability. There is equally no question that any adverse impact he suffered is related to his membership in this group. The question then is whether Jeffrey has been denied access to the general education available to the public in B.C. based on his disability.

The answer is informed by the mandate and objectives of public education in B.C. during the relevant period. Educational policies often contemplate that students will achieve certain results. But the fact that a particular student has not achieved a given result does not end the inquiry. In some cases, the government may well have done what was necessary to give the student access to the service, yet the hoped-for results did not follow.

But if the evidence demonstrates that the government failed to deliver the mandate and objectives of public education such that a given student was denied meaningful access to the service based on a protected ground, this will justify a finding of prima facie discrimination.

The mandate and objectives for public education during the relevant period were set out in the School Act, which stated that "the purpose of the British Columbia school system is to enable all learners to develop their individual potential and to acquire the knowledge, skills and attitudes needed to contribute to a healthy, democratic and pluralistic society and a prosperous and sustainable economy". A related policy document, the 1989 Mandate for the School System, O.I.C. 1280/89, said that the government was "responsible for ensuring that all of our youth have the opportunity to obtain high quality schooling that will assist in the development of an educated society".

These education goals in B.C. informed the Tribunal's conclusion that the District did not take the necessary steps to give Jeffrey the education to which he was entitled. Prima facie discrimination was made out based on two factors: the failure by the District to assess Jeffrey at an earlier stage; and the insufficiently intensive remediation provided by the District for Jeffrey's learning disability in order for him to get access to the education he was entitled to. Only the second is in issue before us, since the conclusions about early assessment which were quashed by the reviewing court, were not appealed to this Court. That leaves only the issue of the sufficiency of the services given to Jeffrey by the District.

There is no doubt that Jeffrey received some special education assistance until Grade 3, but the Tribunal's conclusion that the remediation was far from adequate to give Jeffrey the education to which he was entitled was fully supported by the evidence. To start, the Tribunal found that the Moores were told by District employees that Jeffrey required intensive remediation which, as a result of the closing of the Diagnostic Centre, would only be available outside of the public school system. After Jeffrey's psycho-educational assessment in April 1994, Ms. Tennant concluded that he "needed more intensive remediation than he had been receiving" and recommended that he be considered for the Diagnostic Centre program. The Tribunal accepted the Moores' evidence that at a meeting with Ms. Tennant after this assessment, they were advised that since the Diagnostic Centre was not an option because of its pending closing, Kenneth Gordon School "was the only alternative that would provide the intense remediation that Jeffrey required".

The Tribunal also put great reliance on the views of Ms. Tennant and Ms. Waigh, whose "professional judgment" it accepted. It found that Ms. Tennant had "recognized that Jeffrey needed intensive remediation in an alternate setting", and recommended that he look at the Diagnostic Centre. This recommendation was made "in addition to the Aide time to which Jeffrey was entitled under the provisions of the Collective Agreement". The Tribunal found that "Ms. Waigh agreed that [Diagnostic Centre] would have been beneficial to Jeffrey", and noted that Ms. Tennant described Jeffrey's case as one of the worst she had ever seen in her many years of experience. According to her, Jeffrey needed a high degree of intensive one-on-one instruction in a setting designed to minimize distractions. Her opinion was that Jeffrey needed intensive remediation which, in the District, was only offered by the Diagnostic Centre.

The Tribunal concluded that "[w]hile it is clear that the one-on-one attention he received was unusual, the services were not intensive enough to meet his disability-related needs."

The Tribunal found that when the decision to close the Diagnostic Centre was made, the District did so without knowing how the needs of students like Jeffrey would be addressed. The Tribunal noted that at the Board meeting on April 26, 1994, when the budget closing the Diagnostic Centre was approved, the Minutes stated that "[a]ll Trustees indicated in this discussion that they were adopting the bylaw as it was required by legislation and not because they believed it met the needs of the students." It concluded that the District in general "did not know how many students would be affected" by the closure.

Nor did the District consult Ms. Waigh or Ms. Tennant, despite their role in providing services to Severe Learning Disabilities students and their opposition to the closure. As a result, the Tribunal concluded that "nothing was in place in September when schools opened, other than what the schools already provided".

In brief, the Tribunal found that when the decision to close the Diagnostic Centre was made, the District's motivations were exclusively financial, and it had failed to consider the consequences.

This failure was crucial considering the expert evidence that intensive supports were needed generally to remedy Jeffrey's learning disability, and that he had not received the support he needed in the public school system. The Tribunal accepted the evidence of two experts who found that he "would have benefited from more intensive remediation earlier and from attending at the [Diagnostic Centre]".

It was therefore the combination of the clear recognition by the District, its employees and the experts that Jeffrey required intensive remediation to have meaningful access to education, the closing of the Diagnostic Centre, and the fact that the Moores were told that these services could not otherwise be provided by the District, that justified the Tribunal's conclusion that the failure of the District to meet Jeffrey's educational needs constituted prima facie discrimination.

The next question is whether the District's conduct was justified. A service provider must show "that it could not have done anything else reasonable to avoid the negative impact on the individual".

The District's justification centred on the budgetary crisis it faced during the relevant period, leading to the closure of the Diagnostic Centre. It is undoubtedly difficult for administrators to implement education policy in the face of severe fiscal limitations, but accommodation is not a question of "mere efficiency", since "[i]t will always seem demonstrably cheaper to maintain the status quo and not eliminate a discriminatory barrier".

In Jeffrey's case, the Tribunal accepted that the District faced financial difficulties during the relevant period. Yet it also found that cuts were disproportionably made to special needs programs. Despite their similar cost, the District retained some discretionary programs, such as the Outdoor School.

More significantly, the Tribunal found that the District undertook no assessment, financial or otherwise, of what alternatives were reasonably available to accommodate special needs students if the Diagnostic Centre were closed. The failure to consider financial alternatives completely undermines what is the District's argument, namely that it was justified in providing no meaningful access to an education for Jeffrey because it had no economic choice. To decide that it had no other choice, it had at least to consider what those other choices were.

Given the Tribunal's findings that the District had other options for addressing its budgetary crisis, its conclusion that the District's conduct was not justified should not be disturbed. The finding of discrimination is thereby confirmed.

This brings us to the Province's role. The District's budgetary crisis was created, at least in part, by the Province's funding shortfalls. But in light of the Tribunal's finding that it was the District which failed to properly consider the consequences of closing the Diagnostic Centre or how to accommodate the affected students, it seems that the conclusion that the Province was liable for the District's discriminatory conduct towards Jeffrey cannot be sustained.

This leads to considering the remedies imposed by the Tribunal which have been appealed to this Court. A remedial decision by the Tribunal is subject to a standard of patent unreasonableness according to s. 59 of the Administrative Tribunals Act, S.B.C. 2004, c. 45.

The Tribunal awarded the Moores the amount of tuition paid for Jeffrey to attend Kenneth Gordon School and Fraser Academy, up to and including Grade 12, half of the costs incurred for his transportation to and from those schools, and $10,000 for "the injury to [Jeffrey's] dignity, feelings and self-respect". This order is sustainable given the actual scope of the complaint.

But the Tribunal's systemic remedies are so remote from the scope of the complaint, that they reach the threshold set out in s. 59 of the Administrative Tribunals Act.

Having first found that Jeffrey had suffered discrimination at the hands of the District, the Tribunal then considered whether the broader policies of the District and the Province constituted systemic discrimination.

But the remedy must flow from the claim. In this case, the claim was made on behalf of Jeffrey, and the evidence giving concrete support to the claim all centred on him. This does not in any way detract, however, from the cogency of the Tribunal's core analysis. Its finding of discrimination against Jeffrey Moore by the District should be upheld, as should the individual orders, which reimburse the Moores for the cost of private schooling and award them damages. These orders properly seek to compensate them for the harm that Jeffrey suffered and were well within the Tribunal's broad remedial authority. Given my earlier comments on the liability of the Province, however, the order for reimbursement and damages should apply only against the District. I would, however, set aside the remaining orders.

The appeal is therefore substantially allowed as discussed, with costs to the Moores throughout since they were successful in upholding the central finding that there was discrimination.

Appeal substantially allowed with costs throughout.

When considering whether to put a student in a special education classroom or an integrated classroom, the ultimate principle to follow is the best interests of the child. In this respect the decision on the case of *Eaton v. Brant Board of Education* (1997) the Supreme Court of Canada delivered helps us have a better understanding of how this principle should be applied.

Eaton v. Brant County Board of Education

Date: 1997-02-06

The Brant County Board of Education
and the Attorney General for Ontario Appellants
v.
Carol Eaton and Clayton Eaton Respondents
Reasons delivered: February 6, 1997.
on appeal from the court of appeal for Ontario

Constitutional law -- Charter of Rights -- Equality rights -- Physical disability -- Child with physical disabilities identified as being an "exceptional pupil" -- Child placed in neighbourhood school on trial basis -- Child's best interests later determined to be placement in special education class -- Whether placement in special education class and process of doing so absent parental consent infringing child's section 15 (equality) Charter rights -- If so, whether infringement justifiable under section 1 -- Whether Court of Appeal erred in considering constitutional issues absent notice required by Courts of Justice Act -- Canadian Charter of Rights and Freedoms, sections. 1, 15 -- Courts of Justice Act, R.S.O. 1990, c. C.43, section 109(1) -- Education Act, R.S.O. 1990, c. E.2, sections. 1(1), 8(3) -- R.R.O. 1990, Reg. 305, section 6.

The respondents are the parents of a 12-year-old girl with cerebral palsy who is unable to communicate through speech, sign language or other alternative communication system, who has some visual impairment, is mobility impaired and mainly uses a wheelchair. Although identified as an "exceptional pupil" by an Identification, Placement and Review Committee (IPRC), the child, at her parents' request, was placed on a trial basis in her neighbourhood school. A full-time assistant, whose principal function was to attend to the child's needs, was assigned to the classroom. After three years, the teachers and assistants concluded that the placement was not in the child's best interests and indeed that it might well harm her. When the IPRC determined that the child should be placed in a special education class, the decision was appealed by the child's parents to a Special Education Appeal Board which unanimously confirmed the IPRC decision. The parents appealed again to the Ontario Special Education Tribunal (the "Tribunal"), which also unanimously confirmed the decision. The parents then applied for judicial review to the Divisional Court, Ontario Court of Justice, which dismissed the application. The Court of Appeal allowed the subsequent appeal and set aside the Tribunal's order. At issue here are whether the Court of Appeal erred (1) in proceeding in the absence of the required notice under s. 109 of the Courts of Justice Act, to review the constitutional validity of the Education Act, and (2) in finding that the decision of the Tribunal contravened s. 15 of the Canadian Charter of Rights and Freedoms.

Held: The appeal should be allowed.

In our constitutional democracy, it is the elected representatives of the people who enact legislation. While the courts have been given the power to declare invalid laws that contravene the Charter and are not saved under s. 1, this is a power not to be exercised except after the fullest opportunity has been accorded to the government to support its validity. To strike down by default a law passed by and pursuant to act of Parliament would work a serious injustice not only to the elected representatives who enacted it but also to the people. Moreover, this Court has the ultimate responsibility of determining whether an impugned law is constitutionally infirm and it is important that the Court, in making that decision, have the benefit of a record that is the result of thorough examination of the constitutional issues in the courts from which the appeals arise.

The decision of the Court of Appeal is invalid. No notice was given in this case and in fact the Attorney General and the courts had no reason to believe that the Act was under attack. Clearly, s. 109 was not complied with and the Attorney General was seriously prejudiced by the absence of notice.

The s. 15 Charter issue can be resolved on the basis of principles in respect of which there is no disagreement. Before a violation of s. 15 can be found, the claimant must establish that the impugned provision creates a distinction on a prohibited ground which withholds an advantage from, or imposes a disadvantage on, the claimant.

The principal object of certain of the prohibited grounds is the elimination of discrimination resulting from the attribution of untrue characteristics based on stereotypical attitudes relating to immutable conditions such as race or sex. In the case of disability, this is one of the objectives. The other equally important objective seeks to consider the true characteristics of this group which act as headwinds to the enjoyment of society's benefits and to accommodate them. Exclusion from the mainstream of society results from the construction of a society based solely on "mainstream" attributes to which the disabled will never be able to gain access. It is the failure to make reasonable accommodation, to fine-tune society so that its structures and assumptions do not prevent the disabled from participation, which results in discrimination against the disabled. It is recognition of the actual characteristics and reasonable accommodation of these characteristics which is the central purpose of s. 15(1) in relation to disability.

Disability, as a prohibited ground, differs from other enumerated grounds such as race or sex because there is no individual variation with respect to these grounds. Disability means vastly different things, however, depending upon the individual and the context. This produces the "difference dilemma" whereby segregation can be both protective of equality and violative of equality depending upon the person and the state of disability.

The Tribunal set out to decide which placement was superior, balanced the child's various educational interests considering her special needs, and concluded that the best possible placement was in the special class. It also alluded to the requirement of ongoing assessment of the child's best interests so that any changes in her needs could be reflected in the placement. A decision reached after such an approach could not be considered a disadvantage imposed on a child.

For a child who is young or unable to communicate needs or wishes, equality rights are being exercised on that child's behalf, usually by parents. Moreover, the requirements for respecting these rights in this setting are decided by adults who have authority over this child. The decision-making body, therefore, must further ensure that its determination of the appropriate accommodation for an exceptional child be from a subjective, child-centred perspective -- one which attempts to make equality meaningful from the child's point of view as opposed to that of the adults in his or her life. As a means of achieving this aim, it must also determine that the form of accommodation chosen is in the child's best interests. A decision-making body must determine whether the integrated setting can be adapted to meet the special needs of an exceptional child. Where this is not possible, the principle of accommodation will require a special education placement outside of this setting. For younger children and for persons who are either incapable of making a choice or have a very limited means of communicating their wishes, the decision-maker must make this determination based on the other evidence before it.

The child's placement confirmed by the Tribunal did not constitute the imposition of a burden nor did it constitute the withholding of a benefit. Neither the Tribunal's order nor its reasoning can be construed as a violation of s. 15.

The issue in this case is whether a decision of the Ontario Special Education Tribunal (the "Tribunal") confirming the placement of a disabled child in a special education class contrary to the wishes of her parents contravenes the equality provisions of s. 15(1) of the Canadian Charter of Rights and Freedoms. The Court of Appeal held that it did. I have concluded that the decision of the Tribunal was based on what was in the best interests of the child and that in the circumstances no violation of s. 15(1) of the Charter occurred.

Facts

The respondents, Carol and Clayton Eaton, are the parents of Emily Eaton, a 12-year-old girl with cerebral palsy. Emily is unable to speak. She has no established alternative communication system. She has some visual impairment. Although she can bear her own weight and can walk a short distance with the aid of a walker, she mostly uses a wheelchair.

When she began kindergarten, Emily attended her local public school. The Identification, Placement and Review Committee ("IPRC") of the Brant County Board of Education (the "appellant") identified Emily as an "exceptional pupil" and, at the request of her parents, determined that she should be placed on a trial basis in her neighbourhood school. A full-time educational assistant, whose principal function was to attend to Emily's special needs, was assigned to her classroom. At the end of the school year, the IPRC determined that Emily would continue in kindergarten for the following year. This arrangement was continued into Grade 1. A number of concerns arose as to the appropriateness of her continued placement in a regular classroom. The teachers and assistants concluded, after three years of experience, that the placement was not in Emily's best interests and might well harm her.

The IPRC determined that Emily should be placed in a special education class. Emily's parents appealed this decision to a Special Education Appeal Board, which unanimously confirmed the IPRC decision. The parents appealed again to the Tribunal, which also unanimously confirmed the decision. The Tribunal heard from a large group of witnesses and made numerous findings of fact which are described below. The parents then applied for judicial review to the Divisional Court, Ontario Court of Justice, which dismissed the application. However, the Court of Appeal allowed the subsequent appeal and set aside the Tribunal's order. The court held that s. 8 of the Act should be read to include a direction that, unless the parents of a disabled child consent to the placement of that child in a segregated environment, the appellant must provide a placement that is the least exclusionary from the mainstream and still reasonably capable of meeting the child's special needs. The court also ordered that the matter be remitted to a differently constituted Tribunal for rehearing. With leave of this Court, the appellant appealed from that decision. Shortly after the conclusion of argument, the Court gave judgment allowing the appeal with costs and with reasons to follow.

In the Education Act, exceptional pupils are defined as follows:

"exceptional pupil" means a pupil whose behavioural, communicational, intellectual, physical or multiple exceptionalities are such that he or she is considered to need placement in a special education program by a committee of the board.

Section 8(3) sets out the Minister of Education's responsibility for the provision of special education in Ontario:

8(3) The Minister shall ensure that all exceptional children in Ontario have available to them, in accordance with this Act, appropriate special education programs and special education services without payment of fees by parents or guardians resident in Ontario, and shall provide for the parents or guardians to appeal the appropriateness of the special education placement, and for these purposes the Minister shall,

(a) require school boards to implement procedures for early and ongoing identification of the learning abilities and needs of pupils, and shall prescribe standards in accordance with which such procedures be implemented; and
(b) in respect of special education programs and services, define exceptionalities of pupils, and prescribe classes, groups of exceptional pupils, and require boards to employ such definitions or use such prescriptions as established under this clause.

Regulation 305 (Special Education Identification Placement and Review Committees and Appeals), R.R.O. 1990, under the Education Act, requires that every board of education set up an IPRC and establishes the process by which exceptional students are identified and placed, and the process by which parents may appeal the IPRC's decision.

6(1) An exceptional pupil shall not be placed in a special education program without the written consent of a parent of the pupil.

(2) Where a parent of an exceptional pupil,
(a) refuses or fails to consent to the placement recommended by a committee and to give notice of appeal under section 4; and
(b) has not instituted proceedings in respect of the determinations of the committee within 30 days of the date of the written statement prepared by the committee,

The board may direct the appropriate principal to place the exceptional pupil as recommended by the committee and to notify a parent of the pupil of the action that has been taken.

The Courts of Justice Act, section 109(1), states that:

109(1) Where the constitutional validity or constitutional applicability of an Act of the Parliament of Canada or the Legislature or of a regulation or by-law made thereunder is in question, the Act, regulation or by-law shall not be adjudged to be invalid or inapplicable unless notice has been served on the Attorney General of Canada and the Attorney General of Ontario in accordance with subsection (2).

The Canadian Charter of Rights and Freedoms, s. 15, states that:

15. (1) Every individual is equal before and under the law and has the right to the equal protection and equal benefit of the law without discrimination and, in particular, without discrimination based on race, national or ethnic origin, colour, religion, sex, age or mental or physical disability.

(2) Subsection (1) does not preclude any law, program or activity that has as its object the amelioration of conditions of disadvantaged individuals or groups including those that are disadvantaged because of race, national or ethnic origin, colour, religion, sex, age or mental or physical disability.

Judgments in Appeal

Tribunal

The respondents requested that the Tribunal set aside the placement decision of the IPRC, and asked that the Tribunal direct that Emily be placed full time, in a regular, age-appropriate class, with full accommodation of her special needs. The Tribunal heard from the respondents, speech, occupational and physical therapists familiar with Emily, parents of some of Emily's classmates, a witness who, himself, had received a segregated education before high school, Emily's teachers, special assistants and principal at Emily's school, the Board Superintendent, and a special education teacher with the Board.

The Tribunal stated the principal question as "whether Emily Eaton's special needs can be met best in a regular class or in a special class". The Tribunal considered the wishes of Emily's parents; the empirical evidence available from Emily's three school years in a regular classroom setting; the evidence from the literature on placement; the testimony of experts in the matter of classroom placement; the Ontario Ministry of Education and Training's proposed directions regarding the integration of exceptional pupils; and the Charter and Ontario Human Rights Code, 1990, in reaching its conclusion that the IPRC placement decision was the best placement for Emily.

The Tribunal observed at the outset that it is the extent of Emily's special needs which provokes consideration of a special placement, and not the fact that her needs are different from the mainstream. The Tribunal then reviewed Emily's needs under a number of headings and made numerous findings of fact upon which it based its decision.

Intellectual and Academic Needs: Despite the difficulty in assessing Emily's intellectual abilities owing to her inability to communicate, the Tribunal nevertheless found that there was considerable evidence that Emily had a profound learning deficit, and that there was a wide and significant intellectual and academic gap between her and her peers. The Tribunal concluded that it was clear from the evidence that "a 'parallel' learning program specifically designed to meet [Emily's] intellectual needs, isolates her in a disserving and potentially insidious way".

Communication Needs: Emily has very limited abilities to communicate. Carol Eaton and Emily's educational assistants testified "that to learn sign, Emily needs repetitive, hand-over-hand instruction". The evidence suggested that despite this approach, Emily cannot yet communicate using sign. The importance of communication was emphasized by the Eatons' witness, Robert Williams, an adult with cerebral palsy who communicates by means of assistive technology. The Tribunal concluded that "Emily's need to communicate is going to be met only with very individualized, highly specialized, extremely intense, one-on-one instruction. Because this need is of such over-riding importance for Emily, it makes sense to address it in a setting where there will be maximum opportunity for such instruction".

Emotional and Social Needs: The Tribunal relied on the testimony of Emily's parents, teachers, and educational assistants in assessing these needs. The teachers and educational assistants testified that Emily's classmates tend not to involve themselves with Emily. The Tribunal concluded that "although the empirical evidence is that there is limited, if any, interaction between Emily and her classmates, it may be possible that some of her social and emotional needs are nevertheless being met. However, her classroom behaviours -- the increasing incidents of crying, sleeping and vocalization -- suggest that this is not the case. There appears to be little if any, social interaction between Emily and her peers in the regular class".

Physical and Personal Safety Needs: The Tribunal was concerned with Emily's tendency to place objects in her mouth. Emily's parents asserted that they were not concerned and were confident that Emily would not swallow harmful objects. The Tribunal found that "a home setting that is adjusted to a child with pervasive muscular dysfunction, and idiosyncratic communication abilities, and who regularly mouths objects, is significantly different from a regular classroom setting". The Tribunal found that it was not reasonably possible to cleanse the classroom of mouthable materials or to establish the level of adult supervision necessary in the regular, integrated classroom.

The Tribunal then considered Emily's three years of experience in the integrated classroom. The Tribunal found "that the desired outcome of integration for an exceptional child, namely, fulfilment of intellectual and especially social and emotional needs through regular and natural interaction, has not been realized in Emily's case". It observed that the frequency and intensity of Emily's expressions of discontent __ crying, sleeping, vocalizing __ had been increasing over the three-year period.

The Tribunal stated that the three years of experience in the regular classroom with the adult intervention necessary to meet her profound needs even minimally has the counter-productive effect of isolating her in the theoretically integrated setting. The Tribunal found that "this is a far more insidious outcome than would obtain in a special class".

Accordingly, the Tribunal concluded that "[i]t is our opinion that where a school board recommends placement of a child with special needs in a special class, contrary to the wishes of the parents, and where the school board has already made extensive and significant effort to accommodate the parents' wishes by attempting to meet that child's needs in a regular class with appropriate modifications and supports, and where empirical, objective evidence demonstrates that the child's needs are not being met in the regular class, that school board is not in violation of the Charter or the Ontario Human Rights Code".

Ontario Divisional Court (1994)

The respondents applied for judicial review of the Tribunal's decision and sought to quash it on several grounds. First, they argued that the Tribunal was not expert since it was protected by a privative clause of the "final and binding" style only. Second, the Tribunal committed the following errors: it conducted its own literature search after the hearing, and it failed to place a legal burden (arising from the Charter and Ontario Human Rights Code) on the Board to establish that a special education class was clearly better than a regular class for Emily.

The court found that the specialized Tribunal had dealt comprehensively and thoughtfully with all the issues raised before it and with the central focus being what was best for Emily.

There was no error of law. The court held that the Tribunal's post-hearing review of "the literature" to which the experts generally referred did nothing more than confirm its assessment of the evidence before it and the various admissions of the applicants' experts with regard to that research. Accordingly, there was no denial of natural justice.

Court of Appeal (Appeal Judge Arbour for the court) (1995)

The respondents raised several issues on appeal before the Ontario Court of Appeal. First, they contended that the Divisional Court erred in its application of the Charter to the process of placing disabled students in appropriate educational settings. Second, they raised a number of legal errors committed by the Tribunal which, they submitted, ought to have been reviewed by the Divisional Court.

Appeal Judge Arbour discussed the scope of judicial review appropriate in this case. Owing to the privative clause, the subject matter of the legislation, and the composition of the Tribunal, she held that the Tribunal was worthy of curial deference. However, in constitutional matters, she held that the standard of review was one of correctness.

Arbour J.A. dealt with the alleged errors of law first and concluded that although the Tribunal erred in conducting its own review of the literature after the hearing, this error of law "does not come within the ambit of reviewable error within the standard set out above since the analysis conducted by the Tribunal does little more than confirm that there is an ongoing pedagogical debate about the various models for the placement of disabled students, and that, solely from the pedagogical point of view, integration has not yet been proven superior". Consequently, even if the error was reviewable it would not result in the invalidation of the decision.

Arbour J.A. then turned to the constitutional issue. She noted that the respondents submitted that the Charter and the Ontario Human Rights Code both require a presumption in favour of the integration of disabled students, and that, therefore, the Board had to establish why Emily's needs would be better met in a segregated classroom.

Arbour J.A. held that the Tribunal clearly rejected any notion of a presumption in favour of inclusion, and that the Tribunal simply found that the integrated classroom had not been successful. The Tribunal never answered the question as it framed it, namely, whether Emily's needs could be met best in a regular class or a special class.

The respondents stated that there ought to be a presumption in favour of integration. Accordingly, Arbour J.A. looked at whether Emily's placement in a special classroom amounted to discrimination within the meaning of s. 15 of the Charter. She found that Emily was prevented from attending the regular class because of her disability. Thus, a distinction had clearly been made on a prohibited ground. Arbour J.A. then turned to the question of whether the distinction resulted in the imposition of a burden. She found that the history of disabled persons is a history of exclusion from the mainstream of society. In fact, "[i]n all areas of communal life, the goal pursued by and on behalf of disabled persons in the last few decades has been integration and inclusion". She concluded that, when analysed in its larger context, a segregated educational placement is a burden, and is therefore discriminatory within the meaning of s. 15.

Arbour J.A. stated:

Inclusion into the main school population is a benefit to Emily because without it, she would have fewer opportunities to learn how other children work and how they live. When a measure is offered to a disabled person, allegedly to provide that person with her true equality entitlement, and that measure is one of exclusion from the mainstream, that measure, in its broad social and historical context, is properly labelled a burden.

The School Board suggested that distinctions based on disability are not like those based on race or sex in the context of access to education because equality in education requires that the students be treated according to their actual abilities or disabilities. Arbour J.A. criticized this argument saying that although it may be easier to justify differences in access to educational facilities based on disability than it would be if differences were based on race, this analysis must belong to s. 1. There is no reason to create a hierarchy of prohibited grounds within s. 15 which would elevate distinctions based on some to a more suspect category than others. She stated that "[i]f anything, one should be wary of accepting as inevitable and innocuous a classification on the basis of . . . disability, without the rigorous analysis required by s. 15".

Arbour J.A. went on to consider s. 1 of the Charter and concluded that, "[s] ince it [the Education Act] permits a Charter infringement, … I cannot say that the Act infringes the equality rights of disabled students as little as possible".

She found that the appropriate remedy was to declare that s. 8 of the Act should be read to include a direction that, unless the parents of a disabled child consent to the placement of that child in a segregated environment, the school board must provide a placement that is the least exclusionary from the mainstream and still reasonably capable of meeting the child's special needs.

She held that the Tribunal would not have inevitably arrived at the same conclusion had it appreciated that the Charter required that segregated placement be used only as a last resort. Therefore, Arbour J.A. directed that the matter be remitted to a differently constituted tribunal for re-hearing in accordance with the constitutional principles set out in her reasons.

Issues

This appeal raises the following issues:

1. Did the Court of Appeal err in proceeding in the absence of the required notice under s. 109 of the Courts of Justice Act to review the constitutional validity of the Education Act?
2. Did the Court of Appeal err in finding that the decision of the Tribunal contravened s. 15 of the Charter?

Analysis

The Constitutionality of the Education Act

Section 109(1) of the Courts of Justice Act provides that:

109(1) Where the constitutional validity or constitutional applicability of an Act of the Parliament of Canada or the Legislature or of a regulation made thereunder is in question, the Act, regulation shall not be adjudged to be invalid or inapplicable unless notice has been served on the Attorney General of Canada and the Attorney General of Ontario in accordance with subsection (2).

No notice in compliance with this section was given either in the Divisional Court or in the Court of Appeal and no issue was raised with respect to the constitutionality of the Act. Moreover, in the Court of Appeal the respondents expressly disavowed any intention of attacking the Act or the Regulations. The Attorney General for Ontario relied on the respondents' position in the courts below and made no submissions on the constitutionality of the Act and had no opportunity to adduce evidence or make submissions to support the Act under s. 1 of the Charter. I am satisfied that the Attorney General for Ontario was prejudiced by the absence of notice.

In the order of the Chief Justice of this Court dated February 13, 1996, he stated:

As the law as it now stands has been amended through reading in, to salvage the restriction to s. 15, it is for this reason and this reason only that I will state the following constitutional questions:

1. Do s. 8(3) of the Education Act as amended, and s. 6 of Regulation 305 of the Education Act, infringe Emily Eaton's equality rights under s. 15(1) of the Canadian Charter of Rights and Freedoms?
2. If the answer to question 1 is in the affirmative, are s. 8(3) of the Education Act, and s. 6 of Regulation 305 of the Education Act, justified as a reasonable limit under s. 1 of the Canadian Charter of Rights and Freedoms?

In our constitutional democracy, it is the elected representatives of the people who enact legislation. While the courts have been given the power to declare invalid laws that contravene the Charter and are not saved under s. 1, this is a power not to be exercised except after the fullest opportunity has been accorded to the government to support its validity. To strike down by default a law passed by and pursuant to the act of Parliament or the legislature would work a serious injustice not only to the elected representatives who enacted it but to the people. Moreover, in this Court, it is important that in making that decision, we have the benefit of a record that is the result of thorough examination of the constitutional issues in the courts or tribunal from which the appeals arise.

I am respectfully of the opinion that Arbour J.A. erred in this regard. If she had concluded, as I do, that the reasoning and decision of the Tribunal did not discriminate contrary to s. 15 of the Charter, it would have been unnecessary for her to consider the constitutional validity of the Act.

I will turn to the issue of the validity of the decision of the Tribunal.

Does the Decision of the Tribunal Contravene s. 15 of the Charter?

The placement of children in special education programs and services is carried out pursuant to the provisions of s. 8 of the Education Act and the Regulations thereunder. The current legal framework for the education of exceptional pupils was adopted on December 12, 1980. The Act and Regulations made it mandatory for all school boards to provide special education programs and services for exceptional pupils. The policy of the Ministry of Education is that "[e]very exceptional child has the right to be part of the mainstream of education to the extent to which it is profitable" (Special Education Information Handbook (1984)).

Ontario Regulation 305, R.R.O. 1990, adopted as O. Reg. 554/81, deals exclusively with Special Education Identification Placement and Review Committees and appeals. It provides for the identification of exceptional pupils, a determination of their needs and placement into an educational setting where special education programs and services can be delivered. The specific program modification and services required by each exceptional pupil are outlined in the pupil's education plan. Parents and guardians are involved in the identification and placement process and provision is made for appeal of the identification with a placement decision of the board.

This is the process that culminated in a decision by the Tribunal in the present case. After a three-year trial period in a regular class, the IPRC, after consultation with teacher assistants and Emily's parents, determined that she should be placed in a special education class. Emily's parents appealed to a Special Education Appeal Board which unanimously confirmed the IPRC decision. The parents appealed again to the Ontario Special Education Tribunal which unanimously confirmed the decision of the Special Education Appeal Board.

While there has not been unanimity in the judgments of the Court with respect to all the principles relating to the application of s. 15 of the Charter, I believe that the issue in this case can be resolved on the basis of principles in respect of which there is no disagreement. There is general agreement that before a violation of s. 15 can be found, the claimant must establish that the impugned provision creates a distinction on a prohibited ground which withholds an advantage from, or imposes a disadvantage on, the claimant.

The principle that distinctions based on presumed rather than actual characteristics are the hallmarks of discrimination has particular significance when applied to physical and mental disability. Avoidance of discrimination on this ground will frequently require distinctions to be made considering the actual personal characteristics of disabled persons. The purpose of s. 15(1) of the Charter is not only to prevent discrimination by the attribution of stereotypical characteristics to individuals, but also to ameliorate the position of groups within Canadian society who have suffered disadvantage by exclusion from mainstream society as has been the case with disabled persons.

The principal object of certain of the prohibited grounds is the elimination of discrimination by the attribution of untrue characteristics based on stereotypical attitudes relating to immutable conditions such as race or sex. In the case of disability, this is one of the objectives. The other equally important objective seeks to consider the true characteristics of this group which act as headwinds to the enjoyment of society's benefits and to accommodate them. Exclusion from the mainstream of society results from the construction of a society based solely on "mainstream" attributes to which disabled persons will never be able to gain access. Whether it is the impossibility of success at a written test for a blind person, or the need for ramp access to a library, the discrimination does not lie in the attribution of untrue characteristics to the disabled individual. The blind person cannot see and the person in a wheelchair needs a ramp. Rather, it is the failure to make reasonable accommodation, to fine-tune society so that its structures and assumptions do not result in the relegation and banishment of disabled persons from participation, which results in discrimination against them. It may be seen rather as a case of reverse stereotyping which, by not allowing for the condition of a disabled individual, ignores his or her disability and forces the individual to sink or swim within the mainstream environment. It is recognition of the actual characteristics, and reasonable accommodation of these characteristics which is the central purpose of s. 15(1) in relation to disability.

The interplay of these objectives relating to disability is illustrated by the evolution of special education in Ontario. The earlier policy of exclusion was influenced in large part by a stereotypical attitude to disabled persons that they could not function in a system designed for the general population. No account was taken of the true characteristics of individual members of the disabled population, nor was any attempt made to accommodate these characteristics. With the change in attitude and other developments, the policy shifted to one which assessed the true characteristics of disabled persons with a view to accommodating them. Integration was the preferred accommodation but if the pupil could not benefit from integration a special program was designed to enable disabled pupils to receive the benefits of education which were available to others.

It follows that disability, as a prohibited ground, differs from other enumerated grounds such as race or sex because there is no individual variation with respect to these grounds. However, with respect to disability, this ground means vastly different things depending upon the individual and the context. This produces the "difference dilemma" whereby segregation can be both protective of equality and violative of equality depending upon the person and the state of disability. In some cases, special education is a necessary adaptation of the mainstream world which enables some disabled pupils access to the learning environment they need to have an equal opportunity in education. While integration should be recognized as the norm of general application because of the benefits it generally provides, a presumption in favour of integrated schooling would work to the disadvantage of pupils who require special education to achieve equality. Schools focussed on the needs of the blind or deaf and special education for students with learning disabilities indicate the positive aspects of segregated education placement. Integration can be either a benefit or a burden depending on whether the individual can profit from the advantages that integration provides.

These are the basic principles in respect of which the Tribunal's decision should be tested to determine whether that decision complies with s. 15(1). In applying them, I do not see any purpose in distinguishing between the order of the Tribunal and the reasons for that order. That was a distinction that was sought to be made in the Court of Appeal but the reasons and the order are to the same effect and cannot be dealt with separately in this case. Either both are valid, or both are invalid.

The Tribunal's Decision

A Distinction

It is quite clear that a distinction is being made under the Act between "exceptional" children and others. Other children are placed in the integrated classes. Exceptional children, in some cases, face an inquiry into their placement in the integrated or special classes. The distinction between "exceptional" and other children is based on the disability of the individual child.

Burden

The Tribunal sought to determine the placement that would be in the best interests of Emily from the standpoint of receiving the benefits that an education provides. The Tribunal considered Emily's special needs and strove to fashion a placement that would accommodate those special needs and enable her to benefit from the services that an educational program offers. The Tribunal considered the great psychological benefit that integration offers but found that integration had had the counter-productive effect of isolat[ing] her in the theoretically integrated setting.

Moreover, the Tribunal considered each of the various categories of needs relevant to education. It found that it was not possible to meet Emily's intellectual and academic needs in the regular class without "isolating her in a disserving and potentially insidious way". It found that Emily's communication needs would be best met in the special class. It expressed doubt as to whether her emotional and social needs were being met in the regular class. While it is not clear that the special class would meet these particular needs better, it did appear to the Tribunal that there was little, if any, social interaction between Emily and her peers in the regular class. It also found that certain adaptations were reasonable, but that it would not be reasonably possible to accommodate Emily's particular safety needs without radically altering the classroom or establishing a very isolating level of adult supervision.

The Court of Appeal held that the Tribunal ought not to have ordered a segregated placement unless it found that the segregated placement was better than the integrated placement.

In my view, the Tribunal did answer the question which placement was superior. Its findings clearly indicated the conclusion that the segregated placement was superior to the integrated placement. The Tribunal grouped its findings into several categories of needs and interests implicated in education. With respect to Emily's communication needs, the Tribunal clearly found that "[b]ecause this need is of such over-riding importance, it makes sense to address it, at least initially, and until she demonstrates some minimal competence, in a setting where there will be maximum opportunity for [individualized, highly specialized, extremely intense, one-on-one] instruction". It clearly concluded that these needs were not only unsatisfied, but that she was being isolated in a "disserving and potentially insidious way". The Tribunal also found that, with respect to Emily's physical safety, the special classroom was superior to the integrated classroom. The Tribunal looked at several categories of needs and pointed out that some would be better met in the segregated classroom. With respect to the others, the inefficacy of the integrated classroom was established.

The Tribunal, therefore, balanced the various educational interests of Emily Eaton, considering her special needs, and concluded that the best possible placement was in the special class. It is important to note that the placement proposed was in a class located in a regular school where "the special class is integrated with the regular classes through morning circle and a buddy system which may include hand-over-hand art activities, music, reading, outings such as walks and recess, special activities like assemblies, mini olympics, interactive games, including rolling balls and playing catch" according to the testimony of the teacher of the class in which the Board proposed to place Emily. In addition, the Tribunal alluded to the requirement of ongoing assessment of Emily's best interests so that any changes in her needs could be reflected in the placement. Finally, the Tribunal stated:

. . . our decision in favour of a special class placement does not relieve the school board and the parents of the obligation to collaborate creatively in a continuing effort to meet her present and future needs. Emily's is so unusual a case that unusual responses may well be necessary for her. Such achievements can only be realized through cooperation, and most important, compromise.

It seems incongruous that a decision reached after such an approach could be considered a burden imposed on a child.

We cannot forget, however, that for a child who is young or unable to communicate his or her needs or wishes, equality rights are being exercised on his or her behalf, usually by the child's parents. Moreover, the requirements for respecting these rights in this setting are decided by adults who have authority over this child. For this reason, the decision-making body must further ensure that its determination of the appropriate accommodation for an exceptional child be from a subjective, child-centred perspective, one which attempts to make equality meaningful from the child's point of view as opposed to that of the adults in his or her life. As a means of achieving this aim, it must also determine that the form of accommodation chosen is in the child's best interests. A decision-making body must determine whether the integrated setting can be adapted to meet the special needs of an exceptional child. Where this is not possible, the principle of accommodation will require a special education placement outside of this setting. For older children and those who can communicate their wishes and needs, their own views will play an important role in the determination of best interests. For younger children, and those like Emily, who are either incapable of making a choice or have a very limited means of communicating their wishes, the decision-maker must make this determination based on the other evidence before it.

The Court of Appeal was of the view that the Tribunal's reasoning infringed s. 15(1) because the Charter mandates a presumption in favour of integration. This presumption is displaced if the parents consent to a segregated placement. This is reflected in the remedy that the Court of Appeal found to be appropriate. Section 8 of the Act was to be read to include a direction that, unless the parents of a disabled child consent to the placement of the child in a segregated environment, the presumption applies.

The application of a test designed to secure what is in the best interests of the child will best achieve that objective if the test is unencumbered by a presumption. The operation of a presumption tends to render proceedings more technical and adversarial. Moreover, there is a risk that in some circumstances, the decision may be made by default rather than on the merits as to what is in the best interests of the child. I would also question the view that a presumption as to the best interests of a child is a constitutional imperative when the presumption can be automatically displaced by the decision of the child's parents. Such a result runs counter to decisions of this Court that the parents' view of their child's best interests is not dispositive of the question.

I conclude that the placement of Emily which was confirmed by the Tribunal did not constitute the imposition of a burden nor did it constitute the withholding of a benefit from the child. Neither the Tribunal's order nor its reasoning can be construed as a violation of s. 15. The approach that the Tribunal took is one that is authorized by the general language of s. 8(3) of the Act. I have concluded that the approach conforms with s. 15(1) of the Charter. In the circumstances, it is unnecessary and undesirable to consider whether the general language of s. 8(3) or the Regulations would authorize some other approach which might violate s. 15(1).

In the result, the appeal is allowed, the judgment of the Court of Appeal is set aside and the judgment of the Divisional Court is restored. The appellants are entitled to costs in this Court. I would not award any costs in the Court of Appeal.

Appeal allowed with costs.

REFERENCES

Accessibility for Ontarians with Disabilities Act. SO 2005, C11. https://www.canlii.org/en/on/laws/stat/so-2005-c-11/latest/so-2005-c-11.html

California Legislative Information. (n.d.). *Education Code.* https://leginfo.legislature.ca.gov/faces/codesTOCSelected.xhtml?tocCode=EDC

Eaton v. Brant County Board of Education, 1997 CanLII 366 (SCC). https://www.canlii.org/en/ca/scc/doc/1997/1997canlii366/1997canlii366.html?

Education Act. RSO 1990, c E.2. https://www.canlii.org/en/on/laws/stat/rso-1990-c-e2/latest/rso-1990-c- e2.html

European Agency for Special Needs and Inclusive Education. (2015). *Agency position on inclusive education systems*. https://www.europeanagency.org/sites/default/files/PositionPaper-EN.pdf

Identification and Placement of Exceptional Pupils. O Reg 181/98. https://www.canlii.org/en/on/laws/regu/o-reg-181-98/latest/o-reg-181-98.html

Imazeki, J., & Reschovsky, A. (2006). Does No Child Left Behind place a fiscal burden on states? *Education Finance and Policy, 1*(2), 217–246. doi:10.1162/edfp.2006.1.2.217

Li, X. (2016). Ontario, Canada and Hawaii, USA: Who makes stronger vertical equity efforts? *International Studies in Educational Administration, 44*(1), 71–84.

Li, X. (2023). Special education grant in Ontario, how is it determined? *Brock Education, 32*(1), 83–98. doi:10.26522/brocked.v32i1.963

Luke, R., Bennett, S., Specht, J., White, R., Somma, M., Li, X., Lattanzio, R., Gavan, K., Kyle, G., Porter, G., & Patel, A. (2018). *If inclusion means everyone, why not me?* Community Living Ontario, Western University, Brock University, ARCH Disability Law Centre, Brockville and District Association for Community Involvement, and Inclusive Education Canada. https://www.inclusiveeducationresearch.ca/docs/why-not-me.pdf

Manley-Casimir, M., & Manley-Casimir, K. (2009). *The Courts, the Charter, and the Schools: The Impact of the Charter of Rights and Freedoms on Educational Policy and Practice 1982-2007*. University of Toronto Press.

Meijer, C., & Watkins, A. (2019). Financing special needs and inclusive education – from Salamanca to the present. *International Journal of Inclusive Education, 23*(7-8), 705–721. doi:10.1080/13603116.2019.1623330

Moore v. British Columbia (Education) [2012] 3 SCR 360, SCC 61 (CanLII). https://www.canlii.org/en/ca/scc/doc/2012/2012scc61/2012scc61.html

Ontarians with Disabilities Act, SO 2001, C32. https://www.canlii.org/en/on/laws/stat/so-2001-c- 32/latest/so-2001-c-32.html

Ontario Human Rights Commission. (2018). *Policy on Accessible Education for Students with Disabilities*. https://www.ohrc.on.ca/en/policy-accessible-education-students-disabilities

Ontario Human Rights Commission. (n. d.). *Accommodating students with disabilities - Principles (fact sheet).* https://www.ohrc.on.ca/en/accommodating-students-disabilities-principles-fact-sheet

Ontario Ministry of Education. (2009). *Realizing the promise of diversity—Ontario's equity and inclusive education strategy.* https://collections.ola.org/mon/23004/290471.pdf

Ontario Ministry of Education. (2014). *Equity and inclusive education in Ontario schools: Guidelines for policy development and implementation.* https://collections.ola.org/mon/28011/328556.pdf

Ontario Ministry of Education. (2018). *2018-19 Education funding: A guide to the special education grant.* https://files.ontario.ca/edu-gsn-2018-19-special-education-guide-en-2022-03-03.pdf

Ontario Ministry of Education. (2022). *Education Funding: Grants for Student Needs Projections for the 2022-23 School Year.* https://files.ontario.ca/edu-2223-gsnprojections- en- 2022-04-20.pdf

Ontario Ministry of Education. (n.d.). *Guidelines for approval and provision of an education and community partnership program (ECPP) 2021-22.* https://efis.fma.csc.gov.on.ca/faab/Section_23/21-22/ECPP Guidelines 2021-22 April8_21 FINAL_EN.pdf

Operation of Schools. Ontario Regulation 298. (1990). https://www.canlii.org/en/on/laws/regu/rro-1990- reg-298/latest/rro-1990-reg-298.html

Osgoode Hall Law School, York University. (2020, December 9). *Advanced issues in special education law.* https://osgoodepd.ca/professional-development/short-courses-andconferences/advanced-issues-in-special-education-law-2020/

People for Education. (2019). *2019 Annual report on schools: What makes a school?* https://peopleforeducation.ca/report/2019-annual-report-on-schools-what-makes-a-school/

Special Education Programs and Services. RRO 1990, Reg 306. https://www.canlii.org/en/on/laws/regu/rro-1990-reg-306/latest/rro-1990-reg-306.html

Statistics Canada. (2023). *Consumer Price Index, annual average, not seasonally adjusted.* https://www150.statcan.gc.ca/t1/tbl1/en/tv.action?pid=1810000501&pickMembers%5B0%5D=1.14&cubeTimeFrame.startYear=2002&cubeTimeFrame.endYear=2022&referencePeriods=20020101%2C20220101

The Chinese People's Congress. (2018). *The Chinese Compulsory Education Act*. https://baike.baidu.com/item/

United Nations Educational, Scientific and Cultural Organization. (2017). *A guide for ensuring inclusion and equity in education*. https://unesdoc.unesco.org/ark:/48223/pf0000248254

Chapter 6
Principal's Statutory Responsibilities

ABSTRACT

This chapter concerns school principals' responsibilities according to the law. While mentioning the California Education Code and the Chinese Compulsory Education Act, the chapter focuses on the Ontario Education Act. It lists the sections in the Education Act and Regulation 298/1990 Operation of Schools, which prescribe principals' specific responsibilities. The chapter contains Policy/Program Memorandum (PPM) No. 145 and Policy/Program Memorandum (PPM) No. 120 promulgated by the Ministry of Education, which deal with factors principals shall consider when they discipline students who have engaged in inappropriate activities in schools. In addition, it has the Provincial Model for a Local Police/School Board Protocol by the Ministry of Education stipulating that it is mandatory to report to police certain types of incidents.

The principal of a school has an important influence on the learning of the students in that school. California Education Code Title 2 Division 3 Part 25 Chapter 4 Article 1 sections 44817 and 44818 stipulate that the principal of each school when directed by the district superintendent of schools shall submit an annual report to such superintendent on forms furnished by the Superintendent of Public Instruction. Article 2 section 44860 states that no person shall be employed as principal of a school of six or more certificated employees unless he or she holds a valid school administration credential

DOI: 10.4018/978-1-6684-4163-3.ch006

and at least one of the required additional credentials. Section 44861 presents that a substitute principal holding a valid teacher's credential of the same grade as the school to be administered may be employed without meeting the requirements of section 44860 to meet an emergency for not more than five months. The Chinese Education Act does not mention principals, but the Chinese Compulsory Education Act Chapter 3 Article 26 prescribes that the principal of a school is responsible for that school. The principal shall meet the requirements made by the state. Principals shall be appointed by the education bureau of the people's government at the county level according to the law.

In Ontario principals are appointed by district school boards. Education Act section 265 stipulates that it is the duty of a principal of a school, in addition to the principal's duties as a teacher,

(a) to maintain proper order and discipline in the school;
(b) to develop co-operation and co-ordination of effort among the members of the staff of the school;
(c) to register the pupils and to ensure that the attendance of pupils for every school day is recorded either in the register supplied by the Minister in accordance with the instructions contained therein or in such other manner as is approved by the Minister;
(d) in accordance with this Act, the regulations and the guidelines issued by the Minister, to collect information for inclusion in a record in respect of each pupil enrolled in the school and to establish, maintain, retain, transfer and dispose of the record;
(e) to prepare a timetable, to conduct the school according to the timetable and relevant school year calendar, to make the timetable and calendar accessible to pupils, teachers, designated early childhood educators and supervisory officers, to assign classes and subjects to teachers and to assign junior kindergarten or kindergarten classes or extended day program units to designated early childhood educators;
(f) to hold, subject to the approval of the appropriate supervisory officer, such examinations as the principal considers necessary for the promotion of pupils or for any other purpose and report as required by the board the progress of the pupil to his or her parent or guardian where the pupil is a minor and otherwise to the pupil;
(g) subject to revision by the appropriate supervisory officer, to promote such pupils as the principal considers proper and to issue to each such pupil a statement thereof;

(h) to ensure that all textbooks used by pupils are those approved by the board and, in the case of subject areas for which the Minister approves textbooks, those approved by the Minister;
(i) to furnish to the Ministry and to the appropriate supervisory officer any information that it may be in the principal's power to give respecting the condition of the school premises, the discipline of the school, the progress of the pupils and any other matter affecting the interests of the school, and to prepare such reports for the board as are required by the board;
(j) to give assiduous attention to the health and comfort of the pupils, to the cleanliness, temperature and ventilation of the school, to the care of all teaching materials and other school property, and to the condition and appearance of the school buildings and grounds;
(k) to report promptly to the board and to the medical officer of health when the principal has reason to suspect the existence of any communicable disease in the school, and of the unsanitary condition of any part of the school building or the school grounds;
(l) to refuse admission to the school of any person who the principal believes is infected with or exposed to communicable diseases requiring an order under section 22 of the Health Protection and Promotion Act until furnished with a certificate of a medical officer of health or of a legally qualified medical practitioner approved by the medical officer of health that all danger from exposure to contact with such person has passed;
(m) subject to an appeal to the board, to refuse to admit to the school or classroom a person whose presence in the school or classroom would in the principal's judgment be detrimental to the physical or mental well-being of the pupils; and
(n) to maintain a visitor's book in the school when so determined by the board.

Section 266 subsection (2) states that a record is privileged for the information and use of supervisory officers and the principal, teachers and designated early childhood educators of the school for the improvement of instruction and other education of the pupil, and such record,

(a) subject to subsections (2.1), (3), (5), (5.1), (5.2) and (5.3), is not available to any other person; and
(b) except for the purposes of subsections (5), (5.1), (5.2) and (5.3), is not admissible in evidence for any purpose in any trial, inquest,

inquiry, examination, hearing or other proceeding, except to prove the establishment, maintenance, retention or transfer of the record,

without the written permission of the parent or guardian of the pupil or, where the pupil is an adult, the written permission of the pupil.

Subsection (2.1) prescribes that the principal of a school shall, upon request by the medical officer of health serving the area in which the school is located, give that medical officer the following information in respect of pupils enrolled in the school:

1. The pupil's name, address and telephone number.
2. The pupil's birthdate.
3. The name, address and telephone number of the pupil's parent or guardian.

Subsection (3) presents that a pupil, and his or her parent or guardian where the pupil is a minor, is entitled to examine the record of such pupil.

Subsection (4) states that where, in the opinion of a pupil who is an adult, or of the parent or guardian of a pupil who is a minor, information recorded upon the record of the pupil is,

(a) inaccurately recorded; or
(b) not conducive to the improvement of instruction of the pupil,

Such pupil, parent, or guardian, may, in writing, request the principal to correct the alleged inaccuracy in, or to remove the impugned information from, such record.

Subsection (5) indicates that if the principal refuses to comply with a request under subsection (4), the pupil, parent or guardian who made the request may, in writing, require the principal to refer it to the appropriate supervisory officer.

Subsection (5.1) specifies that the supervisory officer shall consider the request and shall,

(a) require the principal to comply with the request; or
(b) submit the record and the request to a person designated by the Minister.

Subsection (5.2) stipulates that subject to subsection (5.3), on receiving the record and request under clause (5.1) (b), the designated person shall hold a hearing, at which the principal and the person who made the request have the rights of parties, and the designated person shall decide the matter, and the person's decision is final and binding.

Subsection (5.3) stipulates that the designated person may refuse to hold a hearing if,

(a) in his or her opinion, the request is trivial, frivolous or vexatious; or
(b) the request is for the removal of information from a record and, in his or her opinion, a guideline made under paragraph 27 of subsection 8 (1) requires that the information be included in the record.

Subsection (6) states that nothing in subsection (2) prohibits the use by the principal of the record in respect of a pupil to assist in the preparation of,

(a) a report required by this Act or the regulations; or
(b) a report,
    (i) for an educational institution or for the pupil or former pupil, in respect of an application for further education, or
    (ii) for the pupil or former pupil in respect of an application for employment,

where a written request is made by the former pupil, the pupil where he or she is an adult, or the parent or guardian of the pupil where the pupil is a minor.

Subsection (7) prescribes that nothing in this section prevents the compilation and delivery of such information as may be required by the Minister or by the board.

Subsection (8) provides that no action shall be brought against any person in respect of the content of a record.

Subsection (9) presents that except where the record has been introduced in evidence as provided in this section, no person shall be required in any trial or other proceeding to give evidence in respect of the content of a record.

Subsection (10) indicates that except as permitted under this section, every person shall preserve secrecy in respect of the content of a record that comes to the person's knowledge in the course of duties, and no such person shall communicate any such knowledge to any other person except,

(a) as may be required in the performance of duties; or
(b) with the written consent of the parent or guardian of the pupil where the pupil is a minor; or
(c) with the written consent of the pupil where the pupil is an adult.

Subsection (13) stipulates that nothing in this section prevents the use of a record in respect of a pupil by the principal of the school or the board that operates the school for the purposes of a disciplinary proceeding instituted by the principal in respect of conduct for which the pupil is responsible to the principal.

In addition to the Education Act, Regulation 298/1990 Operation of Schools stipulates duties of principals and vice-principals. Section 11 subsection (1) indicates that the principal of a school, subject to the authority of the appropriate supervisory officer, is in charge of,

(a) the instruction and the discipline of pupils in the school; and
(b) the organization and management of the school.

Subsection (2) states that where two or more schools operated by a board jointly occupy or use in common a school building or school grounds, the board shall designate which principal has authority over those parts of the building or grounds that the schools occupy or use in common.

Subsection (3) prescribes that in addition to the duties under the Act and those assigned by the board, the principal of a school shall, except where the principal has arranged otherwise under subsection 26 (3),

(a) supervise the instruction in the school and advise and assist any teacher in co-operation with the teacher in charge of an organizational unit or program;
(b) assign duties to vice-principals and to teachers in charge of organizational units or programs;
(c) retain on file up-to-date copies of outlines of all courses of study that are taught in the school;
(d) upon request, make outlines of courses of study available for examination to a resident pupil of the board and to the parent of the pupil, where the pupil is a minor;
(e) provide for the supervision of pupils during the period of time during each school day when the school buildings and playgrounds are open to pupils;
(f) provide for the supervision of and the conducting of any school activity authorized by the board;
(g) where performance appraisals of members of the teaching staff are required under a collective agreement or a policy of the board, despite

anything to the contrary in such collective agreement or board policy, conduct performance appraisals of members of the teaching staff;

(h) subject to the provisions of the policy of the board or the provisions of a collective agreement, in respect of reporting requirements for performance appraisals, report thereon in writing to the board or to the supervisory officer on request and give to each teacher so appraised a copy of the performance appraisal of the teacher;

(i) where the performance appraisals of members of the teaching staff are not required by board policy, report to the board in writing on request on the effectiveness of members of the teaching staff and give to a teacher referred to in any such report a copy of the portion of the report that refers to the teacher;

(j) make recommendations to the board with respect to,
  - (i) the appointment and promotion of teachers, and
  - (ii) the demotion or dismissal of teachers whose work or attitude is unsatisfactory;

(k) provide for instruction of pupils in the care of the school premises;

(l) inspect the school premises at least weekly and report forthwith to the board,
  - (i) any repairs to the school that are required, in the opinion of the principal,
  - (ii) any lack of attention on the part of the building maintenance staff of the school, and
  - (iii) where a parent of a pupil has been requested to compensate the board for damage to or destruction, loss or misappropriation of school property by the pupil and the parent has not done so, that the parent of the pupil has not compensated the board;

(m) where it is proposed to administer a test of intelligence or personality to a pupil, inform the pupil and the parent of the pupil of the test and obtain the prior written permission for the test from the pupil or from the parent of the pupil, where the pupil is a minor;

(n) report promptly any neglect of duty or infraction of the school rules by a pupil to the parent or guardian of the pupil;

(o) promote and maintain close co-operation with residents, industry, business and other groups and agencies of the community;

(p) provide to the Minister any information that may be required concerning the instructional program, operation or administration of the school and inform the appropriate supervisory officer of the request;

(q) assign suitable quarters for pupils to eat lunch.

Subsection (4) stipulates that a principal shall only make a recommendation to the board under subclause (3) (j) (ii) after warning the teacher in writing, giving the teacher assistance and allowing the teacher a reasonable time to improve.

Subsection (5) indicates that a principal of a school,

(a) in which there is a French-language instructional unit, who does not hold qualifications to teach in the French language; or
(b) in which pupils receive instruction in the English language, who does not hold qualifications to teach in the English language as required,

Shall notify the appropriate supervisory officer in writing of the impracticability of the duty placed on the principal, having regard to the qualifications of the principal, to supervise the instruction, to conduct performance appraisals and to assist and advise the teachers referred to in the notice.

Subsection (8) stipulates that the outlines of the courses of study mentioned in clause (3) (c) shall be written and provided,

(a) in the French language in the case of courses of study provided in a French-language instructional unit operated under Part XII of the Act; and
(b) in both the English and French languages in the case of a course of study in a program established in the school under paragraph 25 of subsection 8 (1) of the Act.

Subsection (9) prescribes that where, after reasonable notice by the principal, a pupil who is an adult, or the parent of a pupil who is a minor, fails to provide the supplies required by the pupil for a course of study, the principal shall promptly notify the board.

Subsection (10) indicates that a principal shall transmit reports and recommendations to the board through the appropriate supervisory officer.

Subsection (11) presents that a principal may arrange for home instruction to be provided for a pupil where,

(a) medical evidence that the pupil cannot attend school is provided to the principal; and
(b) the principal is satisfied that home instruction is required.

Subsection (12) states that the principal of a school shall provide for the prompt distribution to each member of the school council of any materials received by the principal from the Ministry identified as being for distribution to the members of school councils and shall post any materials distributed to members of the school council in the school in a location that is accessible to parents.

Subsection (13) stipulates that in each school year, the principal of a school shall make the names of the members of the school council known to the parents of the pupils enrolled, by publishing those names in a school newsletter or by such other means as is likely to bring the names to the attention of the parents. The principal shall meet these requirements each school year not later than 30 days following the election of parent members of the school council.

Subsection (15) prescribes that the principal of a school shall promptly provide the names of the members of the school council to a supporter of the board that governs the school or to a parent of a pupil enrolled in the school, on the request of the supporter or the parent.

Subsections (16) and (17) state that the principal of a school shall attend every meeting of the school council, unless he or she is unable to do so by reason of illness, shall act as a resource person to the school council, and shall assist the council in obtaining information relevant to the functions of the council.

Subsection (18) indicates that the principal of a school shall consider each recommendation made to the principal by the school council and shall advise the council of the action taken in response to the recommendation.

Subsection (19) presents that in addition to his or her other obligations to solicit the views of the school council under the Act, the principal of a school shall solicit the views of the school council with respect to the following matters:

1. The establishment or amendment of school policies and guidelines that relate to pupil achievement or to the accountability of the education system to parents, including,
   i. a local code of conduct governing the behaviour of all persons in the school, and
   ii. school policies related to policies and guidelines established by the board respecting appropriate dress for pupils in schools within the board's jurisdiction.
2. The development of implementation plans for new education initiatives that relate to pupil achievement or to the accountability of the education system to parents, including,

   i. implementation plans for a local code of conduct governing the behaviour of all persons in the school, and
   ii. implementation plans for school policies related to policies and guidelines established by the board respecting appropriate dress for pupils in schools within the board's jurisdiction.

3. School action plans for improvement, based on the Education Quality and Accountability Office's reports on the results of tests of pupils, and the communication of those plans to the public.

Subsection (20) provides that subsection (19) does not limit the matters on which the principal of a school may solicit the views of the school council.

Section 11.1 stipulates that for any pupil who is enrolled in or seeks to be admitted to the secondary school's day program and requires less than three credits to qualify for an Ontario secondary school diploma, or who is enrolled in or seeks to be admitted to the secondary school's day program and has qualified for an Ontario secondary school diploma, the principal of the school shall inform the pupil of ways to earn a credit that are alternatives to enrolment as a full-time pupil, such as enrolment as a part-time pupil, enrolment in a continuing education course or class, or enrolment in a course of study provided by electronic means, but not including enrolment in a private school.

Section 12 prescribes that board may appoint one or more vice-principals for a school and a vice-principal shall perform such duties as are assigned to the vice-principal by the principal. In the absence of the principal, a vice-principal shall oversee the school and shall perform the duties of the principal.

According to Education Act subsection 265. (1) clause (a) the first duty of a principal of a school is to maintain proper order and discipline in the school. Education Act Part xiii section 300.3 stipulates that when students are engaged in an activity that results in harm, the principal shall notify parents.

Section 300.3 subsection (1) stipulates that subject to subsections (2) and (3), if the principal of a school believes that a pupil of the school has been harmed because of an activity described in subsection 306 (1) or 310 (1), the principal shall notify,

(a) the parent or guardian of the pupil who the principal believes has been harmed; and
(b) the parent or guardian of any pupil of the school who the principal believes has engaged in the activity that resulted in the harm.

Subsection (2) specifies that a principal shall not, without the pupil's consent, notify a parent or guardian of a pupil who is,

(a) 18 years or older; or
(b) 16 or 17 years old and has withdrawn from parental control.

Subsection (3) indicates that a principal shall not notify a parent or guardian of a pupil if in the opinion of the principal doing so would put the pupil at risk of harm from a parent or guardian of the pupil, such that the notification is not in the pupil's best interests.

Subsection (4) prescribes that when notifying a parent or guardian of a pupil under clause (1) (a), the principal shall disclose,

(a) the nature of the activity that resulted in harm to the pupil;
(b) the nature of the harm to the pupil;
(c) the steps taken to protect the pupil's safety, including the nature of any disciplinary measures taken in response to the activity; and
(d) the supports that will be provided for the pupil in response to the harm that resulted from the activity.

Subsection (5) stipulates that when notifying a parent or guardian of a pupil under clause (1) (a), the principal shall not disclose the name of or any other identifying or personal information about a pupil who engaged in the activity that resulted in the harm, except in so far as is necessary to comply with subsection (4).

Subsection (6) states that when notifying a parent or guardian of a pupil under clause (1) (b), the principal shall disclose,

(a) the nature of the activity that resulted in harm to the other pupil;
(b) the nature of the harm to the other pupil;
(c) the nature of any disciplinary measures taken in response to the activity; and
(d) the supports that will be provided for the pupil in response to his or her engagement in the activity.

Subsection (7) prescribes that when notifying a parent or guardian of a pupil under clause (1) (b), the principal shall not disclose the name of or any other identifying or personal information about a pupil who has been harmed as a result of the activity, except in so far as is necessary to comply with subsection (6).

Subsection (8) indicates that when notifying a parent or guardian, the principal shall invite the parent or guardian to have a discussion with the principal about the supports that will be provided for his or her child.

After the province implemented Bill 81, Safe Schools Act 2000, there were criticisms that Ontario schools disproportionately punished special needs students, racialized groups, and English language learners. In 2012, the Ministry announced Policy/Program Memorandum (PPM) No. 145 to direct district school boards to develop progressive discipline policies. The Memorandum states that a progressive discipline approach combines prevention and intervention strategies and discipline with opportunities for students to continue their education. Today a principal must consider progressive discipline when contemplating disciplinary measures. The following is a paragraph from PPM No. 145.

For students with special education needs, interventions, supports, and consequences must be consistent with the student's strengths and needs, as well as program goals and learning expectations documented in his or her Individual Education Plan (IEP). Both school boards and schools are expected to actively engage parents in the progressive discipline approach. Boards and schools should also recognize and respect the diversity of their parent communities and reach out to parents to partner with them in addressing complex and challenging issues (p. 4).

On page 6, PPM No. 145 states:

The range of interventions, supports, and consequences used by the board and all schools must be clear and developmentally appropriate, and must include learning opportunities for students to reinforce positive behaviours and help students make good choices.

Information in the student's IEP must be considered in the determination of interventions, supports, and consequences for students with special education needs.

The following paragraphs on pages 12 and 13 of PPM No. 145 direct what a principal must do when the principal has decided that action must be taken because of a serious student incident.

If the principal has decided that action must be taken as a result of a serious student incident, he or she will file a copy of the reporting form with documentation indicating the action taken in the OSR (Ontario student record) of the student whose behaviour was inappropriate. The names of all other students that appear on the form – both students who engaged in the activity and students who have been harmed – must be removed from the form before it is filed.

Where the principal has acted in the case of more than one student, a copy of the reporting form with documentation indicating the action taken must be filed in the OSR of each student whose behaviour was inappropriate. The names of all other students that appear on the form must be removed from the form before it is filed. In the case of the student who has been harmed, no information about the incident must be placed in his or her OSR, unless that student's parents expressly request that it be placed in the OSR.

In situations where the student who has been harmed has also engaged in a serious student incident, information regarding the incident and the action taken will be placed in the student's OSR.

The form and documentation must be kept in the OSR for a minimum of one year.

If the principal has identified the incident as violent, and if the student engaged in the incident is a student at the school, the reporting form must be retained in that student's OSR for:

- one year, if the student's suspension was quashed or withdrawn and the record of suspension expunged. Documentation of any other action taken (other than suspension or expulsion) must also be retained for this period;
- three years, if the student was suspended for the violent incident;
- five years, if the student was expelled for the violent incident.

For non-violent incidents, if no further action is taken by the principal, the principal is not required to retain the report.

Policy/Program Memorandum No. 120 defines the term of violent incident as the occurrence of any one of the following or the occurrence of a combination of any of the following:

possessing a weapon, including possessing a firearm,
physical assault causing bodily harm requiring medical attention,
sexual assault,
robbery,
using a weapon to cause or to threaten bodily harm to another person,
extortion,
hate and/or bias-motivated occurrences.

The Provincial Model for a Local Police/School Board Protocol (Ministry of Education, 2015) stipulates that it is mandatory to report to police certain types of incidents. The following are the incidents that require mandatory reporting to police.

- all deaths;
- physical assault causing bodily harm requiring treatment by a medical practitioner;
- sexual assault;
- robbery;
- criminal harassment;
- relationship-based violence;
- possessing a weapon, including possessing a firearm;
- using a weapon to cause or to threaten bodily harm to another person;
- trafficking in weapons or in illegal drugs;
- possessing an illegal drug;
- hate and/or bias-motivated occurrences;
- gang-related occurrences;
- extortion;
- non-consensual sharing of intimate images; and
- bomb threats.

The Model further prescribes that police response may also be needed in connection with the following types of incidents:

- giving alcohol to a minor;
- being under the influence of alcohol or illegal drugs;
- threats of serious physical injury, including threats made on social networking sites or through instant messaging, text messaging, email, and so on;
- incidents of vandalism; and
- incidents of trespassing.

Principals should consider mitigating and other factors when deciding whether to call the police in these discretionary situations. It is expected that all other school-related occurrences not specified in the protocol will be dealt with by the principal on a case-by-case basis, and that police will be notified at the principal's discretion. For students with special education needs, school boards should identify circumstances where a police response is neither necessary nor appropriate.

The Model also stipulates particular attention a principal must pay to procedures when investigating an incident together with police.

a) Legal Rights

In the investigation of school-related incidents where a young person is a suspect, particular attention should be given by the principal and police to procedures that are consistent with the following provisions:

- parental notification upon arrest (s. 26, Youth Criminal Justice Act);
- right to counsel (s. 25, Youth Criminal Justice Act);
- right not to make a statement (s. 146, Youth Criminal Justice Act); and
- protection of privacy (s. 110, Youth Criminal Justice Act).

b) Search and Seizure

where investigations involve search and seizure, the police and the principal should pay particular attention to the following procedures and responsibilities:

- procedures to be followed in personal and premise searches, in accordance with the Ministry of Community Safety and Correctional Services' Guidelines LE-011 on search of premises and LE-012 on search of persons, and relevant federal legislation;
- roles and responsibilities of police and school personnel in conducting searches of persons or property;
- the requirement that police notify the principal before conducting searches on school premises. (Under some exigent circumstances, police may execute a search without a warrant and without notice to the principal.); and
- the continuing responsibility of the principal for students even when police are on school premises.

For a principal the Model lists the following general procedures, requirements, and considerations related to police interviews of students:

- the need for the principal to make best efforts to contact parents as soon as possible before the interview;

- the requirement that a parent/legal guardian, third-party adult, or the principal, if no alternative is available, be present when students under the age of 18 are being interviewed at school;
- the requirement, in cases where a student aged 12 to 17 waives the right to have an adult present at the interview, that the principal consider the most appropriate location for conducting the interview and take steps to ensure that the student's rights are respected during the interview;
- factors to consider in determining the most appropriate time and place to conduct a student interview;
- procedures for including the local children's aid society (CAS) in a joint interview if the child is suspected to be in need of protection;
- the need for school personnel to assist police in making the required preparations (e.g., securing a quiet room and establishing a time for the interview);

It is the principal's responsibility to contact parents:

- of all students being interviewed by police during an investigation, except:
- if the principal is otherwise directed by police because of exigent circumstances or where the police believe the parent may be implicated;
- if the student is 18 years of age or older (unless the student consents to or requests such contact or is incapable of providing consent); or
- if the student is 16 or 17 years of age and has withdrawn from parental control (unless the student consents to or requests such contact or is incapable of providing consent).

If a CAS (children's aid society) is involved, school and police officials should discuss and come to agreement with the CAS regarding the timing and procedure for notifying the parents.

In cases involving students with special education needs, the principal should review the student's Individual Education Plan (IEP) and other relevant student records to identify whether further intervention strategies and/or resources are required for the student. These may include the development of and/or revisions to a behaviour management plan or a safety plan.

Providing accommodation to students with disabilities is related to their human rights. Ontario Human Rights Commission states on its website:

Once a disability-related need has been identified, or a case of discrimination has been established, education providers have a duty to accommodate the needs of students with disabilities, unless to do so would cause undue hardship. Accommodation is a means of preventing and removing barriers that impede students with disabilities from participating fully in the educational environment. Accommodation involves three principles: dignity, individualization and inclusion.

1. Respect for Dignity: Students with disabilities have the right to receive educational services in a manner that respects their dignity. Human dignity encompasses individual self-respect and self-worth. It involves physical and psychological integrity and empowerment. It is harmed when individuals are marginalized, stigmatized, ignored or devalued. Accommodation solutions should therefore respect the dignity of students with disabilities, and those that do not will not be considered appropriate.
2. Individualized Accommodation: Each student's needs are unique and must be considered afresh when an accommodation request is made. At all times, the emphasis must be on the individual student and not on the category of disability. Blanket approaches to accommodation that rely on labels and generalizations are not acceptable.
3. Inclusion and Full Participation: In some circumstances, the best way to ensure the dignity of persons with disabilities may be to provide separate or specialized services. However, education providers must first try to build or adapt educational services to accommodate students with disabilities in a way that promotes their inclusion and full participation and enables barrier-free access.

Education Act subsection 306. (1) stipulates that a principal shall consider whether to suspend a pupil if the principal believes that the pupil has engaged in any of certain activities while at school, at a school-related activity, or in other circumstances, where engaging in the activity will have an impact on the school climate. It is easy to understand at school or at a school related activity, but it is not always easy to agree on what a school climate is, let alone an activity that has an impact on the school climate. PPM No. 145 states that the school climate may be defined as the learning environment and relationships found within a school and school community. A positive school climate exists when all members of the school community feel safe, included, and accepted, and actively promote positive behaviours and interactions. One example of an activity that has a negative impact on school climate is cyberbullying committed by students occurring outside school but targeting individual students and causing them to be afraid to come to school.

REFERENCES

California Legislative Information. (n.d.). *Education Code*. https://leginfo.legislature.ca.gov/faces/codesTOCSelected.xhtml?tocCode=EDC

Education Act. RSO 1990, c E.2. https://www.canlii.org/en/on/laws/stat/rso-1990-c-e2/latest/rso-1990-c- e2.html

Ontario Ministry of Education. (2015). *The Provincial Model for a Local Police/School Board Protocol*. http://www.edu.gov.on.ca/eng/document/brochure/protocol/locprote.pdf

Operation of Schools. Ontario Regulation 298. (1990). https://www.canlii.org/en/on/laws/regu/rro-1990- reg-298/latest/rro-1990-reg-298.html

Policy/Program Memorandum No. 120. (2011). http://www.edu.gov.on.ca/extra/eng/ppm/120.html#_ftnref5

Policy/Program Memorandum No. 145. (2018). http://www.edu.gov.on.ca/extra/eng/ppm/145.pdf

Safe Schools Act, SO 2000, c 12. https://www.canlii.org/en/on/laws/astat/so-2000-c-12/latest/so-2000-c-12.html?autocompleteStr=Bill%20 81&autocompletePos=8

The Chinese People's Congress. (2018). *The Chinese Compulsory Education Act* [中华人民共和国 义务教育法]. https://baike.baidu.com/item/中华人民共和国义务教育法/2342357

The Chinese People's Congress. (2021). *The Chinese Education Act* [中华人民共和国教育法]. http://www.moe.gov.cn/jyb_xxgk/xxgk_jyfl/flfg_jyfl/202107/t20210730_547843.html

Chapter 7
Collective Bargaining

ABSTRACT

Chapter 7 is about collective bargaining, which decides the working conditions of teachers in publicly funded schools in both California and Ontario, but not in China. The chapter presents a brief history and discussion of how collective bargaining developed in the last three decades in Ontario, when significant shifts transpired in the education system. It refers to the relevant literature on the issue of teacher collective bargaining. At the time of writing this book, collective bargaining is still going on between four Ontario teachers' unions and the provincial government, but unlike previous bargaining, there is little report from the media on what happens during the bargaining.

Nearly all California's school districts have a teachers' union affiliated with either the California Teachers Association or the California Federation of Teachers. The primary activity of a union is to represent the teachers in negotiating the terms of employment contracts in collective bargaining. School boards and unions must meet at least once every three years. The results of negotiating determine the salaries and benefits, hours, calendar, and most aspects of teachers' working conditions—as well as attempting to solve problems and address new issues that have arisen during the period of the contract (Evergreen Teachers Association, n.d.). There is no collective bargaining in China for teachers, whose salaries are decided by the government.

In Ontario, although district school boards are corporations, their powers and duties come from the provincial legislature and government. Before a Conservative government introduced the current funding formula in 1997,

DOI: 10.4018/978-1-6684-4163-3.ch007

Ontario's education funding model was a guaranteed tax-base grant plan in which local municipalities and the provincial government determined revenues for school boards (Lawton, 1996). There were significant differences in funding per pupil at different school boards, because of variation in wealth among municipalities. Historically, school boards had exclusive authority for levying education property taxes (Garcea & Munroe, 2014), and they had the power to decide how to pay their teachers. When the funding was not enough, they could approach their corresponding municipal councils to increase education tax. In 1997, local support to education was greater than that from the province (Gidney, 1999).

Since 1997 when the Conservatives passed Bill 160, the Education Quality Improvement Act, which took away school boards' power of deciding local education tax, there has been a significant change in the relationship between the Ministry of Education and district school boards. When the provincial legislature passed Bill 160, Ontario English Catholic Teachers' Association and other organizations challenged the legislation on a number of constitutional grounds. The case went all the way to the Supreme Court of Canada, which determined that the Education Act, as amended by Bill 160, the Education Quality Improvement Act 1997, did not prejudicially affect rights held under s. 93(1) of the Constitution Act, 1867 (Supreme Court of Canada, 2001).

Today district school boards must meet all the needs within their jurisdictions with the funding determined by the Ministry of Education. A provincial formula decides education funding, and school boards must make their annual financial statements public. District school boards receive revenues from both the provincial government and their own municipal governments. However, municipal governments across the province provide the same percentage of their income to school boards as education tax, and the provincial Finance Minister decides this percentage; with the consideration of the funding formula, the provincial government provides the balance. In 2020-2021 the provincial government provided approximately 70% of the education funding and 30% was from local property tax (author's calculation based on information from T. Dias, Team Lead, Funding, Special Education / Success for All Branch, Ontario Ministry of Education, personal communication, March 16, 2021).

Ontario teachers' collective agreements used to be negotiated by school boards and teacher union locals. In the 1990s there was a concern that school board trustees seemed unwilling to restrain ever-rising spending and taxation (Bedard & Lawton, 1998). Since 1997 the province determined the foundation on which the negotiations were conducted (Education Improvement Commission, 2000). As part of the provincial centralizing process, in 2005 the government discussed directly with provincial teacher unions and provincial school board associations in renewing teacher contracts, going around local boards, although legally it was the local boards that should negotiate with union locals. In 2008 the government discussed a funding framework for renewing teacher contracts again directly with provincial unions and provincial school board associations to reach agreements (Rushowy & Ferguson, 2009).

Four years later, teachers' collective agreements expired at the end of August 2012. This time the government wanted a freeze of public sector salaries for two years because of a $14 billion provincial deficit. The government started talking to provincial unions in February 2012, and school boards were left out of negotiations (Kane, 2013). Of the four unions in the province, Ontario English Catholic Teachers Association (OECTA) and Association des Enseignantes et des Enseignants Franco-Ontariens (AEFO) signed a memorandum of understanding with the government in July (Rushowy & Benzie, 2012) and August (Talaga & Rushowy, 2012), respectively. The Elementary Teachers' Federation of Ontario (ETFO) and the Ontario Secondary School Teachers' Federation (OSSTF), with approximately 60 percent of all Ontario teachers, refused to accept the government's proposal (Ferguson, 2012).

In September, the legislature passed Bill 115, Putting Students First Act, which would impose on ETFO and OSSTF contracts similar to those for OECTA and AEFO that would freeze salaries for two years and take away teachers' strike right pre-emptively if ETFO and OSSTF did not reach agreements with school boards by the end of December. There was no agreement by the end of the year and contracts were imposed in January 2013. ETFO and OSSTF launched a legal challenge against Bill 115, and they were also engaged in other activities of protest. These activities only stopped after a new premier took over in February and made some amendments to the contracts (Ferguson, 2014). Throughout the whole process, school boards were shut out of negotiations (Rushowy, Brown, & Ferguson, 2013). Later in 2016 Ontario Superior Court of Justice judge Lederer found that violation of the freedom of association of the unions had not been demonstrably justified in accordance with section 1 of the Canadian Charter of Rights and Freedoms (ETFO, 2023).

On August 31, 2014, teachers' agreements expired. This time collective bargaining was conducted under a more formal provincial system passed into law through Bill 122, School Boards Collective Bargaining Act 2014, which established a framework of two-level bargaining: central bargaining and local bargaining. The Ministry of Education, ETFO, and Ontario Public School Boards' Association had their preliminary meeting on September 3,

2014. By November 2015 eight of nine central deals — which covered costly items such as salary and benefits — were reached and most were ratified. However, local negotiations dragged on. Even in the third year of Bill 122 in implementation 13 union locals were still talking to their school boards (Rushowy, October 15, 2016).

In 2017 collective bargaining between the government and provincial teachers' unions were conducted quietly with little reporting from the media. Both the government and unions said little, and they reached agreements, extending the previous agreements for two more years. These agreements expired on August 31, 2019.

In the last round of collective bargaining across the province in 2019 and 2020, the bargaining was conducted with two sides far apart regarding their proposals. At the beginning teacher unions wanted an annual salary increase of 2%, but the government was willing to give only 1%. The government wanted to increase class size. The government also wanted 4 mandatory online courses for secondary students to graduate, but teacher unions pointed out that the purpose of 4 mandatory online courses was to save money by going around the class size limit. Teachers started job actions. Polls conducted at the time indicated that the majority of Ontarians supported teachers' request of salary increase, but not at 2%. The majority of Ontarians did not like class size increase and the 4 mandatory online courses idea. Eventually an agreement was reached with a compromise: Teachers would have an annual salary increase of 1%, and class size would increase, but not as the government originally sought. There would be 2 online courses for secondary students, and they could opt out of these two courses (Alphonso, 2020; "Elementary Teachers' Federation", 2020).

Currently the government and the four provincial teacher unions are still engaged in collective bargaining as the last collective agreements already expired on August 31, 2022. Karen Littlewood, President of the 60,000-member Ontario Secondary School Teachers' Federation, speaking on March 11, 2023 to members gathered in downtown Toronto for their annual provincial meeting, warned that privatization of education could be next, after the Conservative government allowed more private health care in the province. She said the recent union solidarity during Canadian Union of Public Employees education worker talks with the government, as well as big union wins in court, showed the "extent of this collective power" in fighting the provincial government (Rushowy, March 11, 2023). On March 21, 2023 Martha Hradowy, vice-president of the same union, said, "We call on the Ford government to make investing in public education a priority in this budget," at a news conference at Queen's Park, where the Ontario legislature was located, adding that the province had shortchanged education in successive budgets. She also said that the government needed to provide additional mental health help and supports to deal with violence in schools in the upcoming Ontario budget (Rushowy, March 21, 2023).

With legislation, the government acts as an enforcer to compel district school boards to follow provincial policies more closely. The government makes more decisions regarding education funding and delivery in the name of consistency, effectiveness, and efficiency. What has happened in Ontario in the last two decades can be described as consistency achieved through centralized control, from taking away school boards' taxing power with a provincial funding formula under Bill 160 in 1997 to negotiating teacher contracts directly with provincial teacher unions without real participation from school boards under Bill 122 in 2014, to agreements made between the government and provincial teacher unions in 2017 and 2020. It seems that the provincial government will keep its increased powers in collective bargaining as it provides more funding to education than local municipalities.

Bill 122, School Boards Collective Bargaining Act 2014, established a bargaining framework with two levels of bargaining: central bargain and local bargaining. Central bargaining refers to collective bargaining between an employer bargaining agency, one of the school board associations in the province, and an employee bargaining agency, one of the provincial teacher unions, for central terms to be included in a collective agreement. Central terms are general raises in teacher salaries and benefits. Local bargaining refers to collective bargaining between a district school board and bargaining agents for the locals of teacher unions, for local terms to be included in a collective agreement. Local terms are salaries scales, working rules, etc. The actual central bargaining happens between the provincial government and provincial teacher unions, as school board associations have little influence since funding is determined by the provincial formula with complete government control. Local bargaining, after central bargaining is completed, happens between each district school board and the corresponding locals of teacher unions. The provincial government is usually not involved in local bargaining, but the government and school board associations may require a district school board to provide information on the status and progress of local bargaining.

REFERENCES

Alphonso, C. (2020, April 20). Ontario high school teachers reach tentative deal with province. *The Globe and Mail*. https://www.theglobeandmail.com/canada/article-ontario-high- school-teachers-reach- tentative-deal/

Bedard, G., & Lawton, S. (1998, July). The battle over Ontario's Bill 160 and the shape of teacher collective bargaining. *Policy Options*, 49–54.

California Legislative Information. (n.d.). *Education Code*. https://leginfo.legislature.ca.gov/faces/codesTOCSelected.xhtml?tocCode=EDC

Education Act. RSO 1990, c E.2. https://www.canlii.org/en/on/laws/stat/rso-1990-c-e2/latest/rso-1990-c- e2.html

Education Improvement Commission. (2000). *The road ahead IV: A report on improving schools through greater accountability*. http://www.edu.gov.on.ca/eng/document/reports/eic/road4/eic4.pdf

Elementary Teachers' Federation of Ontario. (2023). *ETFO's Charter Challenge Against Bill 115 and Remedy Decision*. https://www.etfo.ca/etfo-action/bills/etfo-s-unfair-labour-practice-complaint-against-the-government-of-ontario

Elementary Teachers' Federation of Ontario (ETFO) Central Agreements Now Ratified. (2020). https://news.ontario.ca/en/backgrounder/56788/elementary-teachers-federation-of-ontario-etfo-central-agreements-now-ratified

Evergreen Teachers Association. (n.d.). *Bargaining*. https://www.etanews.org/page3/

Ferguson, R. (2012, August 17). Liberals lay down the hammer with teachers' bill. *Toronto Star*, p. A6.

Ferguson, R. (2014, November 20). Reopening teachers' contracts cost $468M. *Toronto Star*, p. A1.

Garcea, J., & Munroe, D. (2014). Reforms to funding education in four Canadian provinces. *Canadian Journal of Educational Administration and Policy*, 159.

Gidney, R. (1999). *From Hope to Harris: The reshaping of Ontario's schools*. University of Toronto Press. doi:10.3138/9781442675087

Kane, L. (2013, August 16). High school teachers threaten new protests. *Toronto Star*, p. A1.

Lawton, S. (1996). *Financing Canadian Education*. Canadian Education Association.

Ontario English Catholic Teachers' Assn. v. Ontario (Attorney General) [2001] 1 SCR 470, SCC 15 (CanLII). https://www.canlii.org/en/ca/scc/doc/2001/2001scc15/2001scc15.html?resultIndex=3

Rushowy, K. (2016, October 15). Peel school board settles its final education contract. *Toronto Star*, p. GT10.

Rushowy, K. (2023, March 11). Privatization of education could be next, warns head of Ontario high school teachers union. *Toronto Star*. https://www.thestar.com/politics/provincial/2023/03/11/privatization-of-education-could-be- next-warns-head-of-ontario-high-school-teachers-union.html

Rushowy, K. (2023, March 21). Ford government needs to boost funding amid education 'crisis,' t teachers' union says. *Toronto Star*. https://www.thestar.com/politics/provincial/2023/03/21/ford- government-needs-to-boost-funding-amid-education-crisis-teachers-union-says.html

Rushowy, K., & Benzie, R. (2012, July 6). Catholic teachers, province forge deal. *Toronto Star*, p. A1.

Rushowy, K., Brown, L., & Ferguson, R. (2013, June 14). Elementary teachers get 2% wage increase. *Toronto Star*, p. GT1.

Rushowy, K., & Ferguson, R. (2009, February 15). Teachers accept 4-year deal. *Toronto Star*, p. A4.

Talaga, T., & Rushowy, K. (2012, August 10). French teachers' union seals deal. *Toronto Star*, p. A12.

Chapter 8
Framework of Education Governance

ABSTRACT

How the public education system is governed has an impact on how students learn in schools. This chapter describes and discusses how the governance of Ontario education system changed in the last three decades, when significant reforms were implemented by different provincial governments. The chapter also briefly mentions the governance of education systems in California and China. It contains sections in the Ontario Education Act and Regulation 298/1990 Operation of Schools on the governance of education in the province. In addition, the chapter offers some reflections from the author regarding the changes in Ontario education governance since the 1990s.

How public education is governed has an important impact on how well students learn in schools. California Education Code Title 2 Division 2 Part 20 Chapter 1 Article 1 section 33000 stipulates that there is a state board of education, consisting of 10 members and a student member, appointed by the governor with the advice and consent of two-thirds of the senate. Article 2 section 33031 states that the board shall adopt rules and regulations (a) for its own government, (b) for the government of its appointees and employees, (c) for the government of the day and evening elementary schools, the day and evening secondary schools, and the technical and vocational schools of the state, and (d) for the government of other schools, … as may receive in whole or in part financial support from the state. Section 33032 presents that

DOI: 10.4018/978-1-6684-4163-3.ch008

the board shall make plans for the improvement of the administration and efficiency of the public schools. Chinese Education Act Chapter 2 Article 17 specifies that the establishment, format, duration, expected students, and education aims of schools and other educational institutions shall be determined by the State Council and the educational administrative department the State Council authorizes. The general understanding of the educational administrative department is the national Ministry of Education.

Started in 1807, when the provincial legislature passed the first Public Schools Act, the Ontario publicly funded education system has a history of 215 years. The current framework of education governance has been established by the Education Act, its predecessors, regulations made under the Education Act, and other related laws.

In 1807 there were only eight publicly funded schools in Ontario (Ross, 1896), all of which provided religious education. In those days all European settlers in Ontario were Christians, mainly of two denominations: Protestants and Catholics. The Protestants were the majority and the Catholics were the minority. Catholics in Ontario wanted their own schools so that their children would not be subject to instruction by teachers of the majority denomination. This right of having denominational minority schools was protected by section 93 of the Canadian Constitution (The Parliament of the United Kingdom, 1867).

The provincial government provided funding to these schools for them to hire teachers and appointed trustees to operate the schools (Ross, 1896). All the publicly funded schools could be categorized into two groups: one Protestant group and the other Catholic group. As the number of settlers in Ontario increased and they had children, more children went to school, children went to school for longer periods of time, and more schools were built. The 1816 Common Schools Act indicated that schools would be administered by locally elected trustees (Ross, 1896), which could be considered the beginning of publicly funded school autonomy. More people understood that education was beneficial for individuals as well as society. In 1841 Ontario Legislature passed the Education Act, which authorized residents of a municipality, a town, or a place to collect property taxes for building schools, maintaining schools, and hiring teachers (Walker, 1971), which could be considered the beginning of public schools' financial autonomy. While schools were funded both provincially and locally, they were administered by trustees elected in local municipal elections. In 1871 the School Act was passed, which declared free schools by statute (Ross, 1896). Publicly funded schools mainly depended on locally collected education taxes as part of property taxes to operate. An Education Department was established as the provincial legislature amended the School Act in 1876. In 1940 the Ministry of Education objected to the suggestion the Ontario Education Association made that the Ministry increase their portion of education funding to 50 percent to meet the increasing cost of public schools in the province (Guillet, 1960).

For a long time, Ontario school boards were funded mainly through education tax collected by their corresponding municipalities and locally elected trustees made policies concerning how to operate schools in their school boards. While school boards were quite autonomous, their authority was conferred upon them by the provincial legislature and government. School boards existed to act as intermediaries between the provincial government and local community needs and to operate schools. Subsection (58.1) clause 2 in Education Act Part II.2 clearly stated that it was the government that decided the area of a district school board and gave it a name. Clause 1 in subsection (58.5) indicated that "every district school board is a corporation and has all the powers and shall perform all the duties that are conferred or imposed on it under this or any other Act". Before 1997 there was significant variation in per student funding among school boards due to the variation of the wealth among corresponding municipalities. In 1997 local financial contribution to education was greater than that from the province (Gidney, 1999).

The number of school boards was reduced from over 3,000 in the 1960s to 129 in the 1990s. At that time there was also provincial funding for all school boards, which equalized funding across Ontario to a certain extent. This situation changed when the Progressive Conservative party won the election in 1995 and formed a majority government, who changed the funding formula in 1996 to centralize financial allocation and made funding more equitable across the province. They passed Bill 104, the Fewer School Boards Act 1997, in the legislature, and 129 school boards amalgamated into 72 district school boards in January 1998. Bill 104 also established an Education Improvement Commission (EIC). Bill 160, the Education Quality Improvement Act 1997, was passed in the legislature, which took away school boards' power of deciding local education tax. Although education funding still mainly came from municipalities and the provincial government, education tax was determined by the provincial government, and it was the same across the province. Bill 160 amended the Education Act to make it illegal for school boards to operate with a deficit, enhancing the accountability of district school boards. District school boards could no longer operate on a deficit and had to publish their financial statements (Li, 2015). Education funding was completely decided by the government, and so were other areas formerly determined by school boards, such as the length of school year, teacher preparation time, and class size.

The Ministry of Education took full responsibility of education funding and other matters, and there was a significant change in the relationship between the Ministry and new district school boards. The district school boards must meet all student needs within their jurisdictions with the funding and working conditions determined by the Ministry. There was an increased awareness among the public of accountability, mainly focusing on district school boards. District school boards decisions increasingly came under scrutiny. The newly established EIC (2000) outlined an accountability framework that defined who should do what, delineating the responsibilities of the Ministry and school boards, and provided recommendations for the implementation of the accountability framework. EIC (2000) stated that the government reforms focused on inproving student learning, creating greater equity across the province, developing greater accountability, and ensuring more efficient use of education resources. EIC (2000) believed that the restructuring of education governance was successful but incomplete and continued action was needed from all partners in education. EIC claimed that with the recent major changes the Ontario education system needed stability to consolidate gains. EIC stated that the implementation of an accountability framework was the factor that would have the greatest impact in improving the education system, which was the purpose of the commission and Bill 160, the Education Quality Improvement Act 1997. There was still much work to do to make the education system more effective. This work should be done in a more cooperative way than in the past and the government should engage all partners in the education system (EIC, 2000).

To further enhance accountability, the legislature passed Bill 74, the Education Accountability Act 2000, giving the government more powers over district school boards. In such a politicized environment the values against which school board trustees operated were substantively different from those of provincial politicians in power, creating a situation antagonistic to local governance (Galway et al., 2013). Three largest district school boards: Toronto, Ottawa and Hamilton Public Boards submitted a deficit budget in June 2002, insisting that they could not provide adequate services under the funding formula without deficit spending. In response, the government took over governing authority and appointed supervisors to the three district school boards, where trustees lost all decision-making power and had no access to staff services. The supervisors cut the budgets in August, balancing them in Ottawa and Hamilton and significantly reducing the deficit in Toronto. The supervisor in Toronto had a plan to reduce the deficit further in the following years and eventually balance the budget. In December 2002 a government commissioned report was released, recommending a funding increase of $1.8 billion over a three-year period and greater local school board autonomy for expenditure to support at-risk students (Rozanski, 2002). The government increased funding, but no greater local autonomy was granted.

In October 2003 the Liberals formed a new government. One of the first things they did was to remove the supervisors the previous Conservative government had appointed in Toronto, Ottawa and Hamilton and restored local governance. The restoration of local governance to elected trustees was celebrated as a return to democracy (Boyle, 2004), but the expectation that district school boards must balance their budget did not change. After Liberals increased education funding, some district school boards still complained against inadequate funding. Three large district school boards: Toronto Public Board, Toronto Catholic Board and Dufferin-Peel Catholic Board submitted a deficit budget for the school year of 2006-2007. The government appointed auditors for the three boards to review their budgets. Working with auditors, both Toronto Public and Catholic Boards balanced their budgets, but Dufferin-Peel Catholic Board resisted recommendations from the auditor, leading the government to appoint a financial expert to work with the board to eliminate the deficit. In the process, the government did not formally suspend trustees' right to approve the eventual budget. In dealing with deficit budget submitting boards both the Conservatives and Liberals adopted an economic-bureaucratic accountability orientation described by Anderson and Ben Jaafar (2007). The shift in governance structure in Ontario was part of the trend across the country that emphasized school board level accountability for fiscal responsibility (Anderson & Ben Jaafar, 2007).

The conflicts between some district school boards and the provincial government indicated the unhappiness of trustees with the increasing centralized control of decisions that had been considered local: resources, teacher working conditions, and teacher salaries. In Canada the trend of centralization of education governance at the provincial level happened in the 1990s in the name of equity and efficiency. There was a perception that with fewer school boards there would be less resources spent on administration and with provincial governments having more financial allocation power the funding would be more equalized across a province. Provincial governments became more powerful and school boards less so (Galway et al., 2013; Levin, 2005).

In 2003–2004 the total funding for elementary and secondary education in Ontario excluding capital programs was approximately $15.2 billion (Ontario Ministry of Education, 2003). In 2022-2023 it is about $26.1 billion, with an increase of about 72%, even though enrolment dropped approximately 5% since 2003–2004 (author's calculation based on information from Ontario Ministry of Education, 2003, Spring 2022). At about the same time, the consumer price index in Ontario increased almost 53% from 2002 to 2022 (Statistics Canada, 2023), which was the closest matching period the author could find. There is more money per student in 2022-2023 than in 2003–2004 even with inflation considered. The Liberal government and the following Conservative government, which is still in power today, have invested more in education. Although there is more money, there are more restrictions on where the money can be spent, and there are more requirements on district school boards to report how they spend the money. Some grants are specified where they can be spent. For example, the grant for special education can only be spent to assist students with exceptionalities. If a board has not used the special education grant that they receive for the current year, the board must put it away in a reserve fund for next year.

Since the comprehensive reform implemented by the Conservatives in 1997, Ontario elementary and secondary education has been funded completely following a provincial formula, under which the provincial government determines how much funding each district school board needs based on student enrolment, student needs, and district school board needs. There is less flexibility for boards to decide how to spend their funding (Governance Review Committee, 2009) and they must publish their annual financial statements.

In Ontario about 95 percent of school age children go to publicly funded schools (People for Education, 2012), and there are 72 district school boards: 60 English boards and 12 French boards. Of the 60 English boards 31 are public boards and 29 are Roman Catholic separate boards. Of the 12 French boards 8 are Roman Catholic separate boards and 4 are public boards. Approximately 5 percent of school age children go to independent schools, or are home-schooled. Before the Seven Years' War (1756-1763) between France and England, most European settlers in today's Canada were French and British, but the French controlled a larger area which they called New France (Conrad & Finkel, 2006, p. 141). The French were defeated in the war, and New France became part of British North American colonies. In today's Canada, the largest ethnic group is of British origin and the second largest group is of French origin (Statistics Canada, October, 2022). The Canadian

Charter of Rights and Freedoms Article 23 guarantees French Canadians' right to have their own schools, where instruction is provided in French (the Constitution Act, 1982).

The Canadian trend of provincial governments centralizing power was reflected mainly by changes in how education was funded (Galway et al., 2013). In the late 1990s among the educational reforms that had the greatest impact on Ontario district school boards was the introduction of the new funding formula (EIC, 2000). When the formula was implemented, there was resistance from people who disagreed with the provincial government. These people saw three problems with the formula: 1) overall education funding was reduced; 2) one formula was not suitable for all district school boards, who were different; 3) local autonomy was taken away, which was undemocratic. People continue to debate about whether the current funding is adequate, but there is less protest about whether one size can fit all and lost local autonomy. It seems that no one can have both local autonomy and funding equity across a province. Of the ten Canadian provinces seven have centralized their elementary and secondary education funding and only three still have some local autonomy, but even in these three provinces funding is more equitable than before as these provincial governments have been increasing their equalizing funding.

Brimley, Verstegen, and Garfield (2016) suggest that if the per pupil funding gap between high-poverty districts and low-poverty districts is smaller than 10 percent, education finance equity is within acceptable limits. With this standard, Ontario funding formula can be considered equitable, since it determines resources provincially based on student enrolment, student needs, and district school board needs, regardless of local wealth.

District school boards receive allocations from both the provincial government and their corresponding municipal governments, but municipal governments across Ontario provide the same percentage of their income to school boards as education tax, which is decided by the provincial finance minister; calculated based on the funding formula, the balance is provided by the provincial government. The formula's basic structure remains unchanged since 1997 (Garcea & Munroe, 2014). Currently more education funding comes from the provincial government than from local municipalities (author's calculation based on information from T. Dias, Team Lead, Funding, Special Education / Success for All Branch, Ontario Ministry of Education, personal communication, March 16, 2021).

Most funding allocations in the formula can be moved from one grant to another, except for special education funding. District school boards can make some funding decisions after they receive money from the provincial government and their corresponding municipalities. District school boards decide individual schools' budgets and they decide criteria for things like the number of students a school must have to get staff such as librarians. School boards decide funding for number of teachers to schools based on how many students their schools have, and often also on the number of students who may struggle to meet the required learning outcomes. Boards also make important decisions on which schools should stay open and which should be closed because of fluctuating enrolment, as well as how many custodians and other staff schools get (People for Education, 2012).

The Minister of Education established a Governance Review Committee in November 2008 to consult education stakeholders and make recommendations to clarify the duties and accountabilities of district school boards, effective practices in governance, and appropriate content of provincial interest regulations to ensure that school boards meet student learning outcomes. The Committee submitted its report to the Minister in April 2009 with 25 recommendations.

The report described the challenges district school boards faced: losing local taxation power, operating larger organizations, receiving more immigrants who did not speak English, declining enrollment, increased societal expectations on schools and teachers, and increased provincial directions and interventions. The report indicated that the Ministry of Education took an increasingly active role in establishing provincial goals and priorities and supported their achievement through providing expertise and financial resources. The following were the highlights of the recommendations (Governance Review Committee, 2009): including a statement in the Education Act that the mandate of district school boards is to promote student achievement and well-being, deliver effective and appropriate programs, and provide effective stewardship of resources; trustees are responsible for establishing policies to govern the provision of education in their district school board; requirement that trustees act according to their school board policy, bring the interest of local community to the attention of the board, and communicate and uphold board decisions; and six principles guide the designing of provincial interest regulations.

The Ministry of Education introduced Bill 177, the Student Achievement and School Board Governance Act to amend the Education Act in May 2009. Passed in November 2009, the Act further increased the government's powers by stipulating that the government may make regulations governing the roles and responsibilities of district school boards and their trustees. Added was one section on boards' duties and powers that prescribed that every district school board shall promote student learning outcomes, ensure effective stewardship of resources, and deliver effective and appropriate education programs. With increasing provincial centralization of governance, the Ministry of Education came to play a role of quality-control agent responsible for setting policy, goals, and performance standards and for monitoring local compliance in reference to standards centrally decided. Professional support was only provided to district school boards in the interests of provincially determined goals. The responsibilities of boards were mainly to implement provincial policies to achieve provincial goals. With adding a section on the purpose of education, the Act indicated the goals of the provincial government: Working with partners in the education sector to enhance student learning achievement and well-being, close gaps in achievement among different student groups, and maintain confidence of the public in the province's publicly funded education systems. To make district school board policies more consistent across the province, the government issued the Guideline for Fees for Learning Materials and Activities (Ontario Ministry of Education, March 2011) and a Fundraising Guideline to regulate school fundraising activities (Ontario Ministry of Education, 2012).

One important aspect of governance is how education is financed. The most important education expenditure is teacher salaries. Ontario teachers' collective agreements used to be negotiated between 129 school boards and provincial teacher unions' locals. Since the comprehensive reform conducted with the implementation of Bill 160, the Education Quality Improvement Act 1997, the provincial government determined the financial foundation on which the negotiations were conducted between district school boards and teacher unions (EIC, 2000). As part of the ongoing centralizing process first introduced by the Conservative government and followed through by the Liberal government, in 2005 the Liberal government discussed directly with provincial teacher unions and school board associations in renewing teacher contracts, going around local boards, although according to the law at the time it was the local boards that should negotiate with union locals in renewing contracts. The government announced a funding package for teacher salary increases in the negotiation, but district school boards' access to this increased funding was contingent on following provincial guidelines on their respective agreements with union locals. The government also added funding to satisfy teacher unions' specific requests in improving their working conditions. What happened was that the government demanded district school boards and provincial teacher unions to reach new agreements of four years instead of three or two years as in former agreements to minimize education disruptions caused by labor disputes. With increased resources, the government succeeded in keeping the education system in peace for four years, but some district school boards stated that the government funding to meet teacher salaries increases was inadequate to catch up with inflation and they must use money intended for other areas to increase teacher salaries and benefits. It was reported in the news media that one area some district school boards took money from was the allocation intended for English language learners (Kalinowski, 2006).

The government discussed in 2008 an increased funding framework for renewing teacher agreements again directly with provincial teacher unions and school board associations for new teacher contracts (Rushowy & Ferguson, 2009). The government succeeded in keeping labor peace for four years. Before teachers' collective agreements expired at the end of August 2012, the government indicated that it wanted a freeze of teacher salaries and benefits, along with the freezing of all public service employees' salaries and benefits, for two years, because the government was dealing with a $14 billion deficit. Talking between the government and provincial teacher unions started in February 2012, without real district school boards involvement (Kane, 2013). Out of the four Ontario teacher unions, Ontario English Catholic Teachers Association (OECTA) signed a memorandum of understanding with the provincial government in July (Rushowy & Benzie, 2012), and Association des Enseignantes et des Enseignants Franco-Ontariens (AEFO) signed a similar Memorandum in August (Talaga & Rushowy, 2012). The other two unions, Elementary Teachers' Federation of Ontario (ETFO) and the Ontario Secondary School Teachers' Federation (OSSTF), whose members were approximately 60 percent of all Ontario teachers, refused to accept the government's negotiation proposal (Ferguson, 2012; Talaga & Aulakh, 2012).

The provincial legislature passed Bill 115, Putting Students First Act 2012, in September, imposing contracts on ETFO and OSSTF members similar to those of OECTA and AEFO members, freezing salaries for two years, and taking away teachers' strike right preemptively, if ETFO and OSSTF did not reach agreements with district school boards by the end of December. Contracts were imposed on ETFO and OSSTF members in January 2013 when no agreements were reached. ETFO and OSSTF started a legal challenge against Bill 115, and both their members stopped participating in extra-curricular activities. These activities of protest only stopped after a new premier, Kathleen Wynne, took over in February, who made amendments to the imposed contracts (Ferguson, 2014). Labor peace in the education sector was restored in April. Throughout the whole collective bargaining process, district school boards were not involved in negotiations (Rushowy, Brown, & Ferguson, 2013).

Since 2012 there have been four rounds of collective bargaining, including the current one, which is still ongoing. All these negotiations have been conducted mainly between the provincial government and provincial teacher unions with little active participation and little input from provincial school board associations.

The changes in the Ontario framework of education governance since 1995 have happened in the North American social-political context. In the US, a regime of neo-liberal accountability has dominated the governance of education (Ranson, 2003). In Canada accountability has been the trend for over two decades (Anderson & Ben Jaafar, 2007; Levin & Fullan, 2008; Sattler, 2012). In Ontario education governance has gone through a significant transformation in ideas, institutions and practices (Sattler, 2012). This chapter attempts to provide a brief recent history of education governance in Ontario and the shifts in the relationship between district school boards and the government since 1995. It delineates, analyzes, and discusses the changes the Conservatives, Liberals, and then Conservatives again, have made in the governance of education. The general trend we see in education governance is that the government has demanded more accountability from district school boards, made more regulations, and acted in a more centralized fashion. Bill 160, the Education Quality Improvement Act 1997, had enhancing the accountability of district school boards as one of its purposes. EIC (2000) stated that in reforms at the time one focus was on developing greater accountability and ensuring more efficient use of resources, on the part of district school boards. Bill 74, the Education Accountability Act 2000, even had the word accountability in its title. Accountability was a social practice pursuing particular purposes, defined by distinctive relationships and evaluative procedures (Ranson, 2003, p. 462). Since 1995 Ontario education governance has changed with increasing accountability of district school boards. The purpose of accountability legitimated the creation of detailed regulations that ensured the compliance of practitioners (Ranson, 2003). In Ontario accountability ensured more compliance of district school boards, particularly when it came to provincial goals.

With legislation and regulations, the Ontario government has acted as an enforcer to compel district school boards to follow more provincial policies and follow them more closely. The government makes more decisions about education funding, curriculum, program delivery, and learning outcomes in the name of consistency, effectiveness, and efficiency. Consistency in an education system is often described as achieved through centralized control (Ranson, 2003). What has happened in Ontario in over two decades can be described as consistency achieved through centralized control, from school boards' losing education taxing power introduced with a provincial funding formula under Bill 160, Education Quality Improvement Act 1997, to government negotiating teacher contracts directly with provincial teacher unions without active participation from district school board associations under Bill 122, School Boards Collective Bargaining Act 2014. These reforms in Ontario have been part of the Canadian trend in education governance that sees the centralization of power at the provincial level (Galway et al., 2013). They are also part of the international trend that uses educational reforms through accountability measures intended for local school boards (Anderson & Ben Jaafar, 2007).

Some of the reform initiatives were started by the New Democratic Party government before 1995 when New Democrats lost to the Conservatives in the provincial election. Once in power and formed a majority government, the Conservatives made more significant and more comprehensive changes, and the Liberals continued in the same direction, albeit generally with a more collaborative approach. The Conservatives have been in power again since June 2018. They have further strengthened their control of the education system. The changes in education governance, initiated by the New Democrats, implemented by the Conservatives, followed by the Liberals, and then Conservatives again, have increased accountability in Ontario education governance, mainly for district school boards. Ranson (2003) suggested that the structure of goal-setting accountability erected centralized bureaucratic control. Increasing district school board accountability in Ontario, coupled with greater funding from the provincial government and less funding from local municipalities (author's calculation based on information from T. Dias, Team Lead, Funding, Special Education / Success for All Branch, Ontario Ministry of Education, personal communication, March 16, 2021), has made the governance of education more centralized and has created a regime of provincial regulation.

Will district school boards ever take back some powers they have lost since 1995? With the consideration of what have happened over the last two decades, the current education revenue sources, and the provincial, national, and international trends (Anderson & Ben Jaafar, 2007; Ranson, 2003), it seems that the government will keep its increased powers as it provides more funding to education than local municipalities (Osgoode Hall Law School, York University, 2020). To take back some of their lost powers, district school boards must regain their education taxing power and increase local property tax, which is not very likely to happen under the current social, political, and economic circumstances. What is described in this chapter indicates that in Ontario education governance there are more accountability, more regulations, and more centralization that have developed over the last two decades. Changes in the locus of responsibility for the provision of education (e.g., centralization of governance, control over education finances, quality control versus support functions of provincial administration) is one of the four major policy trends across the country (Anderson & Ben Jaafar, 2007).

The changes in education governance since 1995 have increased accountability for district school boards. There are more provincially designed, implemented, and monitored regulations, and decision making is more centralized at the provincial level. Across the province there is more consistency, but there is no evidence to demonstrate whether education provision has become more effective and more efficient. The world around us changes, society changes, citizens' attitudes change, and the governance of education and education law in Ontario are likely to change accordingly. We all understand how different the education system is today from the time when we were in elementary school. There are still significant inequalities in learning outcomes among different student groups, and for public education more is possible. How Ontario education governance develops in the future will depend on the importance Ontarians place on the publicly funded education system, what they consider the education system should do, how much they trust the system, what they believe the most equitable, effective, and efficient way of providing education is, what an economic situation they are in, and what the provincial, national, and international social and political trends are. An understanding of what has happened over the last two decades in Ontario education governance may help us anticipate what is likely to happen in the future.

Religion plays a very important role in some people's life. The early Protestant group of Ontario schools has developed into the current public school system including English and French public schools, where a pupil shall be allowed to receive religious instruction as the pupil's parent or guardian desires, but no pupil in a public school shall be required to read or study in or from a religious book, or to join in an exercise of devotion or religion, objected to by the pupil's parent or guardian, according Education Act section 51. The current general situation is that a public school shall teach about religion, but not teach religion. There have been controversies surrounding religious exercises held in the public school system.

The early Catholic group of schools has developed into the current Roman Catholic separate school system including English and French Roman Catholic separate schools. The Catholic school system may establish and maintain programs and courses of study in religious education for pupils in all schools under its jurisdiction, according to Education Act section 52. All Catholic separate district school boards, English and French, maintain programs and courses of study in Catholicism. The public system has approximately two thirds of the elementary and secondary school students in the province, and the Catholic separate system has about one third of the students.

In addition to the Education Act, Regulation 298/1990 Operation of Schools made under the Act presents how religion is taught about in public schools.

Section 28 of Regulation 289/1990 subsections (1) and (2) stipulate that a public district school board may provide in grades one to eight and in its secondary schools an optional program of education about religion and such a program shall

(a) promote respect for the freedom of conscience and religion guaranteed by the Canadian Charter of Rights and Freedoms; and
(b) provide for the study of different religions and religious beliefs in Canada and the world, without giving primacy to, and without indoctrination in, any particular religion or religious belief.

Subsection (3) prescribes that such a program shall not exceed sixty minutes of instruction per week in an elementary school.

Section 29 subsection (1) states that a public district school board shall not permit any person to conduct religious exercises or to provide instruction that includes indoctrination in a particular religion or religious belief in a school, but section (2) indicates that a public board may enter into an agreement with a Roman Catholic separate board that permits the Roman Catholic board to use space and facilities to conduct religious exercises or provide religious instruction for the purposes of the Roman Catholic board.

Subsection (3) presents that a public board may permit a person to conduct religious exercises or to provide instruction that includes indoctrination in a particular religion or religious belief in a school if,

(a) the exercises are not conducted or the instruction is not provided by or under the auspices of the board;
(b) the exercises are conducted or the instruction is provided on a school day at a time that is before or after the school's instructional program, or on a day that is not a school day;
(c) no person is required by the board to attend the exercises or instruction; and
(d) the board provides space for the exercises or instruction on the same basis as it provides space for other community activities.

Subsection (4) provides that a board that permits religious exercises or instruction shall consider on an equitable basis all requests to conduct religious exercises or to provide instruction.

Sections 28 and 29 do not apply to the Roman Catholic separate school system and the Protestant separate school board. There is only one Protestant separate school board in Ontario with 339 students (The Protestant Separate School Board of the Town of Penetanguishene, 2022).

Today students play a limited role in the governance of education. Section 55 subsection (1) of the Education Act stipulates how student trustees are elected from grades 9-12 to represent the interests of pupils and what they shall do in schools.

Subsection (2) states that a student trustee is not a member of the board and is not entitled to exercise a binding vote on any matter before the board.

Subsection (3) prescribes that a student trustee is entitled to require that a matter before the board or one of its committees on which the student trustee sits be put to a recorded vote, and in that case there shall be,

(a) a recorded non-binding vote that includes the student trustee's vote; and
(b) a recorded binding vote that does not include the student trustee's vote.

Subsection (4) presents that a student trustee is not entitled to move a motion, but is entitled to suggest a motion on any matter at a meeting of the board or of one of its committees on which the student trustee sits, and if no member of the board or committee moves the suggested motion, the record shall show the suggested motion.

Subsection (5) provides that a student trustee is not entitled to be present at a meeting that is closed to the public.

Subsection (7) indicates that a student trustee has the same status as a board member with respect to access to board resources and opportunities for training.

Subsection (8) stipulates that a student trustee is entitled to an honorarium.

Subsection (9) states that a regulation made by the Ministry of Education may,

(a) provide for and govern the student trustee election process, which may be direct or indirect;
(b) specify qualifications for electors of student trustees;
(c) specify qualifications for student trustees and the consequences of becoming disqualified;
(d) govern the number of student trustees who may sit on a board;
(e) govern student trustees' terms of office;
(f) authorize boards to reimburse student trustees for all or part of the out-of-pocket expenses reasonably incurred in connection with carrying out their responsibilities;
(g) provide for transitional matters that are necessary or desirable in connection with the implementation of section 6 of the Education Statute Law Amendment Act (Student Performance),

Subsection (10) specifies that the regulation may,

(a) specify a method for calculating the amount of the honorarium;
(b) specify conditions for the purposes of the honorarium;
(c) provide that the honorarium for a student trustee who serves two or more terms shall be multiplied by the number of terms served or increased in some other way;
(d) relate the amount of the honorarium to the honoraria received by members of the board;
(e) govern the manner and timing of payment of the honorarium;
(f) provide for the payment of the honorarium to a third party on the former student trustee's behalf;
(g) prescribe classes of student trustees or former student trustees and treat the members of different classes differently.

Subsection (11) stipulates that the regulation may provide for and govern,

(a) student trustee elections at different times in the school year; and
(b) by-elections to fill vacancies

Subsection (12) states that in the regulation, the Minister may provide for any matter by authorizing a board to develop and implement a policy with respect to the matter and may require that the policy comply with policies and guidelines established.

In Ontario government funded schools are administered by 72 district school boards: 60 English boards and 12 French boards. Of the 60 English boards 31 are public boards and 29 are Roman Catholic separate boards. Of the 12 French boards 8 are Roman Catholic separate boards and 4 are pubic boards. Education Act part VI section 169.1 subsection (1) stipulates that every board shall,

1. promote student achievement and well-being;
   (a.1) promote a positive school climate that is inclusive and accepting of all pupils, including pupils of any race, ancestry, place of origin, colour, ethnic origin, citizenship, creed, sex, sexual orientation, gender identity, gender expression, age, marital status, family status or disability;
   (a.2) promote the prevention of bullying;
2. ensure effective stewardship of the board's resources;
3. deliver effective and appropriate education programs to its pupils;
4. develop and maintain policies and organizational structures that,
   (i) promote the goals referred to in clauses (a) to (c), and
   (ii) encourage pupils to pursue their educational goals;
5. monitor and evaluate the effectiveness of policies developed by the board under clause (d) in achieving the board's goals and the efficiency of the implementation of those policies;
6. develop a multi-year plan aimed at achieving the goals referred to in clauses (a) to (c);
7. annually review the plan referred to in clause (f) with the board's director of education; and
8. monitor and evaluate the performance of the board's director of education in meeting,
9. his or her duties under this Act or any policy, guideline or regulation made under this Act, including duties under the plan referred to in clause (f), and
10. any other duties assigned by the board.

Section 170 subsection (1) prescribes that every board shall establish a school council for each school operated by the board.

Regulation 612/00, part II, section 2 subsection (1) indicates that the purpose of school councils is to improve pupil achievement and to enhance the accountability of the education system to parents.

Subsection (2) states that a school council's primary means of achieving its purpose is by making recommendations in accordance with this Regulation to the principal of the school and the board that established the council.

Section 3 subsection (1) presents that a school council for a school shall be composed of the following people:

1. The number of parent members determined under subsection (2).
2. The principal of the school.
3. One teacher who is employed at the school, other than the principal or vice-principal, elected in accordance with section 5.
4. One person who is employed at the school, other than the principal, vice-principal or any other teacher, elected in accordance with section 5.
5. In the case of a school with one or more secondary school grades,
   i. one pupil enrolled in the school who is appointed by the student council, if the school has a student council, or
   ii. one pupil enrolled in the school who is elected in accordance with section 5, if the school does not have a student council.
6. In the case of a school with no secondary school grades, one pupil enrolled in the school who is appointed by the principal of the school, if the principal determines, after consulting the other members of the school council, that the council should include a pupil.
7. Subject to subsection (3), one community representative appointed by the other members of the council.
8. One person appointed by an association that is a member of the Ontario Federation of Home and School Associations, the Ontario Association of Parents in Catholic Education or Parent Partenaires en Education, if the association that is a member of the Ontario Federation of Home and School Associations, the Ontario Association of Parents in Catholic Education or Parent Partenaires en Education is established in respect of the school.

Subsection (2) stipulates that for the purposes of paragraph 1 of subsection (1), the number of parent members shall be determined as follows:

1. If the school council has a by-law that specifies the number of parent members, the number specified in the by-law.

2. If the school council does not have a by-law that specifies the number of parent members, the number specified by the board that established the council.

Subsection (3) prescribes that a school council may specify by by-law that the council shall include two or more community representatives, appointed by the other members of the council.

Subsection (4) indicates that in specifying numbers under subsections (2) and (3), the board or the school council shall ensure that parent members constitute a majority of the members of the school council.

Subsection (5) presents that a person who is employed by the board that established a school council cannot be appointed as a community representative on the council unless,

(a) he or she is not employed at the school; and
(b) the other members of the school council are informed of the person's employment before the appointment.

Section 4 subsection (1) stipulates that a person is qualified to be a parent member of a school council if he or she is a parent of a pupil who is enrolled in the school.

However, subsection (2) states that a person is not qualified to be a parent member of a school council if,

(a) he or she is employed at the school; or
(b) he or she is not employed at the school but is employed elsewhere by the board that established the council, unless he or she takes reasonable steps to inform people qualified to vote in the election of parent members of that employment.

Subsection (3) prescribes that a person is qualified to vote in an election of parent members of a school council if he or she is a parent of a pupil who is enrolled in the school.

However, subsection (4) indicates that an election of parent members of a school council shall be held during the first 30 days of each school year, on a date that is fixed by the chair or co-chairs of the school council after consulting with the principal of the school.

Subsection (5) presents that if a new school is established, the first election of parent members to the school council shall be held during the first 30 days of the school year, on a date that is fixed by the board that established the school council.

Subsection (6) provides that the principal of a school shall, at least 14 days before the date of the election of parent members, on behalf of the school council, give written notice of the date, time and location of the election to every parent of a pupil who, on the date the notice is given, is enrolled in the school.

Section 11 stipulates that a person shall not receive any remuneration for serving as a member of a school council. However, every board shall establish policies respecting the reimbursement of members of school councils established by the board, for expenses they incur as members of the council.

Section 12 subsections (1) and (2) indicate that a school council shall meet at least four times during the school year and meet within the first 35 days of the school year, after the elections, on a date fixed by the principal of the school.

Subsection (3) provides that a meeting cannot be held unless,

(a) a majority of the current members of the council are present at the meeting; and
(b) a majority of the members of the council who are present at the meeting are parent members.

Subsections (4), (5), and (6) state that all meetings shall be open to the public, a school council is entitled to hold its meetings at the school, and all meetings shall be held at a location accessible to the public.

Subsection (7) prescribes that the principal of a school shall, on behalf of the school council, give written notice of the dates, times and locations of the meetings of the council to every parent of a pupil who, on the date the notice is given, is enrolled in the school.

Section 16 prescribes that a school council shall keep minutes of all its meetings and records of all its financial transactions. The minutes and records shall be available at the school for examination without charge by any person. However, these stipulations do not apply to minutes and records that are more than four years old.

Section 18 states that the principal of a school may delegate any of his or her powers or duties as a member of the school council, including any powers or duties under this Regulation, to a vice-principal of the school. In addition, the principal shall perform the duties relating to school councils that are imposed on the principal by Regulation 298 of the Revised Regulations of Ontario, 1990 (Operation of Schools — General).

Section 20 indicates that a school council may make recommendations to the principal of the school or to the board that established the council on any matter.

Section 21 presents that the board that established a school council shall consider each recommendation made to the board by the council and shall advise the council of the action taken in response to the recommendation.

Section 22 subsections (1) and (2) provide that a school may engage in fundraising activities if,

(a) the activities are conducted in accordance with any applicable policies established by the board; and
(b) the activities are to raise funds for a purpose approved by the board or authorized by any applicable policies established by the board.

Subsection (3) stipulates that a school council shall ensure that the funds raised by it are used in accordance with any applicable policies established by the board.

Section 23 states that a school council shall consult with parents of pupils enrolled in the school about matters under consideration by the council.

Section 24 subsections (1) and (2) indicate that every school council shall annually submit a written report on its activities to the principal of the school and to the board that established the council. If the council engages in fundraising activities, the annual report shall include a report on those activities.

Subsections (3) and (4) present that the principal shall, on behalf of the council, give a copy of the report to every parent of a pupil who, on the date the copy is given, is enrolled in the school, by

(a) giving the report to the parent's child for delivery to his or her parent; and
(b) posting the report in the school in a location that is accessible to parents.

Section 27 provides that the purpose of a parent involvement committee is to support, encourage and enhance parent engagement at the board level in order to improve student achievement and well-being and that a parent involvement committee of a board shall achieve its purpose by,

(a) providing information and advice on parent engagement to the board;

(b) communicating with and supporting school councils of schools of the board; and
(c) undertaking activities to help parents of pupils of the board support their children's learning at home and at school.

Section 28 stipulates that a parent involvement committee of a board shall,

(a) develop strategies and initiatives that the board and the board's director of education could use to effectively communicate with parents and to effectively engage parents in improving student achievement and well-being;
(b) advise the board and the board's director of education on ways to use the strategies and initiatives referred to in clause (a);
(c) communicate information from the Ministry to school councils of schools of the board and to parents of pupils of the board;
(d) work with school councils of schools of the board and, through the board's director of education, with employees of the board to,
    (i) share effective practices to help engage parents, especially parents who may find engagement challenging, in their children's learning,
    (ii) identify and reduce barriers to parent engagement,
    (iii) help ensure that schools of the board create a welcoming environment for parents of its pupils, and
    (iv) develop skills and acquire knowledge that will assist the parent involvement committee and school councils of the board with their work; and
(e) determine, in consultation with the board's director of education and in keeping with the board's policies, how funding, if any, provided under the Education Act for parent involvement, is to be used.

Section 33 subsection (1) provides that a parent involvement committee of a board shall include the following:

1. The number of parent members specified in the by-laws of the committee.
2. The director of education of the board.
3. One member of the board, appointed by the board.
4. The number of community representatives specified in the by-laws of the committee.

Subsection (2) indicates that subject to the by-laws of the parent involvement committee, a board may appoint one or more of the following individuals to the parent involvement committee:

1. One principal of an elementary school of the board.
2. One principal of a secondary school of the board.
3. One teacher employed, other than a principal or vice-principal, in an elementary school of the board.
4. One teacher employed, other than a principal or vice-principal, in a secondary school of the board.
5. One person employed by the board, other than a principal, vice-principal or teacher.

Subsection (3) presents that a parent involvement committee shall appoint or elect members to the committee before November 15 of the school year and before the first meeting of the committee in the school year.

Subsection (4) provides that in specifying the number of parent members to be appointed or elected to a parent involvement committee in its by-laws, the committee shall ensure that parent members constitute a majority of the members of the committee.

Subsection (5) prescribes that the term of office of the member of the board appointed under paragraph 3 of subsection (1) shall be determined by the board.

Subsection (6) indicates that community representatives appointed to a parent involvement committee shall not be members or employees of the board.

Subsection (7) stipulates that the board shall make any appointments under subsection (2) before November 15 of the school year and before the first meeting of the parent involvement committee in the school year.

Section 34 subsection (1) prescribes that parent members shall be appointed or elected to a parent involvement committee, in accordance with the by-laws of the committee.

Subsections (2) and (3) present that a person is qualified to be appointed or elected as a parent member of a parent involvement committee if he or she is a parent, or if he or she is employed by the board.

Subsection (4) indicates that a parent member employed by the board shall, at his or her first committee meeting, inform the committee of his or her employment with the board.

Section 37 subsection (1) provides that the term of office of some of the parent members of a parent involvement committee shall be one year and the term of office of some of the parent members shall be two years, as provided in the by-laws of the committee.

Subsection (2) stipulates that a member of a parent involvement committee may be reappointed or re-elected to the committee for more than one term unless otherwise provided in the by-laws of the committee.

Section 38 subsection (1) indicates that a parent involvement committee shall have a chair or, if the by-laws of the committee so provide, co-chairs.

Subsection (2) states that the chair or co-chairs of a parent involvement committee must be parent members of the committee and shall be elected for a two-year term by the parent members of the committee at the first meeting of the committee in each school year that there is a vacancy in the office of chair or co-chair.

Subsection (3) presents that only parent members with a two-year term are eligible to be elected to the position of chair or co-chair.

Subsection (4) provides that an individual may not serve more than two consecutive terms as chair or co-chair of a parent involvement committee.

Subsection (5) prescribes that an individual who has served one term or two consecutive terms as chair or co-chair of a parent involvement committee may be re-elected as chair or co-chair of the committee provided at least one two-year term has elapsed since his or her last term as chair or co-chair.

Subsection (6) stipulates that the chair or co-chairs of a parent involvement committee shall act as spokespersons for the committee in communicating with the director of education of the board and the board.

Subsection (7) states that a parent involvement committee may have such other officers as are provided for in the by-laws of the committee.

Subsection (8) presents that a vacancy in the office of chair, co-chair or any office provided for in the by-laws of a parent involvement committee, shall be filled in accordance with the by-laws of the committee.

Section 40 subsections (1) and (2) stipulate that a parent involvement committee shall meet at least four times in each school year, but a meeting of a parent involvement committee cannot be held unless,

(a) a majority of the members present at the meeting are parent members;
(b) the director of education, or the person designated, is present; and
(c) the member of the board who sits on the committee, or the person designated, is present.

Subsection (3) provides that the board shall make available to its parent involvement committee the facilities that the board considers necessary for the proper functioning of the committee, and shall make reasonable efforts to enable members to participate fully in meetings of the committee by electronic means.

Subsection (4) presents that a member of a parent involvement committee who participates in a meeting through electronic means shall be deemed to be present at the meeting.

Subsection (5) prescribes that all meetings of a parent involvement committee shall be open to the public and shall be held at a location that is accessible to the public.

Subsection (6) indicates that the chair or co-chairs of a parent involvement committee shall ensure that notice of each meeting is provided to all members of the committee at least five days before the meeting by,

(a) delivering a notice to each member by e-mail or regular mail; and
(b) posting a notice on the board's website.

Section 43 stipulates that a parent involvement committee,

(a) may make by-laws governing the conduct of the committee's affairs; and
(b) shall make by-laws,
    (i) specifying the number of parent members to be appointed or elected to the committee, governing the process of appointment or election of parent members and governing the filling of vacancies in parent membership,
    (ii) specifying the number of community representatives, up to three, to be appointed to the committee, governing the process of appointment of community representatives and governing the filling of vacancies in community representative membership,
    (iii) governing the election of members of the committee to the offices of chair or co-chair, and any offices provided for in the by-laws, and governing the filling of vacancies in the offices of the committee,
    (iv) specifying the number of parent members of the parent involvement committee that will hold office for one year and the number of parent members that will hold office for two years,
    (v) specifying how many, if any, of the persons may be appointed by the board to the parent involvement committee,

(vi) specifying the length of the term of office for the community representative members of the parent involvement committee and the members appointed by the board, if any,

(vii) establishing rules respecting conflicts of interest of the members of the parent involvement committee, and

(viii) establishing a process for resolving conflicts internal to the committee, consistent with any conflict resolution policies of the board.

Section 44 subsection (1) stipulates that a parent involvement committee shall keep minutes of all of its meetings and records of all of its financial transactions.

Subsection (2) indicates that a parent involvement committee shall retain the minutes of its meetings and the records of its financial transactions in accordance with the policies of the board, if any, respecting the retention of documents by committees of the board.

Subsection (3) prescribes that the minutes of a parent involvement committee of a board shall be,

(a) posted on the website of the board that established the committee; and
(b) sent electronically to the chair or co-chairs of the school council of each school of the board that established the committee.

Subsection (4) presents that the minutes of a committee's meetings and the records of its financial transactions shall be available for examination at the board's office by any person without charge for four years.

Subsection (5) indicates that minutes posted on the website of the board shall remain on the website for four years.

The Education Act has sections on the conduct and duties of school board trustees (called members of a board in the Act), who are elected in municipal elections. Part VI section 171 subsection (1) of the Act stipulates that a board may,

1. establish committees composed of members of the board to make recommendations to the board in respect of education, finance, personnel and property;
2. establish committees that may include persons who are not members of the board in respect of matters other than those referred to in paragraph 1.

Section 191 subsection (1) indicates that a board may pay to each of its members an honorarium in an amount determined by the board.

Subsection (2) prescribes that a board may pay to its chair and vice-chair an additional honorarium in an amount determined by the board.

Subsection (3) states that the amount of the additional honorarium payable to the chair may differ from the one payable to the vice-chair.

Subsection (4) presents that the Minister may make regulations,

(a) setting limits on honoraria paid and providing a method for calculating those limits;
(b) requiring a board to engage in public consultations before adopting or amending a policy providing for the payment of honoraria under this section;
(c) governing the form of the public consultations, the manner in which they are conducted and their timing, including notice requirements;
(d) respecting the establishment of bodies to represent the public for the purpose of the public consultations;
(e) governing the intervals at which a board may adopt a new policy or amend an existing policy providing for the payment of honoraria under this section.

Section 191.2 subsection (1) stipulates that in respect of travel of a member of a board to and from his or her residence to attend a meeting of the board, or of a committee of the board, that is held within the area of jurisdiction of the board, the board may,

(a) reimburse the member for his or her out-of-pocket expenses reasonably incurred or such lesser amount as may be determined by the board; or
(b) pay the member an allowance at a rate per kilometre determined by the board.

Subsection (2) states that a board may by resolution authorize a member, teacher or official of the board to travel on specific business of the board and may reimburse the member, teacher or official for his or her out-of-pocket expenses reasonably incurred or such lesser amount as may be determined by the board.

Subsection (3) prescribes that a board may establish a policy under which a member of the board may be reimbursed for all or part of his or her out-of-pocket expenses reasonably incurred in connection with carrying out the responsibilities of a board member.

Subsection (4) presents that a board may, in accordance with a policy established by it, reimburse a member for his or her out-of-pocket expenses reasonably incurred in connection with carrying out the responsibilities of a board member.

Subsection (5) indicates that a board may provide for a deduction of a reasonable amount from the allowance of a member because of absence from meetings of the board or of a committee of the board.

Section 207 subsection (1) provides that the meetings of a board and the meetings of a committee of the board shall be open to the public, and no person shall be excluded from a meeting that is open to the public except for improper conduct, subject to the following subsections.

Subsection (2) states that a meeting of a committee of a board, including a committee of the whole board, may be closed to the public when the subject-matter under consideration involves,

(a) the security of the property of the board;
(b) the disclosure of intimate, personal or financial information in respect of a member of the board or committee, an employee or prospective employee of the board or a pupil or his or her parent or guardian;
(c) the acquisition or disposal of a school site;
(d) decisions in respect of negotiations with employees of the board; or
(e) litigation affecting the board.

Subsection (2.1) specifies that a meeting of a board or of a committee of a board shall be closed to the public when the subject-matter under consideration involves an ongoing investigation under the Ombudsman Act respecting the board.

Subsection (3) prescribes that the presiding officer may expel or exclude from any meeting any person who has been guilty of improper conduct at the meeting.

Subsection (4) stipulates that any person may, at all reasonable hours, at the head office of the board inspect the minute book, the audited annual financial report and the current accounts of a board, and, upon the written request of any person and upon the payment to the board at the rate of 25 cents for every 100 words or at such lower rate as the board may fix, the secretary shall furnish copies of them or extracts therefrom certified under the secretary's hand.

Section 208 subsection (1) prescribes that a board shall be deemed to be constituted when a majority of the members to be elected or appointed has been elected or appointed.

Subsection (2) indicates that a board elected at a regular election under the Municipal Elections Act 1996 and a board appointed or elected other than at a regular election under the Municipal Elections Act 1996 shall hold its first meeting not later than seven days after the day on which the term of office of the board commences on such date and at such time and place as the board determines and, failing such determination, at 8 p.m. at the head office of the board on the first Wednesday following the commencement of the term of office.

Subsection (3) presents that on the petition of a majority of the members of a newly elected or appointed board, the appropriate supervisory officer may provide for calling the first meeting of the board at some other time and date.

Subsection (4) stipulates that at the first meeting in December of each year, the chief executive officer shall preside until the election of the chair or, if there is no chief executive officer or in his or her absence, the members present shall designate who shall preside at the election of the chair and if a member of the board is so designated, he or she may vote at the election of the chair.

Subsection (5) prescribes that at the first meeting in December of each year and at the first meeting after a vacancy occurs in the office of chair, the members shall elect one of themselves to be chair.

Subsection (6) states that subsequent meetings of the board shall be held at such time and place as the board considers expedient.

Subsection (7) presents that the members of the board may also elect one of themselves to be vice-chair and he or she shall preside in the absence of the chair.

Subsection (8) provides that in the case of an equality of votes at the election of a chair or vice-chair, the candidates shall draw lots to fill the position of chair or vice-chair.

Subsection (9) stipulates that if at any meeting there is no chair or vice-chair present, the members present may elect one of themselves to be chair for that meeting.

Subsection (10) prescribes that in the absence of the secretary from any meeting, the chair or other member presiding may appoint any member or other person to act as secretary for that meeting.

Subsection (11) states that the presence of a majority of all the members constituting a board is necessary to form a quorum.

Subsection (12) presents that the presiding officer, except where he or she is the chief executive officer of the board and is not a member, may vote with the other members of the board upon all motions, and any motion on which there is an equality of votes is lost.

Section 208.1 subsection (1) stipulates that the Lieutenant Governor in Council may make regulations respecting the use of electronic means for the holding of meetings of a board and meetings of a committee of a board, including a committee of the whole board.

Subsection (2) states that a regulation may provide that a board member who participates in a meeting through electronic means shall be deemed to be present at the meeting for the purposes of this and every other Act, subject to such conditions or limitations as may be provided for in the regulation.

Subsection (3) presents that a regulation may provide for participation through electronic means by members of the board, student trustees and members of the public.

Subsection (4) indicates that in a regulation, the Lieutenant Governor in Council may provide for any matter by authorizing a board to develop and implement a policy with respect to the matter.

Section 209 subsection (1) provides that every person elected or appointed to a board, on or before the day fixed for the first meeting of the new board, or on or before the day of the first meeting that the person attends, shall make and subscribe the following declaration in English or French before the secretary of the board or before any person authorized to administer an oath or affirmation and in default the person shall be deemed to have resigned:

1. I solemnly declare that I am not disqualified under any Act from being a member of (name of board).
2. I solemnly declare that I will truly, faithfully, impartially and to the best of my ability execute the office of board member, and that I have not received and will not receive any payment or reward or promise thereof for the exercise of any partiality or malversation or other undue execution of the said office and that I will disclose any pecuniary interest, direct or indirect, as required by and in accordance with the Municipal Conflict of Interest Act.

Subsection (2) stipulates that where a person is elected or appointed to fill a vacancy on a board, the person shall make such declaration on or before the day fixed for holding the first meeting of the board after his or her election or appointment or on or before the day of the first meeting that the person attends and in default the person shall be deemed to have resigned.

Section 211 presents that every person who wilfully makes a false statement in a declaration required to be made under this Act is guilty of an offence and on conviction is liable to a fine of not more than $200.

Section 212 subsection (1) provides that every person who wilfully interrupts or disquiets the proceedings of a school or class is guilty of an offence and on conviction is liable to a fine of not more than $200.

Subsection (2) indicates that every person who, with intent to prevent the discussion of any matter or the passing of any motion at a meeting of a board, or a committee of a board including a committee of the whole board disrupts or endeavours to disturb or interrupt the meeting after having been expelled or excluded from the meeting is guilty of an offence and on conviction is liable to a fine of not more than $200.

Section 213 subsection (1) stipulates that every member of a board who sits or votes at any meeting of the board after becoming disqualified from sitting is guilty of an offence and on conviction is liable to a fine of not more than $200 for every meeting at which he or she so sits or votes.

Subsection (2) presents that every member of a board who knowingly signs a false report and every teacher who keeps a false school register or makes a false return is guilty of an offence and on conviction is liable to a fine of not more than $200.

Section 217 subsection (1) prescribes that no teacher, or other employee of a board or of the Ministry shall, for compensation of any kind other than his or her salary as such employee, promote, offer for sale or sell, directly or indirectly, any book or other teaching or learning materials, equipment, furniture, stationery or other article to any board, provincial school or teachers' college, or to any pupil enrolled therein.

However, subsection (2) provides that subsection (1) does not apply to a teacher, or any other employee in respect of a book or other teaching or learning materials of which he or she is an author where the only compensation that he or she receives in respect thereof is a fee or royalty thereon.

Subsection (3) states that no person or organization or agent thereof shall employ a teacher, or other employee of a board or of the Ministry to promote, offer for sale or sell, directly or indirectly, any book or other teaching or learning materials, equipment, furniture, stationery or other article to any board, provincial school or teachers' college, or to any pupil enrolled therein, or shall, directly or indirectly, give or pay compensation to any such teacher, or employee for such purpose.

Subsection (4) indicates that every person who contravenes any provision of subsection (1) or (3) is guilty of an offence and on conviction is liable to a fine of not more than $200.

Section 218.1 stipulates that a member of a board shall,

(a) carry out his or her responsibilities in a manner that assists the board in fulfilling its duties under this Act, the regulations and the guidelines issued under this Act;
(b) attend and participate in meetings of the board, including meetings of board committees of which he or she is a member;
(c) consult with parents, students and supporters of the board on the board's multi-year plan;
(d) bring concerns of parents, students and supporters of the board to the attention of the board;
(e) uphold the implementation of any board resolution after it is passed by the board;
(f) entrust the day to day management of the board to its staff through the board's director of education;
(g) maintain focus on student achievement and well-being; and
(h) comply with the board's code of conduct.

Section 218.2 subsection (1) states that a board may adopt a code of conduct that applies to the members of the board.

Subsection (2) indicates that the Minister may make regulations,

(a) requiring a board to adopt a code of conduct;
(b) governing codes of conduct that apply to board members, whether permitted or required under this section, including,
    (i) prescribing codes of conduct or parts of codes of conduct, and
    (ii) prescribing matters to be addressed by codes of conduct.

Section 218.3 subsection (1) presents that a member of a board who has reasonable grounds to believe that a member of the board has breached the board's code of conduct may bring the alleged breach to the attention of the board.

Subsection (2) provides that if an alleged breach is brought to the attention of the board, the board shall make inquiries into the matter and shall, based on the results of the inquiries, determine whether the member has breached the board's code of conduct.

Subsection (3) stipulates that if the board determines that the member has breached the board's code of conduct, the board may impose one or more of the following sanctions:

1. Censure of the member.
2. Barring the member from attending all or part of a meeting of the board or a meeting of a committee of the board.
3. Barring the member from sitting on one or more committees of the board, for the period of time specified by the board.

Subsection (5) stipulates that a member of a board who is barred from attending all or part of a meeting of the board or a meeting of a committee of the board under subsection (3) is not entitled to receive any materials that relate to that meeting or that part of the meeting and that are not available to members of the public.

Subsection (6) prescribes that if a board determines that a member has breached the board's code of conduct,

(a) the board shall give the member written notice of the determination and of any sanction imposed by the board;
(b) the notice shall inform the member that he or she may make written submissions to the board in respect of the determination or sanction by a date specified in the notice that is at least 14 days after the notice is received by the member; and
(c) the board shall consider any submissions made by the member in accordance with clause (b) and shall confirm or revoke the determination within 14 days after the submissions are received.

Subsection (7) stipulates that if the board revokes a determination, any sanction imposed by the board is revoked.

Subsection (8) states that if the board confirms a determination, the board shall, within the time referred to in that clause, confirm, vary or revoke the sanction.

Subsection (9) prescribes that if a sanction is varied or revoked, the variation or revocation shall be deemed to be effective as of the date the original determination was made.

Subsection (10) indicates that the part of a meeting of the board during which a breach or alleged breach of the board's code of conduct is considered may be closed to the public when the breach or alleged breach involves any sensitive matters.

However, subsection (11) presents that a board shall do the following things by resolution at a meeting of the board, and the vote on the resolution shall be open to the public:

1. Decide that a member has breached the board's code of conduct.
2. Impose a sanction.
3. Confirm or revoke a determination.
4. Confirm, vary or revoke a sanction.

Subsection (12) stipulate that a member who is alleged to have breached the board's code of conduct shall not vote on a resolution to do any of the things described in paragraphs 1 to 4 of subsection (11).

Section 218.4 presents that in addition to any other duties under the Act, the chair of a board shall,

(a) preside over meetings of the board;
(b) conduct the meetings in accordance with the board's procedures and practices for the conduct of board meetings;
(c) establish agendas for board meetings, in consultation with the board's director of education or the supervisory officer acting as the board's director of education;
(d) ensure that members of the board have the information needed for informed discussion of the agenda items;
(e) act as spokesperson to the public on behalf of the board, unless otherwise determined by the board;
(f) convey the decisions of the board to the board's director of education or the supervisory officer acting as the board's director of education;
(g) provide leadership to the board in maintaining the board's focus on the multi-year plan established;
(h) provide leadership to the board in maintaining the board's focus on the board's mission and vision; and
(i) assume such other responsibilities as may be specified by the board.

Section 219 subsection (1) indicates that a person is qualified to be elected as a member of a district school board if the person is qualified to vote for members of that district school board and is resident in its area of jurisdiction.

Subsection (2) stipulates that a person who is qualified to be elected as a member of a district school board is qualified to be elected as a member of that district school board for any geographic area in the district school board's area of jurisdiction, regardless of which positions on that district school board the person may be qualified to vote for.

Subsection (3) provides that a member of a district school board or school authority is eligible for re-election if otherwise qualified.

Subsection (4) states that a person is not qualified to be elected or to act as a member of a district school board if the person is,

(a) an employee of a district school board;
(b) Repealed.
(c) the clerk or treasurer or deputy clerk or deputy treasurer of a municipality or an upper-tier municipality, all or part of which is included in the area of jurisdiction of the district school board;
(d) a member of the Assembly or of the Senate or House of Commons of Canada; or

Section 229 subsection (1) prescribes that a member of a board shall be physically present in the meeting room of the board for at least three regular meetings of the board in each 12-month period beginning December 1.

Subsection (2) stipulates that for the period beginning when a member of a board is elected or appointed to fill a vacancy and ending on the following November 30, the member shall be physically present in the meeting room of the board for at least one regular meeting of the board for each period of four full calendar months that occurs during the period beginning with the election or appointment and ending on the following November 30.

Section 230 indicates that the Minister may direct an investigation of a board's affairs if the Minister has concerns that the board may have done or omitted to do something and the act or omission,

(a) contravenes, indicates an intention to contravene or might result in a contravention of Ministry guidelines, regulations or board duties;
(b) makes, indicates an intention to make, or may result in the making of a payment of a type that does not comply with Ministry regulations concerning honoraria; or
(c) applies funds, indicates an intention to apply funds or may result in the application of funds in a manner that contravenes a regulation made under legislative and municipal grants.

Section 230.5 subsection 1 states that where the Lieutenant Governor in Council has made an order in respect of a board, the Minister has control and charge over the board generally with respect to any matter in any way affecting the board's affairs.

Section 230.8 stipulates that the Minister may make any orders from time to time that he or she considers advisable to carry out the provisions of this Part or any agreement made under it and may make rules in respect of any thing done under this Part.

Section 230.11 prescribes that where a board has become subject to Minister's vesting order, the Minister shall always have access to all records of the board relating to the board's financial transactions and may inspect and copy them.

Section 230.12 subsection (1) states that where a board fails to comply with any order of the Minister under this Part, the Minister may do or order done all things necessary for compliance with the order and may exercise all the powers of the board for the purpose, under its name.

Subsection (3) presents that if a board that is subject to an order applies any of its funds otherwise than as the Minister orders or authorizes, the members of the board who voted for the application are jointly and severally liable for the amount so applied, which may be recovered in a court of competent jurisdiction.

Subsection (4) indicates that the Minister may dismiss from office any officer or employee of a board who fails to carry out any order of the Minister under this Part and may exercise all the powers of the board for the purpose, under its name.

Section 230.19 subsection (1) provides that nothing in this Part authorizes the Minister to interfere with or control,

(a) the denominational aspects of a Roman Catholic board;
(b) the denominational aspects of a Protestant separate school board; or
(c) the linguistic or cultural aspects of a French-language district school board.

Subsection (2) stipulates that the powers under this Part shall be exercised in a manner that is consistent with,

(a) the denominational aspects of a Roman Catholic board;
(b) the denominational aspects of a Protestant separate school board; or
(c) the linguistic or cultural aspects of a French-language district school board.

Section 257.30 subsection (1) states that the Minister may direct an investigation of the financial affairs of a board if,

(a) the financial statements of the board for a fiscal year, or the auditor's report on the statements, required to be submitted to the Ministry, indicate that the board had an accumulated deficit for that year;
    (a.1) the board was required to submit a financial recovery plan to the Minister within the time specified by the Minister and the board failed to do so;
    (a.2) the board was required to comply with a financial recovery plan and the board failed to do so;
    (a.3) the board was required to comply with a regulation and the board failed to do so;
(b) the board has failed to pay any of its debentures or instruments or interest on them, after payment of the debenture, instrument or interest is due and has been demanded;
(c) the board has failed to pay any of its other debts or liabilities when due and default in payment is occasioned from financial difficulties affecting the board; or
(d) the Minister has concerns about the board's ability to meet its financial obligations.
    (1.1) The Minister may direct an investigation whether or not he or she has ordered the board to submit a financial recovery plan or considered any such plan that has been submitted.

Subsection (2) prescribes that the Minister may appoint as an investigator a person licensed under the Public Accounting Act, 2004 or an employee in the Ministry.

Subsection (3) indicates that an investigator may,

(a) require the production of any records that may in any way relate to the financial affairs of the board;
(b) examine and copy any records required under clause (a); and
(c) require any officer of the board or any other person to appear before him or her and give evidence, on oath or affirmation, relating to the financial affairs of the board.

Subsection (4) stipulates that section 33 of the Public Inquiries Act, 2009 applies to an investigation.

Subsection (5) states that on completion of an investigation, an investigator shall report in writing to the Minister, who shall promptly transmit a copy of the report to the secretary of the board.

Subsection (6) provides that the investigator may not recommend that control and charge over the administration of the affairs of the board be vested in the Ministry unless the investigation discloses evidence of financial default or probable financial default, of an accumulated deficit or a probable accumulated deficit or of serious financial mismanagement.

Section 257.31 subsection (1) prescribes that after reviewing the report on completion of an investigation, the Minister may give any directions to the board that he or she considers advisable to address the financial affairs of the board.

Subsection (2) indicates that if the report recommends that control and charge over the administration of the affairs of the board should be vested in the Ministry, the Lieutenant Governor in Council may make any order that he or she considers necessary or advisable to vest in the Ministry control and charge over the administration of the affairs of the board.

Subsection (3) presents that if the Minister advises the Lieutenant Governor in Council that he or she is of the opinion that the board has failed to comply with a direction given under subsection (1), the Lieutenant Governor in Council may make any order that the Lieutenant Governor in Council considers necessary or advisable to vest in the Ministry control and charge over the administration of the affairs of the board.

Subsection (4) stipulates that the order shall be promptly transmitted to the secretary of the board.

Section 257.32 subsection (1) states that where a board is subject to an order mentioned above,

(a) the Minister shall publish notice of the order in The Ontario Gazette; and
(b) the persons directed by the Minister to do so shall give notice of the order to the persons specified by the Minister, in the form specified by the Minister.

Subsection (2) indicates that after notice has been published in The Ontario Gazette under clause (1) (a),

(a) no proceeding against the board shall be commenced or continued in any court without leave of the Minister; and

(b) no order of any court shall be enforced against the board without leave of the Minister.

Subsection (3) stipulates that where the commencement or continuance of any proceeding or the enforcement of a court order is prevented under this section,

(a) the running of any limitation period relating to the proceeding or enforcement is suspended until the Minister gives leave to commence or continue the proceeding or to enforce the court order; and
(b) the person having the right to commence or continue the proceeding or to enforce the court order shall, immediately after the leave is given, have the same length of time within which to commence or continue the proceeding or enforce the court order, as the person had when the notice was published in The Ontario Gazette.

Section 257.33 subsection (1) indicates that where the Lieutenant Governor in Council has made an order in respect of a board, the Minister has control and charge over the board generally with respect to any matter in any way affecting the board's affairs.

Subsection (2) states that without limiting the generality of subsection (1), where the Lieutenant Governor in Council has made an order, the Minister has control and charge over the exercise and performance by the board of its powers, duties and obligations with respect to all matters, including but not limited to matters respecting,

(a) the appointment and dismissal of the board's officers and employees and their powers, duties, salaries and remuneration;
(b) the board's revenues and expenditures;
(c) the board's sinking funds, retirement funds and the funds prescribed under clause 247 (3) (e) and the money belonging to those funds;
(d) the board's accounting and audit systems and dealings with the board's assets, liabilities, revenues and expenditures;
(e) the yearly or other estimates of the board, financial statements of the board and other reports of the board required by the Minister as well as the form, preparation and completion of them, and the times when they shall be made;
(f) the amounts to be provided for in the yearly or other estimates;

(g) the borrowing of money for the current expenditures of the board until the current revenue has been received;
(h) the imposition, charging and collection of all fees, charges and expenses;
(i) the sale or other disposition of any of the board's assets.

Section 257.36 presents that where a board is subject to an order, the board may, with the approval of the Minister, enter into an agreement with any person with whom the board has previously entered into an agreement or obligation that, or some term or obligation of which, remains in whole or in part or in any manner to be carried out by the board, for the amendment or cancellation of the subsisting agreement or obligation.

Section 257.37 subsection (1) provides that without the approval of the Minister first being obtained, a board subject to an order shall not exercise or be required to exercise any of its powers if that exercise will or may require money to be provided by the issue of instruments of the board.

Subsection (2) states that where a board is subject to an order, the board may, with the approval of the Minister, pass by-laws providing for the issue of instruments or authorizing the sale of such instruments or the offering of such instruments as security, but no such by-law has any force and effect until approved by the Minister.

Section 257.38 subsection (1) prescribes that where a board is subject to an order, the Minister has full charge and control over all money belonging to the board and received by any person for or on its behalf and the money shall be deposited in one of the following institutions, to be designated by the board or, in the absence of designation by the board, by the Minister:

1. A bank listed in Schedule I or II to the Bank Act (Canada).
2. Repealed.
3. A loan or trust corporation registered under the Loan and Trust Corporations Act.
4. A credit union as defined in section 1 of the Credit Unions and Caisses Populaires Act, 1994.

Subsection (2) indicates that when money is deposited as required, it shall only be applied for the purposes, in the manner and at the times that the Minister may approve.

Subsection (3) stipulates that all cheques drawn and issued by the board shall be signed and countersigned by the persons and in the manner that the Minister may authorize.

Subsection (4) presents that no money belonging to or revenues of the board may be applied by any person except with the approval of or otherwise than as directed by the Minister.

Section 257.39 provides that the powers and duties under this or any other Act of a board that is subject to an order shall only be exercised in accordance with and subject to this Division and any order made or agreement entered into under it.

Section 257.40 subsection (1) prescribes that the Minister has exclusive jurisdiction as to all matters arising under this Division or out of the exercise by the board or any person of any of the powers conferred by this Division, and that jurisdiction is not open to question or review in any proceeding or by any court.

Subsection (2) states that the Minister may at any time review any order, direction or decision made by him or her under this Division and confirm, amend or revoke it.

However, subsection (3) stipulates that the Lieutenant Governor in Council has exclusive jurisdiction as to the making of an order, and that jurisdiction is not open to question or review in any proceeding or by any court.

Subsection (4) indicates that the Lieutenant Governor in Council may at any time review any order made by him or her and confirm, amend or revoke it.

Section 257.41 prescribes that the Minister may make any orders from time to time that he or she considers advisable to carry out the provisions of this Division or any agreement made under it and may make rules in respect of any thing done under this Division.

Section 257.42 states that every certificate, notice or other form that is in substantial conformity with the form required for it under this Division is not open to objection on the ground that it is not in the form required by this Division.

Section 257.43 stipulates that where a board has become subject to an order, all things done by or for the Minister under this Division in relation to the affairs of the board shall for all purposes be deemed to have been done by and for the board and in its name.

Section 257.44 prescribes that where a board is subject to an order, the Minister shall always have access to all records of the board relating to the board's financial transactions and may inspect and copy them.

Section 257.45 subsection (1) stipulates that where a board fails to comply with any order of the Minister under this Division, the Minister may do or order done all things necessary for compliance with the order and may exercise all the powers of the board for the purpose, under its name.

Subsection (3) states that if a board subject to an order applies any of its funds otherwise than as the Minister orders or authorizes, the members of the board who voted for the application are jointly and severally liable for the amount so applied, which may be recovered in a court of competent jurisdiction.

Subsection (4) prescribes that the Minister may dismiss from office any officer or employee of a board who fails to carry out any order of the Minister and may exercise all the powers of the board for the purpose, under its name.

Subsection (5) indicates that a board shall not indemnify any of its members, officers or employees with respect to any fine imposed on conviction for an offence under this Division or with respect to any liability under subsection (3).

Section 257.46 presents that the Minister may by injunction proceedings prevent the exercise by or for a board of any of its powers that has not been approved by the Minister, if that approval is required under this Division.

Section 257.47 provides that where a board is subject to an order, the Minister may direct that two or more of the offices of the board shall be combined and held by the same officer, and may subsequently separate any of the offices so combined.

Section 257.48 subsection (1) stipulates that the Minister may direct payment of the fees and expenses reasonably incurred by the Ministry under this Division that he or she may determine.

Subsection (2) presents that the Minister may appoint a person to exercise the powers and perform the duties that the Minister may provide, and the person so appointed shall be paid the salary and allowed the expenses that the Minister may determine.

Subsection (3) provides that the Minister, in determining the salaries to be paid to any person appointed, shall consider any representations that the board may at any time make.

Section 257.49 indicates that the powers contained in this Division shall be deemed to be in addition to and not in derogation of any power of the Minister under this or any other Act but, where the provisions of any Act or any other provision of this Act conflict with the provisions of this Division, the provisions of this Division prevail.

Section 257.50 subsection (1) states that the Lieutenant Governor in Council shall revoke an order if the Lieutenant Governor in Council is of the opinion that the affairs of a board no longer need to be administered under this Division.

Subsection (2) stipulates that the Lieutenant Governor in Council shall revoke an order if the financial statements of a board for a fiscal year and the auditor's report on the statements submitted to the Ministry indicate that the board did not have an accumulated deficit for the fiscal year.

Section 257.52 subsection (1) presents that nothing in this Division or Division C.1 authorizes the Minister to interfere with or control,

(a) the denominational aspects of a Roman Catholic board;
(b) the denominational aspects of a Protestant separate school board; or
(c) the linguistic or cultural aspects of a French-language district school board.

Subsection (2) provides that the powers under this Division and Division C.1 shall be exercised in a manner that is consistent with,

(a) the denominational aspects of a Roman Catholic board;
(b) the denominational aspects of a Protestant separate school board; or
(c) the linguistic or cultural aspects of a French-language district school board.

Section 304 subsection (1) stipulates that every board shall ensure that opening or closing exercises are held in each school under the board's jurisdiction, in accordance with the requirements set out in the regulations.

Subsection (2) indicates that the opening or closing exercises must include the singing of O Canada and may include the recitation of a pledge of citizenship in the form set out in the regulations.

Subsection (3) prescribes that a pupil is not required to participate in the opening or closing exercises in such circumstances as are prescribed by regulation.

Section 305 subsection (1) states that the Minister may make regulations governing access to school premises, specifying classes of persons who are permitted to be on school premises and specifying the days and times at which different classes of persons are prohibited from being on school premises.

Subsection (2) presents that no person shall enter or remain on school premises unless he or she is authorized by regulation to be there on that day or at that time.

Subsection (3) provides that a person shall not enter or remain on school premises if he or she is prohibited under a board policy from being there on that day or at that time.

Subsection (4) stipulates that the principal of a school may direct a person to leave the school premises if the principal believes that the person is prohibited by regulation or under a board policy from being there.

Subsection (5) states that every person who contravenes subsection (2) is guilty of an offence.

The Public Schools Act 1807 had only 3 pages, but the current Ontario Education Act is over 300 pages. The 1807 Act stipulated that teachers should be of good character. Today teachers still shall be of good character. However, other things have changed significantly. The contemporary Ontario publicly funded elementary and secondary education system is far more complicated, and the complexity of the system is likely to increase in the future. In 1807 few people thought education was a right, but today most Ontarians think education, at least elementary and secondary education, is a right, and people debate about whether higher education is a right or privilege. Parents make far more demands than in 1807. Ontario learning outcomes are compared with those in other provinces and nations. In addition, there are international students in Ontario elementary, secondary, and higher education institutions. The number of them, particularly in higher education, has been increasing significantly in recent years. Among the five English speaking countries, the United States, the United Kingdom, Canada, Australia, and New Zealand, Canadian students performed the best, approaching the top of the education systems that participated in the Programme for International Student Assessment (Organization of Economic Co-Operation and Development [OECD], 2019). In Canada, Ontario students performed above the national average (Council of Ministers of Education, Canada, 2019). While Canadian students performed the best among the five English speaking countries, Chinese students performed at the top (OECD, 2019) since 2009, when they started participating in PISA for the first time. American students performed below Canadian students (OECD, 2019).

With the Canadian quality of life and the reputation of Canadian education, the trend seems to be that more international students will come to Canada. Based on study permits issued by Immigration, Refugees, and Citizenship Canada (IRCC), international students coming to Canada have more than recovered from the dip caused by the pandemic. In 2019 IRCC issued in total 400,640 study permits to international students. In 2022 IRCC issued in total 550,505 study permits to international students (Immigration, Refugees, and Citizenship Canada, 2023).

This book introduces and discusses Ontario education law, while mentioning California Education Code and Chinese education law. As the Chinese economy continues to grow faster than that in North America, is it advisable for Chinese to extend compulsory education to the age of 18, as the Ontario

Education Act and California Education Code stipulate? Chinese students have continued to perform at the top of the world since 2009 when they first participated in PISA. Assuming PISA results are reliable and valid, is there something Ontarians and Californians can learn from Chinese?

REFERENCES

Anderson, S., & Ben Jaafar, S. (2007). Policy Trends and Tensions in Accountability for Educational Management and Services in Canada. *The Alberta Journal of Educational Research*, *53*(2), 207–227.

Boyle, T. (2004, December 29). Toronto school board a tricky balancing act. *Toronto Star*.

Brimley, V. Jr, Verstegen, D., & Garfield, R. (2016). *Financing education in a climate of change* (12th ed.). Pearson.

California Legislative Information. (n.d.). *Education Code*. https://leginfo.legislature.ca.gov/faces/codesTOCSelected.xhtml?tocCode=EDC

Conrad, M., & Finkel, A. (2006). *History of the Canadian peoples* (4th ed., Vol. 1). Pearson Longman.

Education Act. RSO 1990, c E.2. https://www.canlii.org/en/on/laws/stat/rso-1990-c-e2/latest/rso-1990-c- e2.html

Education Improvement Commission. (2000). *The road ahead IV: A report on improving schools through greater accountability*. http://www.edu.gov.on.ca/eng/document/reports/eic/road4/eic4.pdf

Ferguson, R. (2012, August 17). Liberals lay down the hammer with teachers' bill. *Toronto Star*, p. A6.

Ferguson, R. (2014, November 20). Reopening teachers' contracts cost $468M. *Toronto Star*, p. A1.

Galway, G., Sheppard, B., Wiens, J., & Brown, J. (2013). The impact of centralization on local school district governance in Canada. *Canadian Journal of Educational Administration and Policy*, 145.

Garcea, J., & Munroe, D. (2014). Reforms to funding education in four Canadian provinces. *Canadian Journal of Educational Administration and Policy*, 159.

Gibney, R. (1999). *From Hope to Harris: The reshaping of Ontario's schools*. University of Toronto Press.

Governance Review Committee. (2009). *School board governance: A focus on achievement*. Author.

Guillet, E. (1960). *In the Cause of Education*. University of Toronto Press.

Immigration, Refugees, and Citizenship Canada. (2023). *Temporary Residents: Study Permit Holders – Monthly IRCC Updates - Canada - Study permit holders by country of citizenship and year in which permit(s) became effective*. https://open.canada.ca/data/en/dataset/90115b00-f9b8-49e8- afa3-b4cff8facaee/resource/b505b9bc-d375-4525-af39-afdf25639acf

Kalinowski, T. (2006, January 18). ESL students shortchanged. *Toronto Star*, p. B5.

Kane, L. (2013, August 16). High school teachers threaten new protests. *Toronto Star*, p. A1.

Levin, B. (2005). *Governing Education*. University of Toronto Press. doi:10.3138/9781442675438

Levin, B., & Fullan, M. (2008). Learning about system renewal. *Educational Management Administration & Leadership*, *36*(2), 289–303. doi:10.1177/1741143207087778

Li, X. (2015). Ontario education governance 1995 to the present: More accountability, more regulation, and more centralization? *Journal of International Education and Leadership*, *5*(1). https://files.eric.ed.gov/fulltext/EJ1135778.pdf

Ontario Ministry of Education. (2003). *Student-focused funding: School board funding projections for the 2003–04 school year*. https://collections.ola.org/mon/6000/10316038.pdf

Ontario Ministry of Education. (2011). *School Fees Guideline*. Retrieved from http://www.edu.gov.on.ca/eng/parents/fundraising.html

Ontario Ministry of Education. (2012). *Fundraising Guideline*. Retrieved from http://www.edu.gov.on.ca/eng/parents/Fund2012Guideline.pdf

Ontario Ministry of Education. (2022). *Education Funding: Grants for Student Needs Projections for the 2022-23 School Year*. https://files.ontario.ca/edu-2223-gsnprojections- en- 2022-04-20.pdf

Operation of Schools. Ontario Regulation 298. (1990). https://www.canlii.org/en/on/laws/regu/rro-1990- reg-298/latest/rro-1990-reg-298.html

Organization of Economic Co-Operation and Development. (2019). *PISA 2018 Results: Combined Executive Summaries*. https://www.oecd.org/pisa/Combined_Executive_Summaries_PISA_2018.pdf

Osgoode Hall Law School, York University. (2020, December 9). *Advanced issues in special education law*. https://osgoodepd.ca/professional-development/short-courses-and-conferences/advanced- issues-in-special-education-law-2020/

People for Education. (2012). *Making Connections Beyond School Walls: People for Education Annual Report on Ontario's Publicly Funded Schools 2012*. https://www.academia.edu/30790074/MAKING_CONNECTIONS_BEYOND_SCHOOL_WALLS_People_for_Education_Annual_Report_on_Ontarios_Publicly_Funded_Scho ols_2012

People for Education. (2019). *2019 Annual report on schools: What makes a school?* https://peopleforeducation.ca/report/2019-annual-report-on-schools-what-makes-a-school/

Putting, S. F. A. 2012, SO 2012, c 11. https://www.canlii.org/en/on/laws/astat/so-2012-c- 11/latest/so-2012-c-11.html?resultIndex=2

Ranson, S. (2003). Public accountability in the age of neo-liberal governance. *Journal of Education Policy*, *18*(5), 459–480. doi:10.1080/0268093032000124848

Ross, G. (1896). *The School System of Ontario*. D. Appleton and Company.

Rozanski, M. (2002). *Invest in Public Education: Advancing the Goal of Continuous Improvement in Student Learning and Achievement*. Academic Press.

Rushowy, K., & Benzie, R. (2012, July 6). Catholic teachers, province forge deal. *Toronto Star*, p. A1.

Rushowy, K., Brown, L., & Ferguson, R. (2013, June 14). Elementary teachers get 2% wage increase. *Toronto Star*, p. GT1.

Rushowy, K., & Ferguson, R. (2009, February 15). Teachers accept 4-year deal. *Toronto Star*, p. A4.

Sattler, P. (2012). Education governance reform in Ontario: Neoliberalism in context. *Canadian Journal of Educational Administration and Policy*, 128.

School Councils. O Reg 612/00. https://www.canlii.org/en/on/laws/regu/o-reg-612-00/latest/o-reg-612- 00.html

Statistics Canada. (2022, October 26). *The Canadian census: A rich portrait of the country's religious and ethnocultural diversity*. https://www150.statcan.gc.ca/n1/daily-quotidien/221026/dq221026b-eng.htm

Statistics Canada. (2023). *Consumer Price Index, annual average, not seasonally adjusted*. https://www150.statcan.gc.ca/t1/tbl1/en/tv.action?pid=1810000501&pickMembers%5B0%5D=1.14&cubeTimeFrame.startYear=2002&cubeTimeFrame.endYear=2022&referencePeriods=20020101%2C20220101

Talaga, T., & Aulakh, R. (2012, August 14). Union turns back on province. *Toronto Star*, p. A6.

Talaga, T., & Rushowy, K. (2012, August 10). French teachers' union seals deal. *Toronto Star*, p. A12.

The Chinese People's Congress. (2021). *The Chinese Education Act* [中华人民共和国教育法]. http://www.moe.gov.cn/jyb_xxgk/xxgk_jyfl/flfg_jyfl/202107/t20210730_547843.html

The Constitution Act, 1982, Schedule B to the Canada Act 1982 (UK), c 11. https://www.canlii.org/en/ca/laws/stat/schedule-b-to-the-canada-act-1982-uk-1982-c- 11/latest/schedule-b-to-the-canada-act-1982-uk-1982-c-11.html

The Parliament of the United Kingdom. (1867). The Constitution Act, 1867 (The British North America Act, 1867).

Walker, A. (1971). *History of Education in Ontario 1791 – 1841* [Master's thesis]. University of Toronto Library.

Compilation of References

Accessibility for Ontarians with Disabilities Act. SO 2005, C11. https://www.canlii.org/en/on/laws/stat/so-2005-c-11/latest/so-2005-c-11.html

Alphonso, C. (2020, April 20). Ontario high school teachers reach tentative deal with province. *The Globe and Mail*. https://www.theglobeandmail.com/canada/article-ontario-high- school-teachers-reach- tentative-deal/

Anderson, S., & Ben Jaafar, S. (2007). Policy Trends and Tensions in Accountability for Educational Management and Services in Canada. *The Alberta Journal of Educational Research*, *53*(2), 207–227.

Appleby, T. (2008, January 8). C.W. Jefferys staff charged with failing to report alleged assault. *The Globe and Mail*. https://www.theglobeandmail.com/news/national/cw-jefferys-staff-charged-w with-failing-to-report-alleged-assault/article666251/

Bedard, G., & Lawton, S. (1998, July). The battle over Ontario's Bill 160 and the shape of teacher collective bargaining. *Policy Options*, 49–54.

Behaviour, Discipline and Safety of Pupils, O Reg 472/07. https://www.canlii.org/en/on/laws/regu/o-reg-472-07/latest/o-reg-472-07.html

Board of Education for Toronto v. Higgs et al. [1960] SCR 174, 1959 CanLII 24 (SCC). https://www.canlii.org/en/ca/scc/doc/1959/1959canlii24/1959canlii24.html

Boyle, T. (2004, December 29). Toronto school board a tricky balancing act. *Toronto Star*.

Brimley, V. Jr, Verstegen, D., & Garfield, R. (2016). *Financing education in a climate of change* (12th ed.). Pearson.

Brown, A. (2009). *Legal Handbook for Educators* (6th ed.). Carswell.

Brown, A., & Zuker, M. (2007). *Education Law* (4th ed.). Thomson Carswell.

California Legislative Information. (n.d.). *Education Code*. https://leginfo.legislature.ca.gov/faces/codesTOCSelected.xhtml?tocCode=EDC

Conrad, M., & Finkel, A. (2006). *History of the Canadian peoples* (4th ed., Vol. 1). Pearson Longman.

Criminal CodeR. S. C. 1985, c C-46. https://www.canlii.org/en/ca/laws/stat/rsc-1985-c-c-46/latest/rsc- 1985-c-c-46.html

Delaney, J. (2018). Teacher misconduct in Canada. In W. Smale (Ed.), Perspectives on Canadian Educational Law and Policy (pp. 43-66). Word & Deed Publishing Inc.

Delaney, J. (2022). *Education Law for Teachers and School Administrators* (2nd ed.). Brush Education Inc.

Eaton v. Brant County Board of Education, 1997 CanLII 366 (SCC). https://www.canlii.org/en/ca/scc/doc/1997/1997canlii366/1997canlii366.html?

Education Act, RSO 1990, c E.2. https://www.canlii.org/en/on/laws/stat/rso-1990-c-e2/latest/rso-1990-c- e2.html

Education Act. RSO 1990, c E.2. https://www.canlii.org/en/on/laws/stat/rso-1990-c-e2/latest/rso-1990-c- e2.html

Education Improvement Commission. (2000). *The road ahead IV: A report on improving schools through greater accountability*. http://www.edu.gov.on.ca/eng/document/reports/eic/road4/eic4.pdf

Elementary Teachers' Federation of Ontario (ETFO) Central Agreements Now Ratified. (2020). https://news.ontario.ca/en/backgrounder/56788/elementary-teachers-federation-of-ontario-etfo-central-agreements-now-ratified

Elementary Teachers' Federation of Ontario. (2023). *ETFO's Charter Challenge Against Bill 115 and Remedy Decision.* https://www.etfo.ca/etfo-action/bills/etfo-s-unfair-labour-practice-complaint-against-the-government-of-ontario

European Agency for Special Needs and Inclusive Education. (2015). *Agency position on inclusive education systems*. https://www.europeanagency.org/sites/default/files/PositionPaper-EN.pdf

Evergreen Teachers Association. (n.d.). *Bargaining*. https://www.etanews.org/page3/

Ferguson, R. (2012, August 17). Liberals lay down the hammer with teachers' bill. *Toronto Star*, p. A6.

Ferguson, R. (2014, November 20). Reopening teachers' contracts cost $468M. *Toronto Star*, p. A1.

Galway, G., Sheppard, B., Wiens, J., & Brown, J. (2013). The impact of centralization on local school district governance in Canada. *Canadian Journal of Educational Administration and Policy*, 145.

Garcea, J., & Munroe, D. (2014). Reforms to funding education in four Canadian provinces. *Canadian Journal of Educational Administration and Policy*, 159.

Gidney, R. (1999). *From Hope to Harris: The reshaping of Ontario's schools*. University of Toronto Press. doi:10.3138/9781442675087

Governance Review Committee. (2009). *School board governance: A focus on achievement*. Author.

Guillet, E. (1960). *In the Cause of Education*. University of Toronto Press.

Hasham, A. (2021). Toronto teacher should have foreseen drowning risk but is not guilty in death of Jeremiah Perry, 15, judge rules. *Toronto Star*. https://www.thestar.com/news/gta/2021/10/06/verdict-coming-in-toronto-teachers-trial-over- drowning-of-jeremiah-perry-15-in-algonquin-park.html

Identification and Placement of Exceptional Pupils. O Reg 181/98. https://www.canlii.org/en/on/laws/regu/o-reg-181-98/latest/o-reg-181-98.html

Imazeki, J., & Reschovsky, A. (2006). Does No Child Left Behind place a fiscal burden on states? *Education Finance and Policy*, *1*(2), 217–246. doi:10.1162/edfp.2006.1.2.217

Immigration, Refugees, and Citizenship Canada. (2023). *Temporary Residents: Study Permit Holders – Monthly IRCC Updates - Canada - Study permit holders by country of citizenship and year in which permit(s) became effective*. https://open.canada.ca/data/en/dataset/90115b00-f9b8-49e8- afa3-b4cff8facaee/resource/b505b9bc-d375-4525-af39-afdf25639acf

Kalinowski, T. (2006, January 18). ESL students shortchanged. *Toronto Star*, p. B5.

Kane, L. (2013, August 16). High school teachers threaten new protests. *Toronto Star*, p. A1.

Lawton, S. (1996). *Financing Canadian Education*. Canadian Education Association.

Levin, B. (2005). *Governing Education*. University of Toronto Press. doi:10.3138/9781442675438

Levin, B., & Fullan, M. (2008). Learning about system renewal. *Educational Management Administration & Leadership*, *36*(2), 289–303. doi:10.1177/1741143207087778

Li, X. (2015). Ontario education governance 1995 to the present: More accountability, more regulation, and more centralization? *Journal of International Education and Leadership*, *5*(1). https://files.eric.ed.gov/fulltext/EJ1135778.pdf

Li, X. (2016). Ontario, Canada and Hawaii, USA: Who makes stronger vertical equity efforts? *International Studies in Educational Administration*, *44*(1), 71–84.

Li, X. (2023). Special education grant in Ontario, how is it determined? *Brock Education*, *32*(1), 83–98. doi:10.26522/brocked.v32i1.963

Luke, R., Bennett, S., Specht, J., White, R., Somma, M., Li, X., Lattanzio, R., Gavan, K., Kyle, G., Porter, G., & Patel, A. (2018). *If inclusion means everyone, why not me?* Community Living Ontario, Western University, Brock University, ARCH Disability Law Centre, Brockville and District Association for Community Involvement, and Inclusive Education Canada. https://www.inclusiveeducationresearch.ca/docs/why-not-me.pdf

Manley-Casimir, M., & Manley-Casimir, K. (2009). *The Courts, the Charter, and the Schools: The Impact of the Charter of Rights and Freedoms on Educational Policy and Practice 1982-2007*. University of Toronto Press.

Meijer, C., & Watkins, A. (2019). Financing special needs and inclusive education – from Salamanca to the present. *International Journal of Inclusive Education*, *23*(7-8), 705–721. doi:10.1080/13603116.2019.1623330

Moore v. British Columbia (Education) [2012] 3 SCR 360, SCC 61 (CanLII). https://www.canlii.org/en/ca/scc/doc/2012/2012scc61/2012scc61.html

Myers v. Peel County Board of Education [1981] 2 SCR 21, CanLII 27 (SCC). https://www.canlii.org/en/ca/scc/doc/1981/1981canlii27/1981canlii27.html

Ontarians with Disabilities Act, SO 2001, C32. https://www.canlii.org/en/on/laws/stat/so-2001-c-32/latest/so-2001-c-32.html

Ontario College of Teachers. (2018). *Ontario College of Teachers Bylaws*. https://www.oct.ca/about-the- college/what-we-do/legislation-regulations-and-bylaws/college-bylaws

Ontario College of Teachers. (2019). *Complaint Process*. https://www.oct.ca/public/complaints-and- discipline/complaints-process

Ontario English Catholic Teachers' Assn. v. Ontario (Attorney General) [2001] 1 SCR 470, SCC 15 (CanLII). https://www.canlii.org/en/ca/scc/doc/2001/2001scc15/2001scc15.html?resultIndex=3

Ontario Human Rights Commission. (2018). *Policy on Accessible Education for Students with Disabilities*. https://www.ohrc.on.ca/en/policy-accessible-education-students-disabilities

Ontario Human Rights Commission. (n. d.). *Accommodating students with disabilities - Principles (fact sheet)*. https://www.ohrc.on.ca/en/accommodating-students-disabilities-principles-fact-sheet

Ontario Ministry of Education. (2003). *Student-focused funding: School board funding projections for the 2003–04 school year*. https://collections.ola.org/mon/6000/10316038.pdf

Ontario Ministry of Education. (2009). *Realizing the promise of diversity—Ontario's equity and inclusive education strategy*. https://collections.ola.org/mon/23004/290471.pdf

Ontario Ministry of Education. (2011). *School Fees Guideline*. Retrieved from http://www.edu.gov.on.ca/eng/parents/fundraising.html

Ontario Ministry of Education. (2012). *Fundraising Guideline*. Retrieved from http://www.edu.gov.on.ca/eng/parents/Fund2012Guideline.pdf

Ontario Ministry of Education. (2014). *Equity and inclusive education in Ontario schools: Guidelines for policy development and implementation*. https://collections.ola.org/mon/28011/328556.pdf

Ontario Ministry of Education. (2015). *The Provincial Model for a Local Police/School Board Protocol*. http://www.edu.gov.on.ca/eng/document/brochure/protocol/locprote.pdf

Ontario Ministry of Education. (2018). *2018-19 Education funding: A guide to the special education grant*. https://files.ontario.ca/edu-gsn-2018-19-special-education-guide-en-2022-03-03.pdf

Ontario Ministry of Education. (2022). *Education Funding: Grants for Student Needs Projections for the 2022-23 School Year*. https://files.ontario.ca/edu-2223-gsnprojections- en- 2022-04-20.pdf

Ontario Ministry of Education. (n.d.). *Guidelines for approval and provision of an education and community partnership program (ECPP) 2021-22*. https://efis.fma.csc.gov.on.ca/faab/Section_23/21-22/ECPP Guidelines 2021-22 April8_21 FINAL_EN.pdf

Operation Of Schools - General. RRO 1990, Reg 298. https://www.canlii.org/en/on/laws/regu/rro-1990- reg-298/latest/rro-1990-reg-298.html

Operation of Schools. Ontario Regulation 298. (1990). https://www.canlii.org/en/on/laws/regu/rro-1990- reg-298/latest/rro-1990-reg-298.html

Organization of Economic Co-Operation and Development. (2019). *PISA 2018 Results: Combined Executive Summaries*. https://www.oecd.org/pisa/Combined_Executive_Summaries_PISA_2018.pdf

Osgoode Hall Law School, York University. (2020, December 9). *Advanced issues in special education law*. https://osgoodepd.ca/professional-development/short-courses-and-conferences/advanced- issues-in-special-education-law-2020/

Osgoode Hall Law School, York University. (2020, December 9). *Advanced issues in special education law*. https://osgoodepd.ca/professional-development/short-courses-andconferences/advanced-issues-in-special-education-law-2020/

People for Education. (2012). *Making Connections Beyond School Walls: People for Education Annual Report on Ontario's Publicly Funded Schools 2012*. https://www.academia.edu/30790074/MAKING_CONNECTIONS_BEYOND_SCHOOL_WALLS_People_for_Education_Annual_Report_on_Ontarios_Publicly_Funded_Scho ols_2012

People for Education. (2019). *2019 Annual report on schools: What makes a school?* https://peopleforeducation.ca/report/2019-annual-report-on-schools-what-makes-a-school/

Policy/Program Memorandum No. 120. (2011). http://www.edu.gov.on.ca/extra/eng/ppm/120.html#_ftnref5

Policy/Program Memorandum No. 145. (2018). http://www.edu.gov.on.ca/extra/eng/ppm/145.pdf

Proudfoot, A., & Hutchings, L. (1988). *Teacher Beware*. Detselig Enterprises Ltd.

Putting, S. F. A. 2012, SO 2012, c 11. https://www.canlii.org/en/on/laws/astat/so-2012-c- 11/latest/so-2012-c-11.html?resultIndex=2

Ranson, S. (2003). Public accountability in the age of neo-liberal governance. *Journal of Education Policy*, *18*(5), 459–480. doi:10.1080/0268093032000124848

Resurfice Corp. v. Hanke [2007] 1 SCR 333, SCC 7 (CanLII). https://www.canlii.org/en/ca/scc/doc/2007/2007scc7/2007scc7.html

Ross, G. (1896). *The School System of Ontario*. D. Appleton and Company.

Rozanski, M. (2002). *Invest in Public Education: Advancing the Goal of Continuous Improvement in Student Learning and Achievement*. Academic Press.

Rushowy, K. (2016, October 15). Peel school board settles its final education contract. *Toronto Star*, p. GT10.

Rushowy, K. (2023, March 11). Privatization of education could be next, warns head of Ontario high school teachers union. *Toronto Star*. https://www.thestar.com/politics/provincial/2023/03/11/privatization-of-education-could-be-next-warns-head-of-ontario-high-school-teachers-union.html

Rushowy, K. (2023, March 21). Ford government needs to boost funding amid education 'crisis,' tteachers' union says. *Toronto Star*. https://www.thestar.com/politics/provincial/2023/03/21/ford-government-needs-to-boost-funding-amid-education-crisis-teachers-union-says.html

Rushowy, K., & Benzie, R. (2012, July 6). Catholic teachers, province forge deal. *Toronto Star*, p. A1.

Rushowy, K., & Ferguson, R. (2009, February 15). Teachers accept 4-year deal. *Toronto Star*, p. A4.

Rushowy, K., Brown, L., & Ferguson, R. (2013, June 14). Elementary teachers get 2% wage increase. *Toronto Star*, p. GT1.

Safe Schools Act, SO 2000, c 12. https://www.canlii.org/en/on/laws/astat/so-2000-c-12/latest/so-2000-c-12.html?autocompleteStr=Bill%2081&autocompletePos=8

Sattler, P. (2012). Education governance reform in Ontario: Neoliberalism in context. *Canadian Journal of Educational Administration and Policy*, 128.

School Bus Fleet Forums. (2006). *Suit in the Works*. https://www.schoolbusfleet.com/forum/topic.asp?TOPIC_ID=12655

School Councils. O Reg 612/00. https://www.canlii.org/en/on/laws/regu/o-reg-612-00/latest/o-reg-612- 00.html

Shum, D. (2018, September 11). Teacher charged in death of teen who drowned in Algonquin Park has court case put over. *Global News*.

Special Education Programs and Services. RRO 1990, Reg 306. https://www.canlii.org/en/on/laws/regu/rro-1990-reg-306/latest/rro-1990-reg-306.html

Statistics Canada. (2022, October 26). *The Canadian census: A rich portrait of the country's religious and ethnocultural diversity*. https://www150.statcan.gc.ca/n1/daily-quotidien/221026/dq221026b-eng.htm

Statistics Canada. (2023). *Consumer Price Index, annual average, not seasonally adjusted*. https://www150.statcan.gc.ca/t1/tbl1/en/tv.action?pid=1810000501&pickMembers%5B0%5D=1.14&cubeTimeFrame.startYear=2002&cubeTimeFrame.endYear=2022&referencePeriods=20020101%2C20220101

Talaga, T., & Aulakh, R. (2012, August 14). Union turns back on province. *Toronto Star*, p. A6.

Talaga, T., & Rushowy, K. (2012, August 10). French teachers' union seals deal. *Toronto Star*, p. A12.

The Chinese Ministry of Education. (2022). *2021 National Education Development Statistics* [2021年全 国教育事业发展统计公报]. http://www.moe.gov.cn/jyb_sjzl/sjzl_fztjgb/202209/t20220914_660850.html

The Chinese People's Congress. (2018). *The Chinese Compulsory Education Act* [中华人民共和国 义务教育法]. https://baike.baidu.com/item/中华人民共和国义务教育法/2342357

The Chinese People's Congress. (2018). *The Chinese Compulsory Education Act*. https://baike.baidu.com/item/

The Chinese People's Congress. (2021). *The Chinese Education Act* [中华人民共和国教育法]. http://www.moe.gov.cn/jyb_xxgk/xxgk_jyfl/flfg_jyfl/202107/t20210730_547843.html

The Constitution Act, 1982, Schedule B to the Canada Act 1982 (UK), c 11. https://www.canlii.org/en/ca/laws/stat/schedule-b-to-the-canada-act-1982-uk-1982-c- 11/latest/schedule-b-to-the-canada-act-1982-uk-1982-c-11.html

The Parliament of the United Kingdom. (1867). The Constitution Act, 1867 (The British North America Act, 1867).

Thomas v. Hamilton (City), Board of Education 1994 CanLII 739 (ON CA). https://www.canlii.org/en/on/onca/doc/1994/1994canlii739/1994canlii739.html

United Nations Educational, Scientific and Cultural Organization. (2017). *A guide for ensuring inclusion and equity in education.* https://unesdoc.unesco.org/ark:/48223/pf0000248254

United Nations. (1989). *Convention on the Rights of the Child.* https://www.ohchr.org/en/professionalinterest/pages/crc.aspx

Waldick v. Malcolm [1991] 2 SCR 456, CanLII 71 (SCC). https://www.canlii.org/en/ca/scc/doc/1991/1991canlii71/1991canlii71.html

Walker, A. (1971). *History of Education in Ontario 1791 – 1841* [Master's thesis]. University of Toronto Library.

About the Author

Xiaobin Li earned his doctoral degree from the Ontario Institute for the Studies in Education of the University of Toronto, Canada. He is associate professor at the Faculty of Education, Brock University, St. Catharines, Ontario, Canada. He teaches education law, education finance, construction of organizations, and quantitative research methods.

Index

www.ingramcontent.com/pod-product-compliance
Lightning Source LLC
LaVergne TN
LVHW061534290926
849162LV00004B/793
* 9 7 8 1 6 6 8 4 4 1 6 3 3 *